**"Eric Svendsen's new work,
Evangelical Answers, is a must-read.**

Drawn from real-life encounters with the most popular Roman Catholic apologists, Svendsen deftly unties the knotty arguments being used to promote the unbiblical and a-historical claims of Roman Catholicism. Christians who want to know why they can indeed trust the Scriptures and not rely solely upon a single bishop in a far-away country for their knowledge of God and His truth will be greatly helped by Svendsen's timely work."

—*James White*

Author, *The Roman Catholic Controversy*

EVANGELICAL ANSWERS

A CRITIQUE OF CURRENT
ROMAN CATHOLIC APOLOGISTS

Evangelical
Answers

ERIC
SVENDSEN

A PUBLICATION OF REFORMATION PRESS

ERIC SVENDSEN holds a Masters Degree in New Testament Studies from Trinity Evangelical Divinity School, a Doctorate in Theological Studies from Columbia Evangelical Seminary, and has recently completed his dissertation for a Ph.D. in Biblical Studies from Greenwich School of Theology, U.K.. He also serves as a professor of Biblical Studies at Columbia Evangelical Seminary. He is the Co-Founder and Co-Director of New Testament Restoration Ministries, an apologetics ministry dedicated to restoring New Testament beliefs and practices to the church. He has authored and contributed to several books, including *The Table of the Lord: An Examination of the Setting of the Lord's Supper in the New Testament and Its Significance as an Expression of Community*, and *Toward a House-Church Theology*. Dr. Svendsen is active in engaging Catholic apologists in public debate, and has appeared as a guest on numerous Christian radio talk shows. You may contact Eric Svendsen through his ministry's web site www.ntrmin.com.

*To my coworkers in Christ who have tirelessly
upheld the truth of the Gospel in the face of much opposition.*

Reformation Press

160 37th Street
Lindenhurst, New York 11701 USA
631. 956. 0998
reformationpress@email.com
www.reformationpress.com
www.greatchristianbooks.com

Svendsen, Eric, 1960-
    Evangelical answers / Eric Svendsen
        p.   cm.
A *"The Apologetics Series by Reformation Press"* book
ISBN 0-9670840-8-3 (pbk.)
Recommended Dewey Decimal Classification: 234
Suggested Subject Headings:
1. Religion—Christian literature—Apologetics.
2. Christianity—Salvation—Eric Svendsen.
3. The Bible—Doctrine—Salvation.
I. Title

The book and cover design for this title are by Michael Rotolo.
It is typeset in the Minion family typeface by Adobe Inc. and is
quality manufactured on archival standard acid-free paper.
To discuss the publication of your Christian manuscript or
out-of-print book, please contact Reformation Press.

MANUFACTURED IN THE UNITED STATES OF AMERICA

2 3 4 5 6 7 8 9 10   00 01 02 03

~ CONTENTS ~

Introduction **5**

1   *Infallibility of the Catholic Church* **9**

2   *The Nature of the Church* **53**

3   *Apostolic Succession* **59**

4   *The Canon* **65**

5   *The Sufficiency of Scripture* **75**

6   *Old Testament Israel—*
    A Story of the Catholic Church **109**

7   *The Myth of Catholic Unity* **119**

8   *Beliefs About Mary* **127**

9   *The Catholic Priesthood* **165**

10 *The Eucharist and the Mass* **171**

Conclusion **189**

Endnotes **191**

Introduction

There is a growing number of conservative Catholics who have taken it upon themselves to defend the Catholic tradition. Vigorous in their defense and confrontational in their approach, they actively pursue debate with non-Catholics in an attempt to answer sixteenth-century Protestant objections and to lead their opponents back to Rome. Many of them are very clever debaters and can articulate their position in an extremely compelling way.

In many cases, however, their tactics are reminiscent of the fundamentalism they so vehemently oppose.[1] Some of these Catholic apologists, such as Karl Keating, betray a certain condescending attitude in their writings, characterizing their opponents arguments as "laughable."[2] Others, such as Patrick Madrid, refer to non-Catholic beliefs as "Evangelical heresies."[3] Such language serves only to fuel the fire rather than to produce constructive dialogue with their opponents. There is nothing necessarily wrong with head-on tactics, so long as the issues are handled in an even-handed way and without ad hominem attacks; all too often, they are not.

What is worse is that in some of these debates the Evangelical side is represented by uninformed fundamentalists who are not focused well enough on the real issues— or, worse yet, not versed well enough in the Catholic apologists' own arguments! The end result is often that the Catholic apologists' real objections are left unanswered.

This book attempts to answer those objections. It serves as a critique of the major issues raised by Catholic apologists, answering their specific claims in regard to *sola scriptura*, the limits of the canon, the sufficiency of Scripture, apostolic succession, infallibility of the pope and of the magisterium, oral church tradition, Mary, the priesthood, and Catholic unity, as well as some other, peripheral issues.

This book is a revised version of the author's earlier manuscript titled *Protestant Answers*. The title of the present book has purposefully avoided the use of the word *Protestant*. Indeed, the word itself is used in this book only a few times, and then usually only to articulate the precise argument of the Catholic apologists. I prefer the word *Evangelical* for several reasons. First, modern Protestantism encompasses many groups that have little in common with the Protestant Reformers themselves, not least of which is the liberal wing of Protestantism. I am certain that my belief in the full inspiration of the Scriptures, for example, is not representative of many within Protestantism, and I certainly do not share the liberal Protestant belief that Scripture contains errors. Second, while many Reformed apologists who write on Catholic issues are comfortable using this nomenclature— and do so with *historic* Protestantism in mind— the Roman Catholic apologist, nevertheless, does not always understand this, and, as a result, often feels justified in painting Protestants with a broad brush.[4]

Third, as one sorts through the Catholic apologists' own materials dealing with these issues, one gets the distinct impression that the material is directed not to *all* Protestants, but in particular to *Evangelical* Protestants[5] — that is to say, those who share the Catholic apologists' own assumptions regarding the full inspiration of the Scriptures, the ability to know truth, the immutable nature of truth, a closed canon of Scripture, and the recognition of historic orthodoxy. I have therefore opted instead to use the word *Evangelical* to represent my own position on these issues.

My goal in writing this book is to deal with the Catholic apologists' arguments in a fair but critical way. There is little to be gained by engaging in the often careless and misinformed tactics that so frequently plague fundamentalists who write against Roman Catholicism.[6] Nor is there much to be gained by glossing over obvious disagreements between Roman Catholics and Evangelicals.[7] Both of these tendencies will be conscientiously avoided in this book. It is hoped that by doing so, the arguments against erroneous Roman Catholic beliefs will be presented with balance and clarity, but without calling into question the integrity or motives[8] — or indeed, the spiritual status— of the Catholic apologists themselves.

It is my hope that by offering some fresh perspectives on each of these issues, Catholic apologists will honestly and openly reevaluate their own positions in light of clear biblical teaching and historical reality. It is further hoped that this book (as well as the Catholic apologists' own materials) will serve as a wake-up call to a more thorough study of the so-far underdeveloped doctrine of *sola scriptura* among Evangelical churches, as well as a deeper understanding of that doctrine within every Christian individually.

Chapter One

Infallibility of the Catholic Church

A good place to start our discussion is with the issue of the infallibility of the church. The more important subsets of this issue— infallibility of the magisterium, apostolic succession, and infallibility of the pope— are examined in depth below. One reason we have chosen this as a starting point is because this is precisely the starting point at which at least one Catholic apologist, Scott Hahn, begins his objections to the Evangelical position.[9]

Hahn, a prominent spokesman for this group, argues vehemently (as do others in his camp) that unless we attribute authority to oral church tradition, we could never know with certainty historical facts such as who wrote Matthew, Mark, and John. The titles of the books were added much later (e.g., "the gospel according to John"), the authors are not named within the books themselves, and there are no other indicators within these books (so Hahn argues) that point in one direction or another as to which book was written by whom. Therefore, if we accept the authority of the Catholic church in its decisions on *these* issues, we have no good reason not to assent to all other decisions made by the same Catholic church.

This same argument is applied to the canon as well; namely, unless we accept the authority of the church on the collection of the canon, we have no right to accept the fruit of that decision (viz., a New Testament that contains twenty-seven books, not to mention the *right* twenty-seven books!). And if we cannot be certain, apart from the decision of the Catholic church, that these books were written by the men purported to have written them, we likewise have no certainty that these writings are apostolic, or, indeed, Scripture.

The Evangelical is thereby in a dilemma; for if the church is not infallible, is there not a chance that it was wrong in its decision of which books should be included in the canon of Scripture? There is no divinely inspired table of contents that would indicate which books the church was to include in the Bible. The church simply made a decision about these books, and Evangelicals accept that decision as *infallible* without ever questioning it. Yet, on what basis do we ascribe infallibility to the church on *this* issue but not other issues?

The Infallible Catholic Magisterium and Apostolic Succession

Many observations can and must be made about Hahn's thesis. First, in regard to the authority of the church in ascertaining historical data such as the authorship of the gospels, Hahn has simply confused *authority* with *historical reliability*. Just because a person living during the Civil War era happens to record through written correspondence that Abraham Lincoln authored the Gettysburg Address, do we thereby attribute *authority* to this person in all historical matters about which he writes? Usually not. Instead, we recognize that there is a high degree of probability that what he writes is true so long as his statements are consonant with all the other facts we have available to us. The fathers have provided us with *one* piece of external evidence[10] to the authorship of the gospels; and if the internal evidence[11] of the gospels themselves indicates that they are likely correct, then we have no good reason to reject their testimony. As it turns out the bulk of the evidence (both internal and external) points to the men who are historically purported to have written the gospels.[12]

Hahn's proposal that we are here implicitly subscribing to the authority of the church for this information is badly uninformed and just a trifle naive. It is rather the combined testimony of the internal and external evidence that leads us to believe that Matthew, Mark, Luke and John wrote the gospels. In fact, the same church that provides us with this testimony also provides us with testimony that contradicts the internal evidence in other matters— such as which gospel was written first. The early church almost unanimously followed Augustine in his view that Matthew was written first. Indeed, until as recently as 1955, Catholics were *required* to believe that Matthew was the first gospel written.[13] However, virtually no Evangelical or Catholic New Testament scholar today believes that it is even plausible that Matthew was written first. Where is the Evangelical (or, indeed, Catholic!) dependence on the authority of the church fathers in this case?

The same point may be made concerning the authorship of Hebrews. Until the latter half of the fourth century the Western church almost unanimously resisted ascribing Pauline authorship to Hebrews.[14] However, both Jerome[15] and Augustine[16] appealed to the Eastern church's view that Paul wrote this epistle, and their view was eventually adopted at the Sixth Synod of Carthage in 419 A.D.[17], and then reaffirmed at the Council of Trent. Yet, the number of New Testament scholars (Catholic or Evangelical) that would defend Pauline authorship today is practically nil.[18]

It is indeed odd that Hahn would insist that Evangelicals must rely on the authority of the Catholic church to be certain of the authorship of the gospels when he knows full well that Evangelicals have no need for this kind of certainty when the issue is the authorship of Hebrews. The fact of the matter is, the authorship of the gospels is simply not a matter of belief that is binding on the conscience of the believer. We may look to the early church fathers for indicators in what they believed about this or that historical fact— but that is a far cry from ascribing authority to church tradition as Hahn would like us to do.

A second observation regarding Hahn's thesis concerns his insistence that if we accept the biblical canon that the early fathers decided upon, then we must subscribe wholesale to all of their beliefs. This, too, is a curious contention. One must ask the question, Did those who decided upon the canon of Scripture (i.e., those involved in the synods of Hippo [393] and Carthage [397]) view themselves as making an infallible decision? Nowhere in any of the ancient documents do we find the slightest suggestion that these men saw themselves as infallible decision makers. In fact, their method for determining the limits of the canon strongly resembles how an Evangelical might have gone about the same task— namely, by examining each book for apostolic genuineness, coming up with a list of likely candidates, and trusting that God would sovereignly direct the effort— rather than the Catholic view that there should be an infallible proclamation (albeit, after much study and prayer).[19]

There is, moreover, good reason that the men in these synods did not view themselves as infallible in their decision— the Roman Catholic doctrine of infallibility was not defined until 1870. While there is evidence to suggest that the early fathers viewed themselves as authoritative in their collective decisions, and that the church itself is indestructible, no church council for the first millennium of Christian history claimed infallibility in its decisions; and the notion of papal infallibility was not proposed until around the fourteenth century.

A third observation concerns some of the evidence Hahn adduces for such a claim. One way that Hahn has argued for the infallibility (or, at the very least, *authority*) of church tradition and apostolic succession, is to point out its supposed antecedents in the gospels. Hahn makes much of Jesus' statement in Matt 23:2-3 that the Pharisees and the teachers of the Law sit in "Moses seat," and that Jesus' disciples were to obey the Jewish leaders but not emulate their practices. He makes a connection between the "cathedra" (seat) of Moses under the Old Covenant and the *ex cathedra* of the Catholic church.[20] Hahn concludes on this basis that just as the Pharisees were successors to Moses, so also the Catholic magisterium make up the successors to the apostles.

Hahn's contention, however, is again badly uninformed. First, there is no formal connection between the Pharisees and any group that came before them, so that some kind of "line of succession" can be established. The Pharisees of the first century were a relatively young group whose beginnings, although somewhat obscure, can safely be traced back to the time of the *Hasmonaean* and *Hasidim* alliance against hellenization of Judaism around the second century BC. The Pharisees were the *Hasidim* who broke away from this alliance. The first mention of the Pharisees appears in Josephus while relating events that occurred around 145 BC.[21]

Second, Hahn attempts to convince us that there is a distinction to be made between the Pharisees, whom Jesus told his disciples to obey, and all other religious groups, such as the Sadducees, of whom Jesus said nothing in regard to obedience. His point for arguing such a case is to establish the Pharisees as the sole occupants of the seat of Moses, paving the way for succession of authority from Moses to the Pharisees. Indeed, in order for Hahn's argument to stand, the Pharisees and Scribes— *and no other group* (such as the Sadducees)— must have sole occupancy of the seat of Moses; for if other religious groups *do* have this same authority, then the modern day ramification is that Evangelicals (as well as Catholics) could legitimately sit in the "seat of Peter" at the same time.

But Hahn's attempt is futile. Jesus gives this same recognition to the priests of his day. When the leprous man was healed by Jesus, he was told to show himself to the priest and to offer the sacrifices commanded by Moses "as a testimony to them"

(Matt 8:4; Mark 1:44; Luke 5:14). The problem for Hahn is that the priests were Sadducees, not Pharisees.[22] Yet it is clear that Jesus wanted the formerly leprous man to obey the mandates of the priests in the same way that he commanded his disciples to obey the mandates of the Pharisees— *only to the extent that the Pharisees and the priests accurately proclaimed and carried out the "commands of Moses."*[23]

Oddly, Hahn also uses the example of Caiaphas as support for an infallible magisterium. Caiaphas, the high priest mentioned in John 11:49-52, is said to have prophesied (unknowingly) because he was high priest that year:

> Then one of them, named Caiaphas, who was high priest that year, spoke up, "You know nothing at all! You do not realize that it is better for you that one man die for the people than that the whole nation perish." He did not say this on his own, but as high priest that year he prophesied that Jesus would die for the Jewish nation.

Hahn contends that Caiaphas was able to prophesy accurately precisely because he had inherent ecclesial authority— not by virtue of his person or rightness before God, but by virtue of his position as a successor to Moses.

But, again, priests belonged to the party of the Sadducees. Hahn has already argued (on the basis of Matt 23:2-3) that Pharisees, not Sadducees, were successors of Moses. Yet Caiaphas was a Sadducee, not a Pharisee.[24] Hahn cannot have it both ways; either the Pharisees sat in Moses' seat (in which case Caiaphas didn't) or Caiaphas sat in Moses' seat (in which case the Pharisees didn't)— otherwise, his argument for a *sole* successor of Moses falls to the ground. Yet, even if we were to accept Hahn's argument that Caiaphas prophesied *ex cathedra*, what is the point in arguing that the Catholic church has this same special ability? Are we to assume that Hahn wants us to interpret the pope's words in double entendre? That although the pope intends evil, we should look for some hidden truth? It is unclear just exactly what Hahn wants us to glean here.

Jesus commanded obedience to the Pharisees and Sadducees only to the extent that they taught the law of Moses. He certainly did not intend to place his disciples in a position, with the Pharisees, of nullifying the word of God (Matt 15:6; Mark 7:7-9). Put another way, Jesus would not have commanded his disciples to do something that he so forcefully condemned the Pharisees for doing. In fact, Jesus makes this very point in Matt 16:6-12 where, far from telling his disciples to *obey* the teachings of the Pharisees, he tells them to *beware* of them! It will not do to suggest, as Hahn does, that Jesus, who *is* the truth, somehow wanted his disciples to submit to error. Hahn's contention simply will not wash.

But let us grant for the moment that Hahn is correct in his assertion that the Pharisees possessed the same ecclesial authority that the Catholic church claims to have, and that their position over Israel serves as a basis for the Catholic church's authority and infallibility over Christianity as a whole. How does the New Testament portray this ecclesial authority?

1) They were condemned by Jesus (Matt 23:13 ff).
2) They were not entering the kingdom of God, and were shutting out those who wanted to enter (Matt 23:13).
3) They made their converts "sons of hell" (Matt 23:15).
4) Jesus told his disciples to beware of their teachings (Matt 16:6-12).
5) Their traditions contradicted the Scriptures (Mark 7:1-13)
6) Jesus denied that they were children of the covenant (John 8:39-41).
7) Jesus called them children of Satan (John 8:44).
8) The majority of them rejected the Messiah.
9) The majority were excluded from the New Covenant and eternal life.

Many of the statements above regarding the Pharisees follow directly on the heels of the "seat of Moses" statement recorded in

Matt 23:2-3. What are we to make of the supposed authority (or indeed, infallibility) of the Pharisees in light of these observations? If this is how Hahn wants us to view authority and infallibility for the Catholic church, then few Evangelicals would have any problem at all affirming (quite enthusiastically in some cases!) that the Catholic church is indeed "authoritative and infallible"!

But can Jesus really be telling his disciples that they are to submit themselves to the authority of the Pharisees (a decidedly corrupt authority, to say the least) based on the notion that the Pharisees are the successors of Moses and therefore the "spokesmen" of God? Can this be the same Jesus who so openly and unreservedly called the Pharisees "whitewashed tombs" which are "full of dead men's bones and everything unclean" (Matt 23:27), and "hypocrites" who "do not enter" the "kingdom of Heaven" (Matt 23:13)?

Even if we were to concede that the "seat of Moses" is a seat of ecclesial authority, it certainly does not follow that those who sat in it were infallible. Nor does it imply some kind of succession of leadership, for in the Old Testament there is no appointed succession. Kings conquered other kings, and hence won authority. Prophets arose and condemned sitting prophets without in any way first being commissioned by anyone other than God; then they simply disappeared from the scene. Authority was granted directly by God randomly, and without respect to current ecclesial authorities. In fact, in most cases the appointed prophet was sent out to proclaim God's displeasure and judgment against the sitting authorities.[25] Even the Pharisees themselves (to whom Jesus refers in this passage) were a group whose origin, as we have seen, dates only from the second century BC, and could not, therefore, legitimately be connected via succession to Moses. In fact, the Pharisees "protested" the corrupt ecclesial authority of their day, and hence came to power. The modern day equivalent, in that regard, would more resemble the Evangelical (whose origin is the result of the Reformation) than the Catholic (who claims unbroken succession from Peter).

The authority about which Jesus speaks cannot therefore refer to what Hahn wants it to; namely, *ecclesial* authority derived from unbroken succession. Rather, (if we are to assume that Jesus' words are not to be taken as irony) it must refer to *theocratic* or governmental authority; that is to say, authority by virtue of the theocracy over which Moses was placed a leader— not derived by virtue of succession, but by virtue of expediency. The Pharisees held theocratic authority simply because they were the ones currently in charge over the religious matters of the Jewish people— nothing more, and nothing less.[26]

This is not unlike the kind of submission that the Apostles entreat us to in Rom 13, Titus 3:1, and 1 Pet 2:13-17. We are told by Paul and Peter to submit ourselves to the "governing authorities," whether good or bad. Jesus' command, therefore, cannot be taken without qualification— submit to ecclesial authorities *provided they are also "governing" authorities.* In fact, this is precisely what Paul taught in his encounter with the Sanhedrin (Acts 23). Paul is at the same time able to call the high priest a "whitewashed wall" (v. 3), and affirm that there is to be respect for the "leader" of the Jewish people (v. 5). The interesting thing about this episode is that Paul was formerly a Pharisee; and yet he still acknowledges the high priest (a Sadducee) as leader of the Jewish people. The only way he could have done this is to recognize the governmental (or theocratic) authority of the high priest without recognizing his ecclesial or spiritual authority. Spiritually he was a "white-washed tomb"; governmentally he was a "leader" of the people.

What then did Jesus mean when he commanded his disciples to obey the Pharisees? Did he mean for his disciples blindly to accept false teachings just because the Pharisees sat in the seat of Moses? Jesus himself said of the Pharisees, "if a blind man leads a blind man, both will fall into a pit" (Matt 15:14). Jesus did not intend for his disciples to practice and propagate error— rather, if the Pharisees demanded a temple tax, his disciples were to pay it (Matt 17:24-27). Hahn's fanciful and highly anachronistic interpretation of Jesus' words says more about Hahn's zeal for Rome than it does about the biblical text.

Infallibility of the Pope

Closely related to the notion of ecclesial infallibility of the Catholic church is the equally important belief in the infallibility of the pope. Keating attempts to defend the Catholic position by postulating several points.[27] He begins by stating that papal infallibility is merely a negative protection against error, not an assurance that whatever the pope says on any issue will be correct. He then attempts to make a distinction between those times that the pope is speaking *ex cathedra* (i.e., infallibly), and those times that the pope is speaking as a "private scholar."[28] Infallibility also belongs to the universal body of bishops (though, theirs is merely a *confirmatory* infallibility of what the pope has already defined, and not an inherent infallibility for defining dogmas). Finally, Keating cites passages of Scripture that he believes supports the doctrine of infallibility.

Among the passages cited in support of papal infallibility are Matt 16:17-19 ("you are Peter . . . on this Rock I will build my church. . . . I will give you the keys of the kingdom. . . . whatever you bind/loose . . . shall be bound/loosed in heaven"), John 21:15-17 (where Jesus tells Peter, "feed my sheep"), and Luke 22:32 (where Jesus says to Peter "I have prayed for you that your faith may not fail . . . strengthen your brothers"). These are the Petrine passages that are alleged to support papal infallibility. Others (including Matt 28:19-20, John 16:13 and 1 Tim 3:15) are said to support church infallibility, but not specifically papal infallibility. What can we say about these passages of Scripture?[29] Do they support papal infallibility? It will be helpful to examine each one in turn.

Matt 16:18 has been a long-disputed passage as to its meaning. According to the Catholic view, Jesus is here proclaiming that Peter is the rock upon which the church is to be built.[30] All but a few Evangelicals reject this view, adopting in its place the view that Jesus is calling Peter's *confession* (not Peter himself) the rock upon which the church is to be built. However, as D. A. Carson has pointed out, this view does not account for all the particulars that need to be considered.[31] Let us therefore concede the point that Peter *is* the rock in this passage.[32] What does it prove? Can Peter and the other apostles be a foundation without being infallible? That seems to be self evident. Foundations do not necessarily require infallibility, and it is a leap of logic to suggest otherwise.

What about the rest of this passage (v. 19), which states "Whatever you shall bind on earth shall be bound in heaven, and whatever you shall loose on earth shall be loosed in heaven"? Does this suggest papal infallibility? At best, all it could suggest is that the pope has the power to forgive sins. There certainly is no hint of infallibility here. But just what does this passage mean? The Greek words translated here respectively as "shall be bound" and "shall be loosed" are dedemenon ($\delta\epsilon\delta\epsilon\mu\acute{\epsilon}\nu o\nu$) and lelumenon ($\lambda\epsilon\lambda\upsilon\mu\acute{\epsilon}\nu o\nu$). Both are future periphrastic perfect participles, which simply means that the action, though future, is prior to the binding and loosing that Peter will do. A more literal translation of this passage would look like this:

> "Whatever you may bind on earth shall already have been bound in heaven, and whatever you may loose on earth shall already have been loosed in heaven."

So far from teaching Peter's infallibility to define dogma (much less, sacerdotalism), this passage teaches that Peter (and the other apostles according to Matt 18:19) will be (unwittingly) carrying out what has already been sovereignly decreed in heaven.

But just what does this binding and loosing entail? Does it, as the Catholic church claims, entail making infallible pronouncements about who should and who should not be absolved from sins? If so, what example is there in Scripture of such a practice?

The passage in question does indeed refer to who is and who is not included in the kingdom via forgiveness of sins; but the focus is exactly the opposite of what the Catholic church thinks it is. It is evident from the parallel passage in Matt 18:19 that "loosing" in the form of church discipline is what is in mind. Verses 15-17 speak of one who refuses to repent of sin. The discipline process involves first a private consultation. Then, if the sinning brother refuses to repent, we are to take one or two more as witnesses and confront him again. Finally, if the sinning brother is still unrepentant, the whole church is to be told. If the sinning brother remains unrepentant, he is then "loosed" from the church. Paul gives us an example of this in 1 Cor 5:1-13, where he tells the Corinthian assembly to "expel the wicked [incestuous] man from among you."

On the other hand, the binding referred to here is nothing more (or less) than a *declarative* authority that one's sins are forgiven. This authority is inherent in the gospel message itself. We as Christians can confidently tell others that if they believe in Jesus Christ, their sins are forgiven. This authority is primarily in the *message*, not in the *messenger*. It is in the messenger only to the extent that the messenger has the right message.[33] When a sinner repents at the reception of the gospel message, that person has been "bound." Examples of this kind of binding are replete in the New Testament.[34] Papal infallibility can be found neither in the text of Matthew 16, nor in any subsequent biblical examples. In any case, we have sufficiently shown that Peter can be the foundation upon which the church is built without ascribing infallibility to him.[35]

But what of Jesus' words to Peter in John 21:15-17? Yes, Jesus does tell Peter to feed his sheep, but the instant Peter inquires about the role of another apostle (John), Jesus tells Peter to mind his own business![36] Hardly a thing to tell the supposed supreme head of the church, under whom every Christian is to submit. Is John not part of the church that is to submit to the pope? Should it not be Peter's prerogative to know what John's ministry will be? Not according to Jesus. Peter's "feeding" of Jesus' sheep is no more important than that of the other elders of the church, with whom Peter saw himself a coworker, nothing more.[37] In any case, this passage certainly does not support papal infallibility.

One more Petrine passage to consider is Luke 22:31-32: "Simon, Simon, Satan has asked to sift you as wheat. But I have prayed for you, Simon, that your faith may not fail. And when you have turned back, strengthen your brothers." The Roman Catholic takes this passage as a statement by Jesus that Peter, as pope (and by extension, his successors), would not err in ex cathedra statements; that is to say, statements made concerning matters of faith and morals that are binding on every believer. The word "faith" is here taken to mean "belief" (at least that is what one must assume if the connection is to be made between this passage and papal infallibility), and the word "fail" is taken to mean "fallible." In this way the Catholic apologist can extend this passage as evidence that a pope, when defining matters of belief, will be infallible.

But such meanings ascribed to these words are untenable in this context. "Faith" here is not Peter's belief system but rather Peter's personal trust in God. Jesus' prayer is for Peter's trust not to falter in an ultimate sense: "What is promised to Peter here is not freedom from error but grace to keep faith to the end."[38] That Peter's faith did indeed falter temporarily is borne out by his triple denial of Jesus— indeed, this is what Jesus himself predicts would happen just two verses later: "And you, *once you have turned*, strengthen your brothers." There can be no *turning* without a prior failing. Clearly then, Jesus' prayer was not here intended to be taken as a statement of papal infallibility.

Other passages that are cited in support of papal or ecclesial infallibility are equally without weight. Each one of them fails to make the Catholic apologist's case for infallibility. Take, for example, Christ's statement in Matt 28:20, "I am with you to the end of the age." Catholic apologists argue on the basis of this passage that the Catholic church is infallible. Yet, one is hard-pressed to find anything remotely resembling infallibility in this passage. Christ does not use the word "infallibility" or any equivalent in this passage; nor is the concept of infallibility present here. Is it possible for Christ to be *with us* without our having to be infallible? That seems obvious; otherwise, we would have to conclude that everyone with whom Jesus associated on earth must have been infallible.

The same may be said about John 16:13, which states that the Holy Spirit would guide the apostles into all truth. Catholic apologists take this to mean that the Roman Catholic church from this point will forever be protected from error. But again, there is no support in this passage for an infallible church.[39] The passage certainly suggests that the apostles would receive an infallible deposit of truth (after all, God is guiding them); but we certainly cannot extrapolate from this passage any ongoing activity of infallibility after that deposit. We must seek that kind of information elsewhere.[40]

Another passage to which Catholic apologists appeal in support of this doctrine is 1 Tim 3:15, which states that the church is the "pillar and foundation of the truth." Roman Catholics focus on the word "foundation" and argue that truth *springs from* the church (as the canon of Scripture sprang from the church). Therefore, the church, and not Scripture per se, is the ultimate source of truth. However, this is based on a dubious translation of the word *hedraiôma* (ἑδραίωμα). This word can equally mean "foundation" (in the sense of the *source* of truth) or "support" (in the sense of the *defender* or *protector* truth).[41] In any case, since this word occurs only once in the entire New Testament it is precarious to build an entire doctrine around it.

Another way that Catholic apologists argue for the legitimacy of a pope who has primacy over the entire church is to engage in what I have termed the Peter-Most/Peter-First/Peter-Only argument. For the sake of brevity, we will not go into detail concerning all the passages that are adduced in support of this thesis— nor is it necessary to do so. The argument may be summarized as follows: (1) Peter is mentioned in the gospels more times than any other apostle; (2) In any list of apostles Peter is always mentioned first (or takes the initiative first in any activity); and (3) there are many instances where Peter alone is designated in a certain way, or stands in a special relationship to Jesus. This is held out as proof that Peter is to be seen as the first pope.[42]

The reason we have not listed all the passages used by Catholic apologists to support the primacy of Peter is that we do not disagree with the major thrust of any of the three points above (though there may be some slight disagreements on some of the details). Peter is indeed listed more times in the gospels than any other apostle. He is also almost always listed first in lists of apostles, and in many cases stands alone in designations and roles given by Jesus. The reader may safely agree with these points and still not accept the Roman Catholic apologists' conclusions regarding these texts; namely, that this evidence supports the notion that Peter held primacy over the entire church, and that the pope, by extension, holds primacy over the entire church today.

While we may concede that Peter was a prominent and outspoken member of the early church, when one considers this evidence compared to the evidence supporting the primacy of Paul, an entirely different picture emerges. Paul wrote half of the books included in the New Testament canon— Peter wrote only two. Paul's life and mission are the focal point in Acts, comprising sixteen of its twenty-eight chapters— Peter's ministry comprises approximately eight chapters. Paul was appointed the apostle to the Gentiles (Acts 9:15, 15:7, Rom 11:13, 15:16, Gal 2:7-9, Eph 3:1, 8, 1 Tim 2:7, 2 Tim 1:11)— Peter is said to be the apostle to the Jews only (Gal 2:7-9). Since the church is made up primarily of Gentiles (not Jews), it is odd that Paul should not have primacy afforded to him by the Catholic church.

Moreover, Paul writes that whatever "pillar" Peter may have been in the church made no difference to him: he did not see Peter as having the slightest primacy over him (Gal 2:6). Paul lumps Peter in with James and John when he speaks of the so-called "pillars" of the church (Gal 2:9), not giving any higher status to Peter than to the others. Indeed, in this passage Paul names James *before* Peter (perhaps then James should have primacy instead of Peter!). Paul rebuked Peter to his face for his hypocrisy (Gal 2:11-14). Paul did not submissively address Peter as "Holy Father," "Supreme Pastor," or "Vicar of Christ" and gently point out his mistake. Instead, he publicly censured him! Paul seems to go out of his way ("I said to Peter in front of them all"— v. 14) to show potential followers of Peter that Peter had no more authority than he himself did. Paul denies that any apostle has pre-eminence over him when he says, "I consider myself not in the least inferior to the most eminent apostle" (2 Cor 11:5; 12:11). Paul seems to claim ecclesial preeminence over all of Christendom when he writes, "This is the *rule I* lay down in *all* the churches" (1 Cor 7:17), and claims responsibility for the spiritual welfare of all Christians in his statement to the Corinthians, "Besides everything else, *I face daily the pressure of my concern for all the churches*" (2 Cor 11:28). Obviously, in light of these points, Paul is at least as qualified as Peter (if not more so) to hold ecclesial primacy. Of course, it would be nonsense to conclude from all this that Paul was a pope. But that is just the point; the Catholic apologist engages in special pleading when he points to all the passages that seem to single out Peter in an attempt to demonstrate Petrine primacy, but concludes something completely different about those passages that single out Paul in a very similar way.

One last passage to which Catholic apologists appeal for support of papal primacy is Acts 15. In this chapter we read that the Gentiles were being disrupted by Judaizers who wanted to impose the Mosaic law on the Gentiles. Paul and Barnabas decide to go to Jerusalem to address the issue, and the Jerusalem council convenes. During this meeting many of the church leaders speak on the issue, including the Judaizers, Paul, Barnabas, Peter and James. Scott Hahn argues that Peter exercises his papal prerogative here and makes the final decision in this passage (vv. 7-11), and that the purpose of James' speech afterward (vv. 13-21) is merely to raise a pastoral concern.[43]

But just how Hahn arrives at this conclusion is rather baffling. Peter's address simply relates an experience he had with the Gentile community which he posits as proof that God had already accepted the Gentiles. James is the one who actually decides what would be done about it. James says, "It is my *judgment*, therefore, that we should not make it difficult for the Gentiles who are turning to God" (15:19). The word translated "judgment" here is the verb *krino* (κρίνω) and means "I decide." Peter was simply stating his view, along with all the others, in an attempt to win adherents— nothing more! It was *James* who made the final decision. Hahn's Petrine allegiance seems to preclude any hope of even-handed exegesis of this or any passage where Peter is mentioned.

We have examined the major passages used by Catholic apologists to support the notion of papal primacy and infallibility, and have found in each case that the passage cited cannot bear the weight of the argument that the Catholic apologist places on it. But if the basis for papal infallibility cannot be found in Scripture, can that basis be found in oral tradition? If so, how can we be certain that the tradition is right to begin with if we cannot first establish the basis for infallibility? It would be circular reasoning to argue that oral tradition is infallible simply because oral tradition says it is so.[44]

Nor does the precedent of Old Testament Israel help the cause of the Catholic apologist. The only precedent we have is a nation that through the ages was highly idolatrous, the leaders of which Jesus unreservedly condemned. So again, any basis for the doctrine of an infallible church is conspicuously absent.

What it ultimately comes down to, then, is that the Catholic church is infallible for no other reason than that it says it is infallible. In other words, if we were to ask a Roman Catholic how he can be certain that the pope is correct in his *ex cathedra* pronouncements, the answer would be that the pope is infallible in such matters. But when pressed on how he can be certain that the pope is infallible, the Roman Catholic must ultimately appeal either to dubious exegesis of select biblical passages, or else to the authority of the Catholic church itself which says he is infallible.

Only the dullest mind could fail to see the circular reasoning at work here. The Catholic church has proclaimed the Catholic church to be infallible. Yet, the only way that any Catholic can be certain that this proclamation is itself infallible is first to assume (on decidedly flimsy evidence) the infallibility of the very institution that made the proclamation in the first place.[45] If it is argued that the Catholic church bases its infallibility on the Scriptures, then we are obliged to ask how the Catholic church can be certain it is interpreting those Scriptures correctly— especially in light of the fact that the church itself, until recent times, did not understand those same passages to be teaching ecclesial infallibility.[46]

Examples of Papal Fallibility

Not only is there no basis for the infallibility of the pope, there are, in fact, many counter-examples throughout history. It is important to point out that there do not have to be many counter-examples— by definition, one case of error devastates the entire argument for infallibility. But, as we shall see, there are indeed many. The definition of papal infallibility is as follows:

> The Roman Pontiff, when he speaks *ex cathedra* (that is, when— fulfilling the office of Pastor and Teacher of all Christians— on his supreme Apostolical authority, he defines a doctrine concerning

faith or morals to be held by the Universal Church), through the divine assistance promised him in blessed Peter, is endowed with that infallibility, with which the Divine Redeemer has willed that His Church— in defining doctrine concerning faith or morals— should be equipped: And therefore, that such definitions of the Roman Pontiff of themselves— and not by virtue of the consent of the Church— are irreformable.[47]

Three examples of popes who have erred in their proclamation of a doctrine can be seen in Victor (189-198), Zephyrinus (198-217) and Callistus (217-222)[48], all of whom embraced Sabellianism (the idea that the Father, the Son and the Holy Spirit are one person manifested in three personalities, rather than the orthodox view that they are three persons in one being). This teaching was subsequently condemned as heretical.

Other examples can be seen in Pope Honorius (seventh century) who taught that the monothelite view of Christ (i.e., that he has one will rather than the orthodox position that he has two wills) was "self-evident and beyond controversy"[49]; Pope Zosimus (fifth century) who received confessions of faith from both Pelagius and Ceolestius, officially declared them orthodox, reproved the African bishops who condemned them, and subsequently changed his mind upon discovering that his predecessor (Innocent I) had also condemned these men.[50] Also, Liberius, the bishop of Rome, gave his official endorsement of the Arian position by signing an Arian decree in 358; Felix II (Liberius' predecessor) was openly Arian; and Sixtus V released an error-filled edition of the Latin Bible. Modern Roman Catholic apologists would no doubt want to argue that infallibility does not extend to versions of the Bible. But Bellarmine certainly thought it did, going so far as to suggest that the printer had erred, not the pope, even though Sixtus V corrected the proofs himself![51]

Even the definition of papal infallibility itself is at odds with other official church documents. Specifically, the words, "such definitions of the Roman Pontiff of themselves— and not by virtue of the consent of the Church— are irreformable," conflict with the councils of Pisa, Constance, and Basel, all of which upheld the authority of ecumenical councils over the pope.[52]

To adduce evidence against the infallibility of the Roman Catholic church as a whole, one need look no further than the case of Joan of Arc. Joan was condemned as a heretic by the Catholic church, and subsequently burned at the stake in 1431. This condemnation was revoked twenty-four years later (1455) by the same Catholic church. The complete reversal came in 1920 when the very same Catholic church that condemned and burned Joan of Arc exalted her to sainthood.[53] Since infallibility extends to the canonization of saints,[54] then it must also effectively prevent the condemnation of saints (since, as Keating has pointed out, infallibility is a *negative* protection against error). Indeed, as we have already seen, the key passage that is used to support the primacy (and infallibility) of Peter as pope (Matt 16:17-19; and its extension to bishops in Matt 18:19) is in a context of church discipline. If Rome wants to use these passages to support primacy and infallibility, then it must allow that disciplinary pronouncements by Popes must be infallible. Yet, it is embarrassingly evident that the Catholic church cannot both "bind" and "loose" Joan of Arc and still be infallible. The same holds true of all other condemnations by popes throughout the ages— including those railed against other popes, and including the condemnation of Galileo in the seventeenth century for postulating the Copernican theory of the solar system (the earth revolves around the sun and not vice versa)[55], which condemnation has only recently been lifted!

One might also mention the period known as The Avignon Captivity when Clement V moved the papal see from Rome to Avignon. This "captivity" lasted most of the fourteenth century. Yet, if the see of Peter is in Rome, then is it not true that succession from Peter ceased for a period of approximately seventy years while the see resided in Avignon? Was not Clement V in error when he made the decision to move the see to Avignon; and was he not, in essence, proclaiming that Rome no longer held primacy? How could a pope, who supposedly cannot err in official proclamations, undercut the very foundation of the papacy and still be viewed as making official decisions infallibly?

It is abundantly clear that the decision to move to Avignon was an official one. No pope could casually move the see of Peter from Rome, especially in light of the fact that there was much opposition to the idea[56] — Clement was pro-active in the face of opposition. Was this an issue that pertained to "faith or morals"? That all depends on whether or not is it a doctrine of the Catholic church that the see of Peter resides in Rome, and that Rome *alone* has primacy over all the faithful.

The most recent edition of the Catholic Catechism makes the following points about Rome:

> Particular Churches [diocese] are fully catholic through their communion with one of them, the Church of Rome "which presides in charity." "For with this church, by reason of its pre-eminence, the whole Church, that is faithful everywhere, must necessarily be in accord." Indeed, "from the incarnate Word's descent to us, all Christian churches everywhere have held and hold the great Church that is here [at Rome] to be their only basis and foundation since, according to the Savior's promise, the gates of hell have never prevailed against her."[57] . . . Just as "by the Lord's institution, St. Peter and the rest of the apostles constitute a single apostolic college, so in like fashion the Roman Pontiff, Peter's successor, and the bishops, the successors of the apostles, are related with and united to one another."[58] . . . The Pope, Bishop of Rome and Peter's successor, "is the perpetual and visible source and foundation of the unity both of the bishops and of the whole company of the faithful." "For the Roman Pontiff, by reason of his office as Vicar of Christ, and as pastor of the entire Church has full, supreme, and universal power over the whole Church, a power which he can always exercise unhindered."[59]

The head of the church, according to the statements above, is the *Roman* Pontiff, who alone is *Peter's successor* and who alone is the *Vicar of Christ*. No church is *fully* catholic without communion with the Roman church. The Roman church alone *presides*, is *pre-eminent*, is the *only basis and foundation* since

Christ to the present day, and its head, the *Roman Pontiff*, is the *perpetual and visible* source of unity.[60]

To reiterate the question, Is it a doctrine of the Catholic church that the see of Peter resides in Rome, and that Rome *alone* has primacy over all the faithful? According to the Catholic Catechism it is. The direct implication of the catechetical statements above is that Clement V did indeed err in his official, definite act to move the see of Peter from Rome to Avignon. While the see of Peter resided in Avignon, there was no *Roman* Pontiff who resided over the church; and since there was a period of time (and a lengthy one at that) during which there was no Roman pontiff, then the unavoidable conclusion is that the Roman Pontiff has *not* been a *perpetual* source of unity within the Catholic church. This also entails that succession from Peter was broken for at least seventy years, since where there is no *Roman* Pontiff, there can be no successor. Here we have yet another instance of a pope who steered the Roman Catholic church into error, opposing an official teaching of the Catholic Faith. The doctrine of the infallibility of the pope is thereby necessarily canceled out.

It is naive to hold, along with the catechetical excerpt above, that "from the incarnate Word's descent to us, all Christian churches everywhere have held and hold the great Church that is here [at Rome] to be their *only basis and foundation*," that "with *this* church, *by reason of its pre-eminence*, the whole Church, that is faithful everywhere, must necessarily be in accord," that the *Roman Pontiff* "is the *perpetual* and *visible* source and foundation of the unity both of the bishops and of the whole company of the faithful [in other words, unbroken succession]," and at the same time acknowledge that there was a span of history when there was no Roman Pontiff and when the Church of Rome held no pre-eminent position.[61] In fact, since this statement itself is an "official" teaching,[62] and since it is clearly contradicted by historical facts, it is itself in error; hence, we have another example of a fallible— indeed, *erroneous*—

"official" church teaching.

Immediately after the papal see moved back to Rome, the Catholic cardinals elected Urban VI to be pope. Because of Urban's tendency to be a dictator, the same cardinals deposed him and elected a second pope (Clement VII). The two popes not only condemned each other but also engaged in warfare against each other. Clement finally settled in Avignon with support from France, Spain and Scotland, while Urban remained in Rome with support from Italy, Hungary and England. Urban (whom Catholics would eventually view as the "true" pope) tortured to death those cardinals that resisted him.

This is merely one instance of many where there have been rival popes, each anathematizing the other. The successors of both Urban and Clement continued into the next century. Finally, the cardinals deposed both rival popes in 1409, and replaced them with Alexander V. Since neither of the other popes (in Avignon and Rome) recognized the new pope, there were now three popes vying for the papal seat. Alexander's successor, John XXIII, was eventually forced to give up his position in 1415 after a council pronounced his papal claim invalid. At the same time one of the other popes, Gregory XII, resigned, again leaving only one pope, Benedict XIII. He was deposed two years later, at which time a new pope, Martin V, was elected.

The point of all of this (and the point which Keating[63] seems to miss) is that the last pope (Martin V) was not a direct successor of *any* of the other popes— all were deposed, or they resigned. In fact, if we trace the schism back to its origin, direct succession had been broken for over one-hundred years! Martin V (the pope from which all subsequent popes descended to the present day) was elected illegally, since Benedict XIII was deposed illegally![64] The Catholic Catechism explicitly states that this is so:

> "The college or body of bishops has *no authority unless united with the Roman Pontiff*, Peter's successor, as its head." As such, this col-

lege has "supreme and full authority over the universal church; *but this power cannot be exercised without the agreement of the Roman Pontiff.*"[65] ..."The college of bishops exercises power over the universal church in a solemn manner in an ecumenical council." *But "there never is an ecumenical council which is not confirmed or at least recognized as such by Peter's successor."*[66] [Italics mine]

Obviously, if we accept the truthfulness of the catechetical statement above, we cannot accept the legitimacy of any pope from Martin V on to the present day. There was an improper, illegal, and illegitimate deposition of Benedict and election of Martin— and Martin's successors cannot claim any more legitimacy than he, since legitimacy cannot increase with the passing of time!

But if we are to accept the legitimacy of the current pope, then we cannot accept the truthfulness of the catechetical statement above, nor the one quoted previously. And if we cannot accept these statements, then the statements must again be in error. Any way one wishes to slice it, the church has erred in "official" statements, or is illegitimate by virtue of an illegitimate pope. But if the latter is true, then the church has erred again by claiming an authority for its pope that he does not have. The Roman Catholic apologist is trapped in a catch-22 situation.

This is not the only example of papal illegitimacy,[67] of course, but it is enough to discount papal infallibility from further consideration, since (by the very definition of infallibility) it takes only one exception to nullify the rule. There is little need to go into detail about all of the corrupt medieval popes who were immoral, not only in their own practice, but also in the rules they imposed on others.[68] It simply will not do to argue (as do most Catholic apologists) that a distinction is to be made between what a pope *practices* and what he *proclaims*. One often "teaches" and "proclaims" much more by his actions than by his words.[69] Popes regularly murdered their predecessors,[70] were caught up in gross immorality[71] and idolatry.[72] Popes were regularly deposed unlawfully and replaced by unlawful successors.[73] Other popes were found guilty of heresy.[74]

In his papal Bull *Unam Sanctam* (1302), Boniface VIII declared:

> We are obliged . . . to believe . . . that outside [the Roman Catholic church] there is neither salvation nor remission of sins. . . . Furthermore we *declare, state, define,* and *pronounce* that it is altogether necessary to salvation for every human creature to be subject to the Roman pontiff.[75] [Italics mine]

There can be no doubt by the language used ("declare, state, define, and pronounce") that this statement must be considered an "official" papal declaration.[76] Notice the parallels with the infallible statement regarding Mary's Immaculate Conception:

> To the glory and adornment of the Virgin Mother of God, . . . we, with the authority of our Lord Jesus Christ . . . do *declare, pronounce* and *define* that the doctrine which holds that the Virgin Mary was, in the first instance of her conception, preserved untouched by any taint of original guilt . . . was revealed by God and therefore is to be firmly and steadfastly believed by all the faithful.[77]

Yet the statement from *Unam Sanctam* is contradicted by another "official" statement by the Catholic church:

> [Protestants] who have been justified by faith in Baptism are incorporated into Christ; they therefore have a right to be called Christians, and with good reason are accepted as brothers in the Lord by the children of the Catholic church. . . . Christ's Spirit uses these Churches and ecclesial communities as *means of salvation.*[78] . . .The church knows that she is joined in many ways to the baptized who . . . do not profess the Catholic faith in its entirety or have not preserved unity of communion under the successor of Peter. Those who believe in Christ and have been properly baptized are put in a certain, although imperfect, communion with the Catholic church. With the Orthodox churches, this communion is so profound that it lacks little to attain the fullness that would permit a common celebration of the Lord's Eucharist.[79]

Add to this the words of Innocent III: "Whatever is done contrary to conscience leads to hell . . . as in this matter no one must obey a judge against God, but rather humbly bear the excommunication."[80] In other words, whenever a Catholic teaching violates one's conscience, one must submit to it to be saved according to *Unam Sanctam* and violate it to be saved according to Innocent III. One must submit to the authority of Rome to be saved according to *Unam Sanctam*, but can be saved apart from Rome according to the official Catechism of the Catholic church.

This evidence notwithstanding, Catholic apologists have a convenient way of ensuring that no pope could ever be indicted with the charge of violating standards of infallibility.[81] They first point out that infallibility and impeccability are not identical. Then, after conceding that many popes were indeed immoral, they conveniently dismiss these instances of immorality as "immaterial" since infallibility does not guarantee impeccability.[82] Yet even in those instances where it is clear that a pope made a proclamation regarding (directly or indirectly) a "right" belief, the Catholic apologist always seems to find some reason why this case does not meet the criteria for infallibility[83]; hence, the dogma of infallibility dies the death of a thousand qualifications. What it comes down to is that no matter what instance we point to where a pope appears to be violating the standards of infallibility, the Catholic apologist will *always* and *automatically* argue that extenuating circumstances disallow the application of the standard, so that the pope was not speaking "officially," or was not speaking in conjunction with the bishops, or some other such qualification.

The Roman Catholic notion of papal infallibility strains credulity because it is engineered in such a way as to be completely unfalsifiable. Ultimately, if the pope speaks "officially" on this or that issue— with all the attendant "proclamation" language— how do we know whether or not it is infallible? What if ten years from now another pope "officially" contradicts an "official" statement of the current pope? What will the Catholic apologists say in that case?[84]

One gets the distinct impression that Catholic apologists will treat this case the same way they have treated all other "apparent" instances of papal error, perhaps countering that the first pope simply lied about his official statement, that it never was "official" to begin with, and that this case (as with all the others) falls under the rubric of the pope's impeccability, not infallibility. The Catholic church never said (they might argue) that the pope could not *lie* about making an infallible statement. And the fact that all bishops agreed with the lie proves nothing. It merely means that bishops are capable of lying along with the pope they support. None of this argues against infallibility, since none of it has to do with "truly official" statements of the church.

It is simply a no-win situation. It is abundantly clear by reading the Catholic apologists that they will not accept any evidence that overturns papal infallibility. No matter how badly a pope has erred— morally, doctrinally, or otherwise— no charge against papal infallibility will ever stick.[85] It would save us a lot of time if Catholic apologists will simply admit this.

In reality, this is nothing short of historical gymnastics and wishful reconstructions at best— and blatant dishonesty at worst. There were no distinctions between "official" and "unofficial" statements made by popes of antiquity— they simply meant what they said and said what they meant. It is only the desire somehow to vindicate papal infallibility that the modern Catholic apologist has introduced the terms "official" and "unofficial."[86]

What About Church Councils?

The Council of Chalcedon, which, it cannot be denied, was certainly an ecumenical council, is often either down-played by Catholic apologists or not mentioned at all in discussions pertaining to infallibility— and for good reason; its canon 28 grants Constantinople (which it calls *New Rome*) equal privilege with Rome itself. Further, it states that the reason the Fathers gave privileges to "Old Rome" in the first place is not because it was the see of Peter, but rather because it was the "imperial city," just as Constantinople was becoming.[87] The difficulty with this canon is that it contradicts the notion of the sole primacy of Rome as currently held by Roman Catholics. Yet Catholics also believe that decisions reached at ecumenical councils are infallible (including those of Chalcedon), and so again find themselves in the precarious position of having to believe two conflicting propositions; namely, (1) that Rome *alone* reigns supreme over the entire church, and (2) that Constantinople has equal privileges with Rome.

On the other hand, it is evident in the early church councils that the primary verification of the truthfulness of each council was not in the infallibility of the decisions reached, but rather in the *acceptance* of those decisions by all the churches. This was true for Athanasius who regarded acceptance by the church as a whole as of "fundamental importance."[88] In sharp contrast, most recent Catholic dogmas (such as the infallibility of the pope and many Marian dogmas) do not have universal acceptance by the church; the majority of the church (Eastern Orthodoxy, Anglicanism, and Protestantism) do not accept these dogmas. As Küng points out:

> The determining factor is not the will to make infallible definitions, but the intrinsic truth of the council's decisions that inevitably imposes itself on the Church's sense of faith.[89]

Councils are therefore not infallible, but useful in defining what Christianity already believes— they are certainly not useful in defining what Christianity *is to* believe![90] Councils have erred, corrected each other, and contradicted each other. As Küng has shown:

> The councils of Nicaea and Sardica assumed . . . there was only one hypostasis of the Godhead . . . [while] the First Council of Constantinople and the Council of Chalcedon assumed . . . there were three . . . . . Chalcedon in 451 rejected the decisions of the Second Council of Ephesus of 449 . . . [and] Constantinople in 754 rejected the veneration of images, which the Second Council of Nicaea in 787 approved. . . . Chalcedon in 451 specifically amended the decision of the First

Council of Ephesus in 431 [which had condemned Nestorianism] . . . [and] recognized the claims of Antioch theology [Nestorius' view] and specifically rejected the central doctrine of Alexandrine christology [Cyril's view] which had dominated the two councils of Ephesus. . . . Thus, the Patriarch Nestorius, who was condemned in 431 and 449, would have been able to subscribe completely to the formulation of faith laid down at Chalcedon in 451, to which Cyril, the leading spirit at Ephesus I, could have subscribed only with open or secret reservations, and to which Dioscorus, the leading spirit at Ephesus II . . . could not have subscribed at all.[91]

To this we might add the voice of Augustine on the infallibility of church councils:

The writings of bishops after the settlement of the canon may be refuted both by the perhaps wiser words of anyone more experienced in the matter and by the weightier authority and more scholarly prudence of other bishops, and also by councils, if something in them perhaps has deviated from the truth; and that even councils held in particular regions or provinces must without quibbling give way to the authority of plenary councils of the whole Christian world; and that even the earlier plenary councils are often corrected by later ones, if as a result of practical experience something that was closed is opened, something that was hidden becomes known.[92]

It is clear by the above statement that Augustine could not have believed in the infallibility of church councils, for something infallible cannot later be corrected.

Alternatives To Infallibility

But if not infallibility, then what standard do we have to measure whether this or that individual or group holds the truth? Not surprisingly, Jesus gave us that very standard before he left this earth.[93] Jesus said in Matt 7:15-23:

Watch out for false prophets. They come to you in sheep's clothing, but inwardly they are ferocious wolves. By their fruit you will recognize them. Do people pick grapes from thornbushes, or figs from thistles? Likewise every good tree bears good fruit, but a bad tree bears bad fruit. A good tree cannot bear bad fruit, and a bad tree cannot bear good fruit. Every tree that does not bear good fruit is cut down and thrown into the fire. Thus, by their fruit you will recognize them. "Not everyone who says to me, 'Lord, Lord,' will enter the kingdom of heaven, but only he who does the will of my Father who is in heaven. Many will say to me on that day, 'Lord, Lord, did we not prophesy in your name, and in your name drive out demons and perform many miracles?' Then I will tell them plainly, 'I never knew you. Away from me, you evildoers!'

Jesus tells us in no uncertain terms how we are to test those who claim to represent him. Even if a group can claim miracles, it is no guarantee it is of God. Even if those in this group prophesy in Christ's name, or convey Christian truth accurately, it is inconsequential. The only criteria Jesus gives here is the bearing of fruit. Just what is this fruit to which Jesus refers?

Jesus himself tells us what this "fruit" is: it is doing "the will of the Father." Those who do not qualify are called "evildoers." Therefore, the "fruit" mentioned here must be of a moral quality. None of the other things mentioned is sufficient according to Jesus. Religious groups can perform miracles, drive out demons and prophesy truth to their heart's content; but if they do not bear good, moral fruit, they are automatically disqualified from further consideration. Jesus never "knew" them, nor has he recognized their authority.

The Catholic church itself must be measured against this standard. Does it pass the test? Yes and no. Until the late Middle Ages, the Catholic church (although aberrant in most of its ecclesiology) could have passed Jesus' moral test. This is not the case, however, for the Roman Catholic church from the late Middle Ages on to the Reformation. With the advent of Indulgences, the Crusades, the Inquisition, multiple popes (each condemning the others to hell), and other such corruption, the Catholic church became disqualified from further consideration. The success and timeliness of the Reformation was God's way of stating that fact.

But what of the scriptural texts that indicate the church will not fail, such as Matt 16:18 where our Lord says: "I will build my church and the gates of hell will not prevail against it"? Or again, Matt 28:20: "I am with you always, even to the end of the age"? If not ecclesial infallibility, what do these passages teach? Both teach simply the *indestructibility* of the church, not its infallibility. They are guarantees that the church will live on, and that there will always be those who make up Christ's body on earth. It does not guarantee, however, that an institution called the Catholic church would always be preserved in the truth. The Holy Spirit "blows where it pleases," and is not obliged to reside in an institution that has strayed so far from the apostolic deposit. He preserves his church through individuals who are eager to do his will. This he has promised, and this he has carried out.

Christianity does not cease to exist simply because a static institution that has outlived its usefulness ceases to maintain the truth of God. Rather, God moves from one movement of the church to the next, appointing whomever he wishes as the guardian of the truth. He resides in Christianity as a whole, not in a denomination called the Catholic church. He resides in his people whether they happen to be Eastern Orthodox, Catholic, or Evangelical. The indestructibility of the church guarantees that truth will be preserved in the hearts of his people, not in papal declarations. It means that the masses of his people will always believe truth, even if mixed in with the truth they also subscribe to some degree of error. Indeed, the truth of the deity of Christ during the Nicaean controversy was not upheld so much by the decision of a council as by the refusal on the part of the laity to accept a low view of Christ.[94] This illustrates nicely how God has preserved his truth through his remnant— not by magisterial decrees, but by general acceptance on the part of his people. Ironically, the majority of Christianity (Eastern Orthodoxy, Reformed churches, the Anglican church, as well as early Christianity) rejects the primacy of Rome and the notion of its infallibility, thereby making such claims suspect as to their truthfulness. Yet, they all (with one voice) believe in the indefectibility of the church universal. Catholic belief in these things must therefore be seen as a mere aberration of normative Christian belief.[95]

Do We Need An Infallible Interpreter?

One of the reasons why the Catholic church sees a need for an infallible pope is so that we may know with certainty what the correct interpretation of any given biblical passage is. With so many conflicting interpretations of Scripture, how else could we be sure of the correct interpretation? Catholic apologists see the Evangelical as being in a dilemma in this regard. True, the Evangelical can defer to the infallibility of the Scriptures, but how does the Evangelical know he is interpreting them correctly? How can he be certain that his interpretation is correct over against, say, the Jehovah's Witness interpretation?[96]

Hahn thinks he has solved this dilemma by introducing an infallible interpreter of Scripture; namely, the pope and the magisterium.[97] But Hahn has merely advanced the dilemma one step. How can Hahn be certain that his interpretation of the infallible interpreter is correct? What makes *his* interpretation of the papal decrees, councils, and encyclicals correct over against a more moderate Catholic understanding of these?[98] Who will infallibly interpret the infallible interpreter? And after that, who will infallibly interpret the infallible interpreter of the infallible interpreter? All Hahn has accomplished with his argument is to postulate the necessity of an endless series of infallible interpreters, so that at the end of the day, each individual needs to be infallible in order to interpret the infallible interpreter.[99]

Patrick Madrid attempts to clarify the need for an infallible interpreter with the statement "I never said you stole money."[100] Madrid points out that this one statement could be interpreted in a number of different ways, depending on the emphasis one gives to each word. For instance, "*I* never said you stole money" would imply that someone else said it, not I. Or, "I never *said* you stole money" might imply that, while I did not explicitly say it, I nevertheless thought it. Or, "I never said you stole *money*" might imply that you stole something else instead of money. Madrid argues on this basis that we need an infallible interpreter who could accurately tell us where the emphasis should be placed. He compares the infallible interpreter to someone who happened to be in the same room with the speaker when the statement was originally given.

But Madrid's analogy breaks down on two points. First, while it is true that if we had only the above statement by itself, there would be some question as to the meaning of the statement; yet rarely is this the case with Scripture. There is always a *context* surrounding each statement, and it is this context that points the way to a correct interpretation. For instance, suppose there were an entire paragraph surrounding Madrid's lone statement: "They asked me several questions about it. But through it all, I never said you stole money. I kept insisting that it was John who stole it." It is clear in such a context (even though none of the words in the original statement is italicized) that it is the word *you* that is to be emphasized here. A different context might demand that another word be emphasized. The point is, while Madrid and others might find it convenient to rely on a supposed infallible interpreter, there is no need to do that. God has given us the tools of thought and understanding (and illumination from the Holy Spirit) to determine the meaning of Scripture.

The second point at which Madrid's analogy breaks down is that no pope was ever in a room with any of the writers of the New Testament. If the pope had been on the scene when Jesus originally spoke his messages to his disciples, Evangelicals might well give due weight to the pope's understanding of those words.[101] But the fact is, neither he nor anyone else living was there.

To What Extent is the Church Infallible?

We need to pause here and examine the Catholic apologists' argument regarding the need of an infallible interpreter more closely. It is very curious indeed that while the Catholic apologist insists that we need (1) the collection of the New Testament books (the canon) to be infallible, and (2) an infallible ruling on the meaning of New Testament Scripture, we somehow do not need an infallible ruling on the Greek manuscripts behind those Scriptures. There are four traditions (or families) of New Testament manuscripts from which to choose, and even within the four traditions there are no two manuscripts completely identical in every reading of the text.[102] The Roman Catholic church for centuries used the Byzantine text type, but now uses the Eclectic text (which is primarily an Alexandrian text type).

Are we to assume, then, that the infallible Roman church was for most of its existence wrong in its choice of manuscript traditions? Moreover, how could an infallible church which requires an infallible canon and an infallible interpretation *not* require an infallible Greek text to be handed down to them from their infallible predecessors? Catholics cannot know for certain which readings are original and which are not. They must simply trust scholars (both Catholic and Protestant) to give their best opinion in such matters— a decidedly *fallible* authority. So, at best, a Catholic can claim to have an infallible canon and an infallible interpretation of a given passage of Scripture, but he cannot be certain that the passage in question is even the correct reading of the original.

But the Catholic apologists' dilemma is even more severe than this. Catholic apologists point to the decisions of Hippo and Carthage in regard to the New Testament canon as infallible decisions of the church whose authority Evangelicals implicitly accept. Yet both Hippo and Carthage were local synods, not councils, and the Roman Catholic church does not officially recognize local synods as being infallible. When the Catholic apologist is presented with this fact, appeal is often made to the "ordinary magisterium" of the church (by which is often meant that local synods *can* be infallible if a thousand years later the church still believes in the doctrines those synods defined).[103] Yet the same synods that defined the New Testament canon for

Rome (and which Catholic apologists claim were infallible) also defined an Old Testament Canon that *differs in content* from the Old Testament canon to which Rome now holds[104]— which means that the Catholic apologist wants us to believe that we must rely on the infallible decision of the church for our New Testament, while at the same time themselves rejecting the decision of that *same* church gathered at the *same* synod in regard to the contents of their Old Testament canon.

The point of all this is to show that of the remaining two infallible pillars to which Rome lays claim (infallible canon and infallible interpretation), the former *cannot* be infallible because it differs with Rome's current position. One may also legitimately ask why the "ordinary magisterium" was not operative in regard to handing down accurate manuscripts of the New Testament. Isn't preserving the content of the word of God at least as important as preserving the content of the canon and the interpretation of that content?

So if those who were entrusted to accurately pass down the manuscripts erred so badly as to have misplaced the best and oldest manuscripts for almost the entire existence of the Roman Catholic church, then what good reason do we have to ascribe infallibility to them in their decision about the canon? Indeed, once we have established that Hippo and Carthage were never infallible decisions to begin with, and that the manuscript tradition passed down by the church was itself decidedly flawed, all we have left of Roman infallibility is the *interpretation* of Scripture— to which we now turn.

The Perspicuity of the Scriptures

Catholic apologists often claim that the Protestant principle of *sola Scriptura* leads to an endless barrage of interpretations about every verse of Scripture. In fact, Catholic apologists have made too much of the differences of interpretations among Protestants. The Catholic church itself has at least as many interpretations of the Scriptures— not to mention official church teachings— as do Protestant denominations.[105] The sword cuts both ways here. If Catholic apologists want to paint a picture of complete confusion of interpretation within Protestantism, they must own up to the fact that Catholics are in just as precarious a situation.[106] It does not help their case in the least to postulate an infallible interpreter. The Catholic apologists' concept of a unity of belief in Catholicism is illusory.

Catholic apologists have attempted to paint the New Testament as a fuzzy, incomprehensible document that is shrouded in fog and muddy symbols— much like an ancient allegory which has no plain meaning but whose signification is comprehensible only to the spiritually elite. Both Paul and Jesus emphatically deny this kind of elitism. Jesus praised his Father because he had not revealed his truth to the "wise" but to "babes" (Matt 11:25; Luke 10:21). Paul insisted that God has confounded the wisdom of the wise with the simplicity of the gospel (1 Cor 1:18-31). The point of both Jesus and Paul is clearly that the average person with average intelligence is capable of understanding the truth of God without the aid of an infallible interpreter.[107]

Indeed, had Jesus and Paul subscribed to anything like the Catholic notion of the necessity of an infallible interpreter, we might expect statements such as: "I praise you Father, because you have not revealed this to the average person, but have revealed it to your appointed spokesman." Or, "God has confounded the wisdom of the simple, and revealed his truth to elite spiritual interpreters." Thankfully, no such teaching may be found in the pages of the New Testament.

All this, of course, is not to say there are no "difficult" passages in the Bible. Clearly there are. But none of these passages adversely affects our understanding of what is clearly proclaimed in the Scriptures. Catholic apologists want a neat, clear-cut way of knowing what every passage of Scripture means. Yet, even the Catholic church does not offer that kind of help (even if one accepts the notion of an infallible interpreter), since there are no "official" interpretations of the Scriptures by the church. Some Catholics are under the impression that there are six, seven, or eight such passages of Scripture. However, Raymond Brown (arguably *the* foremost Scripture scholar in Catholicism today) has written, "In terms of what we might call the literal sense of scripture, i.e., what a verse meant when it was first written, it is doubtful that the Roman Catholic Church has ever defined the meaning of any passage."[108]

With this statement by Brown, the final leg of Roman infallibility crumbles.[109] Every step in the process for which the Catholic apologist must claim infallibility in order to have an advantage over Evangelicalism has been shown to be non-existent: From the infallible passing down of accurate copies of inerrant manuscripts (not to mention infallibly preserving the originals), to the infallible decision about the extent of the canon, to the infallible interpretation of Scripture, to the infallible understanding of all church teachings in each individual Catholic— all have been shown to be severely wanting.

At the end of the day, the Roman Catholic has no advantage over the Evangelical. Both have the infallible Scriptures, both have reasoning faculties, both have the ability to gain biblical knowledge through rigorous study, access to the views of the fathers as well as of current scholars, and, to the extent that each one is open to receiving his ministry of illumination, both have recourse to the Holy Spirit for help in understanding the Scriptures.

But if there is no infallible interpreter, has God then left us completely defenseless in our understanding of Scripture? On the contrary; God has provided his people with a built-in "lie detector" as it were. John speaks of this in his first epistle:

> But you have an anointing from the Holy One, and all of you know the truth. I do not write to you because you do not know the truth, but because you do know it and because no lie comes from the truth. Who is the liar? It is the man who denies that Jesus is the Christ. Such

a man is the antichrist— he denies the Father and the Son. No one who denies the Son has the Father; whoever acknowledges the Son has the Father also. See that what you have heard from the beginning remains in you. If it does, you also will remain in the Son and in the Father. And this is what he promised us— even eternal life. I am writing these things to you about those who are trying to lead you astray. As for you, the anointing you received from him remains in you, and you do not need anyone to teach you. But as his anointing teaches you about all things and as that anointing is real, not counterfeit— just as it has taught you, remain in him (1 John 2:20-27).

John's words make it clear that there is no need for an infallible interpreter. His stated reason for writing this passage is that there are those who are "trying to lead [his readers] astray" (v. 26).[110] His counsel for dealing with these false teachers is simply this: "you do not need *anyone* to teach you" precisely because "his anointing teaches you about all things" (v. 27). The "anointing" to which John refers here is the indwelling of the Holy Spirit, which John believes is sufficient to guard against heresy.

It is rather doubtful that a Catholic apologist would— or, indeed, could— respond to the readers' situation in the same way John has done. The Catholic apologist would instead have to insist that the readers do indeed need the church to teach them, and that they are to submit to its teaching magisterium. The difference between John's answer and the Catholic apologist's answer betrays the vast difference in the underlying assumptions held by each. The Catholic apologist contends that we cannot be certain of the correct interpretation of Scripture— and therefore, truth— unless an infallible interpreter is at hand to inform us. Yet when the question is "how do we know that what any given teacher espouses is the truth," John does not portray the average believer as a defenseless dullard who is unable to stand up against heresy and who is in need of an infallible interpreter. In fact, he says just the opposite: "But you have an anointing from the Holy One, and all of you know the truth."

So far from the Catholic apologists' notion of an impotent believer who encounters only confusion when sorting out truth from error, John insists that we *all know the truth* because of the "anointing" we have received from the "Holy One." This anointing "remains" in us, so that we do not need a human teacher to discern error for us (much less an infallible interpreter).[111] That John is not addressing any so-called magisterium in these verses is evident from 2:12-14, where he addresses spiritual "children," "young men," and "fathers." His words in 2:20-27 apply equally to all three groups.

Paul affirms the same teaching in 1 Cor 2:10-16: "We have... received the Spirit of God, *that we may understand* what God has freely given us... The spiritual man makes judgments about all things." The Catholic apologist, by postulating the need for an infallible interpreter, diminishes the work of the Holy Spirit.

What is the Meaning of 2 Peter 1:20?

Based on 2 Pet 1:20, Catholics believe that the church magisterium alone has the means by which to interpret Scripture correctly. The Roman Catholic rendition of this passage, complete with v. 21, is as follows:

> "Know this first of all, that there is no prophecy of scripture that is a matter of personal interpretation, for no prophecy ever came through human will; but rather human beings moved by the holy Spirit spoke under the influence of God." [112]

Roman Catholics take the view that Peter meant to say in this passage that no Scripture is of any *private* interpretation; that is to say, no one but the magisterium can be assured of an infallible interpretation. Peter then (it is argued) is here laying the foundation that would preclude any attempt to undermine the authority of the church by an appeal to the Scriptures alone.

In his tape series,[113] Scott Hahn notes that some Protestant scholars agree with the Catholic understanding of this passage, citing E. Käsemann as one example. Hahn contends that he is simply being honest with the text when Käsemann notes that 2 Pet 1:20 gives credence to the Catholic notion of "no private interpretations." Hahn drives his point home by reminding us that Käsemann is a *Protestant* scholar.

However, it must be pointed out that Käsemann is a *liberal* Protestant scholar. We have already noted that the Catholic apologists' tendency to lump together all Protestants into one package is illegitimate. Käsemann does not even believe that 2 Peter was written by Peter, even though the author explicitly identifies himself as Peter. Jesus himself stated, "I have spoken to you of earthly things and you do not believe; how then will you believe if I speak to you of heavenly things?" (John 3:12). Käsemann errs on his assessment of *who* wrote 2 Peter (a comparatively historical, earthly question). Is it likely then, based on Jesus' words, that Käsemann will be more accurate when he interprets Scripture (a comparatively spiritual question)?

Hahn is very selective in his use of scholars, and he seems to think that if a professing Protestant agrees with a Catholic teaching, that very fact validates that teaching. Would Hahn also agree with liberal Catholic scholars (such as Pheme Perkins and others) who believe that Jesus was rebuking Mary in John 2:4?[114] Would he agree with Raymond Brown and others who assert that the Catholic church's official teaching on the inspiration of Scripture is that inspiration extends only to those passages which pertain to matters of salvation?[115] It seems unlikely that Hahn would conclude that *these* scholars are simply being honest with the text, and it seems clear that Hahn's criteria for truth is not whether a scholar (Catholic or Evangelical) is being honest with the text, but whether or not that scholar agrees with Hahn and his view of what the Catholic church teaches.

Then, just what is the proper understanding of 2 Peter 1:20? Historically, there have been two schools of thought on this passage. The Catholic school of thought has already been noted. This view sees this passage as referring to the *interpretation* of Scripture. The second school of thought sees this passage as referring to the *origin* of Scripture, not its interpretation. The question at hand is, Which of these interpretations makes the most sense of the context?

Peter has already pointed out that the Messiah has come, and that he (along with others) was an eye-witness: "We did not follow cleverly invented stories when we told you about the power and coming of our Lord Jesus Christ, but we were eyewitnesses of his majesty" (v. 16); and that he (along with others) heard the voice of God confirming it:

> "For he received honor and glory from God the Father when the voice came to him from the Majestic Glory, saying, 'This is my Son, whom I love; with him I am well pleased.' We ourselves heard this voice that came from heaven when we were with him on the sacred mountain (vv. 17-18)."

Because of the coming of the Messiah, all of the Old Testament prophecies made about his coming are thereby proved true. Peter makes this point in v. 19: "And we have the word of the prophets made more certain." But that is not all he says about the word of the prophets. He also exhorts us "to pay attention to it, as to a light shining in a dark place, until the day dawns and the morning star rises" (v. 19). In other words, the Scriptures have been validated as to their truthfulness. As a result, we may now have *full* confidence in them to guide us (if, indeed, there were any reservations to begin with). With this in mind Peter writes vv. 20-21.

The question becomes, Is Peter changing the subject from *confidence* in the Scriptures to *danger* in interpreting them by warning us against private interpretations? Or rather, is he reinforcing the theme of this confidence by stating the reason for such confidence; namely, because no prophesy of Scripture ever originated through man, but rather through the Holy Spirit?[116] The Greek word translated "interpretation" in v. 20 is *epiluseôs* (ἐπιλύσεως), and means literally "an unraveling/a releasing."[117] The question is, what *kind* of "releasing" is Peter writing about? Does he mean the releasing of the *meaning* of the prophecy (i.e., "interpretation," the Catholic understanding)? Or, does he mean the releasing of the *origin* of the prophecy?

The entire Greek text of v. 20 literally reads: "Knowing this first, that no prophecy of Scripture comes about of its own releasing." The problem with the first view above (unraveling or releasing of the *meaning* of Scripture) is that it cannot account for the word *ginomai* (γίνομαι, "becomes/originates"). If we adopt this meaning, the passage would read: "Knowing this first, that no prophecy of Scripture *becomes* (or, originates) of its own interpretation." This is awkward, makes little sense of the text, and makes even less sense of the context. On the other hand, a literal translation of this passage clearly lends support to the view that it is the *origin* of Scripture that is in view here: "Knowing this first, that no prophecy of Scripture *becomes* (or, originates) of its own releasing (i.e., its own origin)." Unlike the Catholic understanding of this passage, this rendition makes good sense of the Greek words used and flows well with all that comes before.

But let us apply still another test to both interpretations. How well does each one stand up when viewed in light of v. 21?

The Catholic View	The Evangelical View
Above all, you must understand that no prophecy of Scripture came about by any private interpretation. *For prophecy never had its origin in the will of man, but men spoke from God as they were carried along by the Holy Spirit.*	Above all, you must understand that no prophecy of Scripture came about of its own (or, of the prophet's own[118]) origin. *For prophecy never had its origin in the will of man, but men spoke from God as they were carried along by the Holy Spirit.*

If we are to adopt the Catholic understanding of this passage, then it must be insisted that v. 21 has very little to do with v. 20.[119] On this view, v. 20 refers to private interpretations of Scripture; but v. 21 clearly refers to the origin of the Scriptures.

This is not to say that Peter cannot address both concepts in the same passage, but it is exceedingly unlikely that he does so.[120] The reason is that Peter begins v. 21 with the word "for" (Gr., *gar* [γαρ]). Exegetes call this an "explanatory for," since it is intended to introduce an explanation of what precedes it. But if v. 21 is an explanation of v. 20, then how does the statement "Scripture never had its origin in man" *explain* why there can be no *private interpretations*? If the Catholic view is adopted, it must also be admitted that these two verses are connected awkwardly at best.

On the other hand, if we adopt the second interpretation of v. 20, then v. 21 follows very naturally. It is easy to see how the statement "Scripture never had its origin in man," explains the statement "no prophecy of Scripture came about of its own (or the prophet's own) origin." Indeed, on this view, it is difficult to see how v. 20 could have been penned without also including v. 21. In any case, the Catholic understanding of this passage is rendered deficient, both contextually and linguistically.

Concluding Remarks

We have spent much time dealing with the issues of papal and ecclesial infallibility and authority; and we have found that the Roman Catholic interpretation of the Scripture passages adduced in support of these teachings is itself deficient. It is not so much that the Catholic interpretation numbers among several good options from which to choose. It is rather the case that the Catholic interpretation does not come close to qualifying as a valid option. We are therefore forced to conclude that the Roman Catholic notion of papal and ecclesial infallibility is without biblical support, and as such must be rejected.

Chapter Two

The Nature of the Church

The history of widespread corruption and abuse in the Catholic church throughout the centuries is well documented, and most Catholic apologists make no attempt to deny it. While most Evangelicals are quick to call into question the legitimacy of an organization so plagued with corruption, Scott Hahn argues that we need not view the Catholic church's corrupt history as an argument against her legitimacy. He marvels at the seeming indestructibility of the Catholic church, pointing out that sometimes the church was without armies, sometimes without scholars, and sometimes *even without saints!* Yet, the church lived on. According to Hahn, all of this serves to illustrate the indestructibility of the Catholic church.[121]

This is an odd contention to say the least. One is left wondering, just what is the church in Hahn's view? Is it, as the New Testament portrays it, a living organism— a body of believers who make up the body of Christ? Or, is it rather a lifeless institution that sometimes consists of believers and other times not? Apparently to Hahn, the church can be a body of unbelievers, so long as God keeps those unbelievers from doctrinal error.

This notion is of course refuted many times over in the New Testament. The writer of Hebrews, for example, makes it clear that while the Old Covenant was based on descent from Abraham (that is, one was born into the covenant), the New Covenant is based on a personal relationship with God: "No longer will a man teach his neighbor, or a man his brother, saying, 'Know the Lord,' because *they will all know me, from the least of them to the greatest*" (Heb 8:11). So far from a church that contains no saints, the writer of Hebrews insists there is no one included in the New Covenant that is not a saint. To postulate a church without saints (as Hahn does) is a concept quite foreign to the New Testament writers.

On the other hand, Hahn's statement is very telling. The church, in Hahn's view, is not necessarily "a chosen people, a royal priesthood, a holy nation, a people belonging to God" (1 Pet 2:9); indeed, it may very well consist of nothing more than "scoundrels" and "infidels." If this is the kind of "church" Hahn has in mind then there certainly can be no objection to a reformation which steers it back to the Scriptures— or, indeed, a complete break with such an institution. Jesus has ensured that his truth would be preserved throughout the ages— but he gave no indication that it would be safeguarded by a lifeless institution that *called itself* "the church."[122] This is not to say that he did not use the Catholic church to accomplish his will until the Reformation. God is flexible, and he can use a number of creative means to guard the truth— including anything from corrupt political power to corrupt ecclesial power.

Yet, somewhat surprisingly, Hahn's view of the church is not the official view of the Catholic church. The Catholic Catechism states:

> "The Church . . . is held, as a matter of faith, to be *unfailingly* holy."... The Church, then, is "*the holy People of God*," and her members are called "saints."[123] [Italics mine]

If this is how the Catholic Catechism defines the church, then Hahn's view must be discounted. If, as the Catechism states, the church *is* the holy people of God, and the church is *unfailingly* holy, then, at the end of the day, where there are no saints, there can be no church. Taking into account what Hahn so obviously points out about church history (viz., there were periods of time when there were no saints in the Catholic church) we must conclude that the Catholic church during those periods was not the church of Jesus Christ. And if this can be confirmed for *any* period of time, then the Catholic church must be disregarded from any further consideration. Why so? Because Jesus himself promised that the "gates of Hell shall not prevail against it" (Matt 16:18). If it can be confirmed by history that the people of God ceased to exist within the Catholic church, then we must look elsewhere for those people of God. The fact is, the aggregate of the people of God who make up the true church transcends any institutional shell, both then and now. Indeed, there have often been reform movements within the Catholic church itself! This is where the true church is to be found during all those years of corruption prior to the Reformation.

Is There a Universal Church?

Catholic apologists make the same mistake about the church that the Jews of Jesus' day made about Israel. The Jews were mistaken in thinking that spiritual heritage comes through physical descent, and that "true" Israel was a visible institution. Paul corrected this error in Romans 9:6-8 where he writes:

> It is not as though God's word had failed. For not all who are descended from Israel are Israel. Nor because they are his descendants are they all Abraham's children. On the contrary, "It is through Isaac that your offspring will be reckoned." In other words, it is not the natural children who are God's children, but it is the children of the promise who are regarded as Abraham's offspring.

Catholic apologists, guilty of the same error, mistakenly think that the church is solely a visible organization.[124] They base this on Jesus' words in Matt 5:13-15:

> You are the salt of the earth. But if the salt loses its saltiness, how can it be made salty again? It is no longer good for anything, except to be thrown out and trampled by men. You are the light of the world. A city on a hill cannot be hidden. Neither do people light a lamp and put it under a bowl. Instead they put it on its stand, and it gives light to everyone in the house.

Does this passage prove what Catholic apologists want it to prove— namely, a church that is visible by virtue of an institution? Even if it does refer to this, the Catholic church would be precluded from consideration. Why so? Because of the rest of the passage, which the Catholic apologist omits. How does Jesus himself apply the principle of this passage? "In the same way, let your light shine before men, that they may see your good deeds and praise your Father in heaven" (v. 16). Contrary to the contention of the Catholic apologist, according to Jesus the church is not visible by virtue of an institution, but by virtue of individual good deeds. But even if this passage did mean what Catholic apologists claim (namely, proof for the legitimacy of an institution), the Catholic church, beset for several centuries by blatant immorality, is disqualified from further consideration in any case.

Catholic apologists misrepresent the Evangelical as teaching only a "spiritual" church, one that is essentially "invisible." However, although the Westminster Confession does use the term "invisible" to describe the universal church, what is meant by the term is not that the church cannot be seen (as so many Catholic apologists mistakenly assume in their arguments against this notion), but that the church transcends time and geographic locale.[125] That is to say, Evangelicals view the church as the body of Christ composed of all believers irrespective of their era, location or denominational affiliation. Paul makes this clear in Eph 5:25-27:

> Husbands, love your wives, just as Christ loved the church and gave himself up for her to make her holy, cleansing her by the washing with water through the word, and to present her to himself as a radiant church, without stain or wrinkle or any other blemish, but holy and blameless.

This cannot refer strictly to a "visible" church, for then how would those who are not yet visible (i.e., those who have not yet been born), or those who are no longer visible (i.e., those who had passed away by the time of this letter) be included in the presentation of Christ's church to himself, or be among those for whom Christ died? Indeed, as we noted earlier, the Catholic Catechism itself insists that the church is much broader than the institution called the Catholic church:

[Protestants] who have been justified by faith in Baptism are incorporated into Christ; they therefore have a right to be called Christians, and with good reason are accepted as brothers in the Lord by the children of the Catholic church... Christ's Spirit uses these Churches and ecclesial communities as means of salvation.[126]

Catholic apologists are in a precarious position; for the instant they deny the concept of a "universal church" (i.e., a church that is comprised of believers regardless of denominational affiliation), they also contradict the words of their own catechism. Their charge that Evangelicals do not make up a "visible" church on the earth is therefore without merit. Even if we were to grant the Catholic apologists' definition of "church," one is left to explain how the Evangelical church is any less visible than the Catholic church. One need merely walk into any meeting of any Evangelical church on any Sunday to be convinced that when the church meets together it is certainly not invisible. Another kind of visibility occurs when the church is taking a stand on the truth of the Gospel message. To the extent that the Christian message does not escape the notice of the unbelieving world, to that extent the Evangelical church is indeed a visible "city on the hill."

Chapter Three

Apostolic Succession

Another issue of importance to this discussion is the Catholic teaching of apostolic succession. Roman Catholics believe that there is an unbroken line of papal succession from Peter to the present. They argue that since the idea of apostolic succession can be found in the writings of the early church fathers, and they themselves claim to be able to trace successors all the way back to Peter, apostolic succession must therefore have been taught by the apostles. This claim is refuted on several points.

To begin with, it does not follow that simply because one can find patristic evidence for apostolic succession, apostolic succession must therefore be of apostolic origin. Hahn, for instance, quotes Irenaeus, who claims that he can name every successor from Peter to his day.[127]

> It is within the power of all, therefore, in every Church, who may wish to see the truth, to contemplate clearly the tradition of the apostles manifested throughout the whole world; and we are in a position to reckon up those who were by the apostles instituted bishops in the Churches, and [to demonstrate] the succession of these men to our own times. . . . [we do this, I say,] by indicating that tradition derived from the apostles, of the very great, the very ancient, and universally known Church founded and organized at Rome by the two most glorious apostles, Peter and Paul; as also [by pointing out] the faith preached to men, which comes down to our time by means of the successions of the bishops. . . . The blessed apostles, then, having founded and built up the Church, committed into the hands of Linus the office of the episcopate. . . . To him succeeded Anacletus; and after him, in the third place from the apostles, Clement was allotted the bishopric. . . . To this Clement there succeeded Evaristus. Alexander

followed Evaristus; then, sixth from the apostles, Sixtus was appointed; after him, Telephorus, who was gloriously martyred; then Hyginus; after him, Pius; then after him, Anicetus. Sorer having succeeded Anicetus, Eleutherius does now, in the twelfth place from the apostles, hold the inheritance of the episcopate. In this order, and by this succession, the ecclesiastical tradition from the apostles, and the preaching of the truth, have come down to us.[128]

Hahn seems to think that this statement provides incontestable proof of his premise that apostolic succession is of divine origin. In fact, it proves nothing of the kind. Hahn first assumes the infallibility of Irenaeus in order to prove the apostolicity of apostolic succession. He then argues that since some of the early fathers believed in apostolic succession (viz., Irenaeus), it must therefore be of apostolic origin. Hahn is guilty of begging the question. He first assumes something that he tries later to prove based on the implications of his previous assumption. He is, in effect, arguing in a circle.

The quote from Irenaeus proves nothing more than that *Irenaeus* held to apostolic succession. Irenaeus was stating his own opinion, and his opinion was wrong on many issues. One such issue is the age of Jesus when he was crucified. The title of his chapter 22, book 2, of *Against Heresies* reads:

> The Thirty Aeons Are Not Typified By The Fact That Christ Was Baptized In His Thirtieth Year: He Did Not Suffer In The Twelfth Month After His Baptism, But Was More Than Fifty Years Old When He Died.

Irenaeus proceeds to defend this thesis against the Gnostic heresies first by using dubious logic, and then by appealing to the tradition of the apostles themselves!

> Being a Master, therefore, [Jesus] also possessed the age of a Master,... sanctifying every age,... For He came to save all... infants, and children, and boys, and youths, and old men. *He therefore passed through every age*, becoming an infant for infants, thus sanctifying infants; a child for children, thus sanctifying those who are of this age,... So likewise He was an old man for old men, that He might be a perfect Master for all, not merely as respects the setting forth of

the truth, but also as regards age, sanctifying at the same time the aged also, and becoming an example to them likewise... [The heretics] are forgetful to their own disadvantage, destroying His whole work, and robbing Him of that age which is both more *necessary* and more *honorable* than any other; that more advanced age, I mean, during which also as a teacher He excelled all others. For how could He have had disciples, if He did not teach? And how could He have taught, unless He had reached the age of a Master?... but from the fortieth and fiftieth year a man begins to decline towards old age, which our Lord possessed while He still fulfilled the office of a Teacher, *even as the Gospel and all the elders testify; those who were conversant in Asia with John, the disciple of the Lord, [affirming] that John conveyed to them that information. And he remained among them up to the times of Trajan. Some of them, moreover, saw not only John, but the other apostles also, and heard the very same account from them, and bear testimony as to the [validity of] the statement. Whom then should we rather believe? Whether such men as these, or Ptolemaeus, who never saw the apostles, and who never even in his dreams attained to the slightest trace of an apostle?* [129] [Italics mine]

It is important to note that Irenaeus speaks here with the same confidence and appeals to the same "authoritative" tradition as when he speaks about apostolic succession. Indeed, if we had only Irenaeus' testimony, we might be compelled to believe that *everyone* in the early church must have believed that Jesus was over fifty years old when he died. Of course, no one today would agree with Irenaeus' position, including Catholic apologists. Yet on what basis can the Catholic apologist reject *this* testimony while simultaneously appealing to the same church father who in the same treatise cites the same "apostolic tradition" in defense of apostolic succession? The Catholic apologist at this point must tacitly abandon his normal criteria for determining truth— namely, testimony from a church father who appeals to tradition handed down unaltered from the apostles themselves— and embrace the decidedly more Evangelical approach of judging the merits of each patristic belief on a case-by-case basis according to how well that belief is supported by the testimony of the Scriptures. In doing so, the Catholic apologist unwittingly demonstrates the deficiency of the Catholic appeal to apostolic tradition, and affirms that neither Irenaeus, nor any church father, can function as the criterion of truth. Only inspired Scripture can be given that status. It is from Scripture alone that we can be certain of apostolic teaching.[130]

But even if we were to concede that Irenaeus is correct in his testimony that the apostles designated successors after them, one must ask the question, Is it possible that each of the apostles could appoint a successor for himself without further thought of an appointed successor to his successor? If one looks at the precedent set in the Old Testament, then one must accept this possibility. God directly appointed Moses to be the leader of Israel, and then named Joshua as his successor. But successors of Joshua are conspicuously absent from Scripture. More significantly, whenever a prophet arose in Israel, he was never told to command Israel to restore a successor of Moses to power. Sometimes Israel had prophets ruling over them, sometimes women, and sometimes kings. But never again is there any hint of a successor of Moses, except for the Messiah himself. Hence, succession from the apostles still does not imply an *ongoing* succession, much less infallible ongoing successors.

Yet, at the end of the day, one must grapple with statements by the New Testament writers that suggest that there would be *no* apostolic succession in the sense that the Catholic church understands it. Both Paul and Peter knew beforehand when they were about to depart this life. Paul wrote Timothy that his time of death was imminent (2 Tim 4:6), and Peter wrote the church that he knew he was about to die (2 Pet 1:13-15). What better time to introduce a new successor than when speaking about one's own death? What's so significant is that neither Peter nor Paul gives even one mention about a successor. What Peter *does* say about spiritual guidance for the church after his death is revealing:

> *So I will always remind you of these things*, even though you
> know them and are firmly established in the truth you now have.
> I think it is *right to refresh your memory* as long as I live in the
> tent of this body, because I know that I will soon put it aside,
> as our Lord Jesus Christ has made clear to me. *And I will make*
> *every effort to see that after my departure you will always be able*
> *to remember these things* (1 Pet 1:12-15).

Far from seeing a need to appoint a successor to lead the
church after his death, Peter thought it more effective simply to
remind the church of the things he had already taught them. He
reminds them of crucial points *by writing it down as Scripture.*
This is what Peter does for the church to ensure that it will
have guidance after his death. The entire letter of 2 Peter *is* that
reminder.

We must not miss the point here. Peter writes these words
based on certain underlying assumptions. One must ask honestly, Are these the words of someone who believed he was going
to appoint another pope as his successor; a person supposedly
infallible, who would then guide the church after his death? If
so, these are strange words indeed! We must conclude that Peter
missed a golden opportunity to appoint his successor. Would it
not have made more sense (assuming a Roman Catholic belief
in apostolic succession) to have given explicit instructions to the
church to obey the new pope, such as one finds in some of the
patristic writings when the author was about to be martyred?[131]
Or, are these rather the words of someone who thought it crucial
to leave a legacy of written instructions to the church that would
then act as a guide in the absence of apostolic authority?

Apostolic succession is simply not taught in the New Testament. While Paul does instruct Timothy to guard the deposit
entrusted to him (1 Tim 6:20; 2 Tim 1:14), and to entrust that
deposit to faithful men who would also be able to teach others
(2 Tim 2:2), this has to do with ensuring there would be capable
teachers who would guard the truth after the apostles passed

on— not that there would be appointed successors. The idea of apostolic succession is a concept that would have been quite foreign to the apostles; it is certainly never reflected in their teachings.

Chapter Four

The Canon

The issue of the definition of the canon is arguably the most important issue for the Catholic apologist when debating the authority of the Catholic church. As we noted in the first chapter of this book, Catholic apologists are fond of arguing that unless we accept the infallibility of the teaching magisterium of the church, we have no way of knowing what books should or should not be included in the canon. After all, it is argued, the canon was not officially recognized by the church until several centuries after it was written. What assurance do we have that the church of that day (if not infallible) was correct in the books it chose to include?

Catholic apologists have tried to impale us on the horns of a dilemma; namely, either the Catholic church is infallible and has *all* of the truth, or it is fallible and has *none* of the truth. If the former, then we as Evangelicals must submit to *all* of the teachings of Rome. If the latter, then we as Evangelicals can have no certainty as to the decisions made by the church, such as in the councils of Hippo and Carthage where the canon of the New Testament was defined. How do we know that the church did not err when it decided which books would be included in the canon and which books would be excluded?

In fact, what the Catholic apologists have postulated is a false dilemma— these are not the only two options. There is a third option that will allow us to go between the horns of this dilemma.[132] We can acknowledge the general reliability of the early church in determining what was accepted and what was not, without ascribing infallibility to it.[133] As we have already seen, the church at that time was not under the impression that its decisions were infallible. We shall see shortly how we can be certain that our Bible contains *all* the right books and *only* the right books.

Before we address that issue, however, we must make a crucial observation, and one that is devastating to the arguments of the Catholic apologists who insist upon these points. The Catholic church *did not* first determine the canon. It was the Eastern Orthodox church that came up with the list of twenty-seven books first. The consensus by the Eastern church was decided in 367, and the twenty-seven books were included in Athanasius' Easter letter from Alexandria.[134] This decision was made twenty-six years *before* Hippo. The Western (Roman) church accepted a canon that did not include the book of Hebrews, but eventually followed the East in including all twenty-seven books. In other words, the Roman church relied upon the Eastern Orthodox church for her canon. Far from making an infallible decision, the Roman church, at Hippo and Carthage, simply adopted the decision of the Eastern church. Therefore, the canon that we currently have is the work of the Eastern Orthodox church, which does not claim magisterial infallibility. Catholics must rely on the decision of the Eastern church and cannot claim to have determined the canon themselves.[135]

Yet, even if the Roman church had first determined the canon, would that thereby make it infallible? The Catholic apologists' argument on this point proves to be baseless— in fact, it backfires. Jesus and the New Testament writers all use phrases such as, "the Scripture says," or "it is written." We might pose the Catholic apologists' question to Jesus and the apostles. How did *they* know that what *they* were quoting was Scripture? There was no council in Israel that declared a "canon" of the Old Testament prior to Jesus and the apostles' use of it. And we certainly cannot conclude that Israel was infallible and infallibly declared what was Scripture *ex cathedra*— one need only read the corpus of Jesus' thoughts about the religious leaders of his day to reject this notion. How then do we explain the confidence with which Jesus and the apostles cited Scripture and prefaced it with the words, "It is written," or "the Holy Spirit says," or "the Scripture says," or other statements to this effect?

These statements carry with them the underlying assumption that Jesus and the apostles knew what books comprised the canon of Scripture, and that their audience would be in agreement with them. In other words, there was confidence on the part of Jesus and the apostles about the canon of Scripture, not because there was an infallible ecclesial authority that declared what the canon was— indeed, it was in spite of the obviously corrupt ecclesial authority of that day— but because there was a *general recognition* of the canon of Scripture.[136]

This is an important point. Catholic apologists have argued that Evangelicals have no right to pick and choose among the practices and beliefs of the early church fathers— that we must either accept all or reject all. Put another way, if we reject *some* practices and beliefs, we have no right to accept the decision of the early church regarding the canon. Conversely, if we accept *that* decision, we must also accept the infallibility of the church in all other decisions (including veneration of Mary, the priesthood, and transubstantiation to name a few).[137]

But was this the view of Jesus and the apostles? Did they ascribe infallible ecclesial authority to the Pharisees or any other religious body of their day? We have already dismissed that possibility— Jesus ascribed *only* governmental authority to these groups. Did Jesus and the apostles accept the same canon of Scripture as did the Pharisees? Obviously so, otherwise they could not have stated with confidence phrases such as "it is written"— nor could they have assumed that their audience would be in agreement with their idea of what Scripture was. Did Jesus and the apostles feel it necessary to accept "all or nothing" from the religious leaders of their day? On the contrary, both Jesus and the apostles rejected the spiritual authority of the Pharisees and other religious leaders of that day while at the same time embracing the same canon of Scripture. Are Evangelicals then in a precarious position when they accept the canon as infallible without ascribing infallibility to the early church fathers? Not if Jesus and the apostles are to be our precedent. The Catholic apologists' contention is, simply put, misinformed; and their objections to the Evangelical confidence in the reliability of the canon are groundless. There can be no objection to holding identical assumptions as those held by Jesus and the apostles.

Evidence For a General Recognition of the Old Testament Canon

It simply cannot be argued that Jesus, being infallible, conveyed the canon of the Old Testament to his disciples. If that were indeed the case, it would be senseless for Jesus and the apostles to use Scripture to argue with those opposing them. How, for instance, could Jesus be certain that his hearers would understand what books he was referencing when making his point about "the Scriptures" which "cannot be broken" (John 10:35)— a statement that makes no sense at all if there were not a recognized collection of writings called "the Scriptures" already in existence? How would one know whether he had "broken" something that does not exist in recognizable form? Or, how would Jesus' hearers have known for certain which "smallest letters" and which "least strokes of a pen" would be preserved until "all is fulfilled" (Matt 5:18; Luke 16:17)? Or again, when he rebuked the Sadducees for not knowing "the Scriptures" (Matt 22:29), how would they have known which writings they were ignorant of? And when he rebuked the Pharisees who searched "the Scriptures" and yet could not recognize him (John 5:39), how would they know where to look? To what collection of books does Luke refer when he praises the Bereans for "searching the Scriptures" to test Paul's teaching? None of these statements from Scripture makes any sense apart from recognizing the underlying presupposition on the part of Jesus and the apostles that there is a collection of books recognized by all as forming the corpus of Scripture.

That the Jews recognized a specific collection of books which they called "Scripture" is virtually beyond dispute.[138] That the New Testament writers refer to this same collection is equally beyond dispute. Both Jesus and the apostles use Scripture freely, calling it Scripture and assuming all along that they and their opponents share at least this much in common. Moreover, there is no attempt by the New Testament writers to justify their version of the canon (as opposed to a hypothetically different "Jewish" version) in any of their writings. At least two of the gospels were likely written for Jewish evangelistic purposes, and Hebrews was almost certainly written to Jews who were deciding between staying in the Christian community and going back into Judaism. Both of these books are replete with citations of Old Testament passages. Yet, there is no thought that the Jews might not accept these quotations.

Paul affirms the Jewish collection of Old Testament books by his statements to Timothy: "All Scripture is God-breathed" (2 Tim 3:16), and "from infancy you have known the holy Scriptures, which are able to make you wise" (2 Tim 3:15). In the latter of the two, Paul makes the point that Timothy has known the Scriptures from "infancy," a time before Timothy was acquainted with Christianity (precluding the notion that Timothy knew the limits of the Old Testament canon only through Jesus or the church). Also significant is Paul's statement in Rom 3:2 where he discusses the benefits of being a Jew: "they have been entrusted with the very words of God." This statement presupposes that Paul believed that the Jews had the right books in their canon. Moreover, he affirms that Israel was the recipient of God's divine revelation (Rom 9:4). All of this confirms that Paul accepted the same canon as did the Jews. There can therefore be no difference between the canon of the Jews and the canon of the early Christians. Rather, a common canon of Scripture is everywhere assumed, both by Jesus and by the New Testament writers.

How Did the Old Testament Canon
Gain General Recognition?

Jesus decried the tradition of the Jewish leaders of his time in no uncertain terms:

> You have a fine way of setting aside the commands of God in order to observe your own traditions! For Moses said, 'Honor your father and your mother,' and, 'Anyone who curses his father or mother must be put to death.' But you say that if a man says to his father or mother: 'Whatever help you might otherwise have received from me is Corban' (that is, a gift devoted to God), then you no longer let him do anything for his father or mother. Thus you nullify the word of God by your tradition that you have handed down. And you do many things like that (Mark 7:9-13).

How was Jesus able to distinguish between Scripture and tradition so that he could at the same time confidently affirm Scripture and condemn the Jews' tradition? Does it sound as though Jesus found difficulty in separating Scripture from tradition, or that he did not know with certainty whether the passage he was quoting should be included in the canon? Does it sound as though Jesus and the apostles required a council to determine what Scripture was before they could be certain of it? It is significant that the Jews themselves never make the point that Jesus' understanding of the canon of Scripture is wrong, and that the "traditions of the elders" are part of Scripture, too. Also significant is Jesus' underlying assumption whereby he is able to give a very high view of Scripture (which to him is completely authoritative and reliable), and at the same time a very low view of extrabiblical religious tradition (whose validity must always be judged by Scripture). The question is, How was Jesus (and later, the apostles and New Testament writers) able to distinguish between Scripture and extrabiblical literature and tradition?

What is so remarkable is that there seems to be an assumption that whatever has always been recognized as Scripture *is*

Scripture. The first-century church made no attempt to redefine what books should be included in the Old Testament canon. Rather, there was a general recognition by both the church and the Jews of the collection of books that comprised Scripture.[139] The assumption of the church was simply that God sovereignly directed the infallible collection of his word so that it would forever be preserved— *in spite of the obviously corrupt and fallible ecclesial authorities he used to collect and preserve it!* First-century Christians had complete confidence in the transmission, authority, reliability, and, indeed, infallibility of the Old Testament Scriptures— yet they had equal confidence in their belief that the agents of this collection (namely, the Jews) were dead wrong in their understanding of it! Such is the case today. We may have complete confidence in our canon, and at the same time recognize that the *collectors* of the canon were completely fallible.

How Do We Define the Limits of the Canon?

How then must we view the collection of the books of the New Testament? Are we to adopt the Catholic apologists' understanding that the canon of Scripture was simply declared *ex cathedra* by an infallible church? Neither Scripture nor history will support an infallible church. What is the alternative? Is it, as Catholic apologists argue, that we simply cannot know the limits of the canon? Or is there another alternative?

The alternative is to take the same view of the development of the canon as did Jesus and the New Testament writers. They were faced with the same situation as Evangelicals are today; namely, adherence to a canon of Scripture preserved until the Reformation by a corrupt ecclesial body. Jesus, the apostles, and the rest of the New Testament writers were able to place complete confidence in such a canon. Yet they would be able to do this only on the assumption that the Holy Spirit occasionally gives infallible guidance, especially where it concerns the recognition and preservation of his word, and in spite of the fallibility of the agents he uses. No other understanding of the canon— least of all the Catholic understanding of an infallible proclamation— adequately explains these assumptions on the part of Jesus and the New Testament writers. We may, therefore, safely assume— indeed, we may have complete confidence in the fact— that the Holy Spirit acted in the same way with regard to the collection of the New Testament writings. It is Evangelicalism, not Catholicism, that holds the same assumptions as did Jesus himself.

Does the Canon Need to be Determined By a Council?

One last question that needs to be addressed along these lines is that of the need of the councils of Hippo and Carthage to determine the canon in the first place. We have already noted that there was no such council to determine the canon of the Old Testament prior to Jesus and the New Testament writers' use of it. Yet they were able to quote it with confidence and ascribe unequivocal authority to it. All of this shows that God's word is self-preserving— that no matter how corrupt the religious authorities are, there would always be a general recognition by the people of God, of what *is* and what is *not* to be included in the canon of Scripture.[140] Yes, some of the books were disputed at times; but there was always final consensus at some point.[141] If Jesus and the New Testament writers did not require a council to determine the canon of the Old Testament before they embraced it as Scripture, neither then does the church require a council to determine the scope and limits of the New Testament canon.

It was inevitable that Scripture be recognized as Scripture— not because of the infallibility of its collectors, but because of the nature of God's word. The councils of Hippo and Carthage were therefore unnecessary in determining the final canon. There would still be a general recognition of the New Testament canon today *even if there had been no council to recognize it!* The councils were nothing more than deviations from normative standards of general recognition. Viewed from this perspective, the Catholic apologists' *coup de grace* argument against the Evangelical confidence in the canon of the New Testament suddenly becomes less pivotal.

Concluding Thoughts

Catholic apologists insist that the New Testament canon is an example of a "doctrine" not found in the pages of Scripture, and that Evangelicals who subscribe to the twenty-seven book canon of the New Testament defined at Hippo and Carthage are inconsistent in their principle of sola Scriptura. However, the issue of the canon is not properly part of the apostolic deposit since according to Jude 3, 1 Tim 6:20, and 2 Tim 1:14 the deposit of faith was "entrusted" and "delivered" (past tense) to the church hundreds of years before Hippo and Carthage met in session. The canon, therefore, is to be seen as a salvation-historical work of God— not as a doctrine *per se*.

There is no reason to suppose that the formation of the New Testament canon would be formally different than that of the Old Testament canon. Although there was no *official* Old Testament canon at the time of Jesus, all of Jesus' statements in this regard reflect the belief that a canon was generally recognized and accepted. As we shall see in the next chapter, the Hebrew canon recognized by Jesus was identical in content to the Evangelical Old Testament canon. Many statements in the New Testament (e.g., John 10:35, "the Scripture cannot be broken"— by which Jesus means that one cannot do away with the verse cited in v. 34 since it belongs to the Scriptures as a whole) make no sense at all if the limits of the Old Testament canon were not well known and generally accepted. This general acceptance certainly does not attest to the notion that the Jewish leaders were somehow infallible, for they are condemned for virtually everything else.

Instead, it attests to God's sovereignty in preserving His word in spite of the fallibility (and error) of Israel and the church.

Chapter Five

The Sufficiency of Scripture

In an attempt to show that Scripture was never sufficient for the early church, Scott Hahn argues that since New Testament writers quote oral Jewish tradition as authoritative, they must have relied on extrabiblical tradition.[142] He adduces examples from Jude 9 ("but even the archangel Michael, when he was disputing with the devil about the body of Moses, did not dare to bring a slanderous accusation against him, but said, 'The Lord rebuke you!'"), Jude 14 ("Enoch, the seventh from Adam, prophesied about these men"), and 1 Cor 10:4 ("for they drank from the spiritual rock that accompanied them, and that rock was Christ"). All of these are authoritative for the New Testament writers, but none is found in the pages of the Old Testament. Hahn thinks that this gives credence to the Catholic notion of placing oral tradition on par with Scripture.

Such is just one example of the rationale behind the Catholic apologists' notion that the Scriptures are insufficient to operate as the final authority for the church. The Scriptures, we are told, are *materially* sufficient— that is to say, all that the Christian must believe is to be found in Scripture, implicitly or explicitly; but they are not *formally* sufficient— that is to say, they must be supplemented by Catholic tradition in order to understand them correctly.

But Hahn's point proves too much. In the first place, Jude is not reciting oral tradition here; instead, he is quoting from the pseudepigraphical books, *The Assumption of Moses* and *1 Enoch*— written, not oral, tradition. If Hahn and the Catholic church really believe these writings to be inspired and authoritative, why are they not found in the Catholic Bible as Scripture? Not only does the Catholic church omit these books as Scripture, it does not even include them among their deuterocanonical books (i.e., the Apocrypha). Hahn uses these quotations in an attempt to trap the Evangelical in an inconsistency, but then makes no attempt to show how the ramifications that he gleans from these quotations apply equally to his own church. But if the Catholic church does not accept these books as inspired writings, then Hahn can no longer argue his point.[143]

New Testament authors often cite non-inspired writers, recognizing the truthfulness of this or that statement without ascribing inspiration or authority to it. Yet whereas these statements were not originally inspired by God— nor a part of divine oral tradition— they became inspired by virtue of being included in Scripture. This is well illustrated by Paul's quotation of Greek poets when speaking with the Athenians in Acts 17:28: "'For in him we live and move and have our being.' As some of your own poets have said, 'We are his offspring.'" The first quote is from the Greek poet Epimenides, while the second is from Aratus. Both quotes by Paul are taken from writings honoring Zeus. Paul quotes the first of these poets again in his letter to Titus: "Even one of their own prophets has said, 'Cretans are always liars, evil brutes, lazy gluttons.' This testimony is true" (1:12-13). Similarly, Paul quotes another Greek writer, Meander, in 1 Cor 15:33: "Bad company corrupts good character."

None of these men was a believer, much less inspired by God— and none of the statements they made can be considered part of any supposed divine oral tradition. Yet it is an interesting fact that in his quote of Epimenides in Tit 1:12-13, Paul calls the Greek writer a "prophet," and confirms that his words are "true." This kind of language is remarkably similar to what we find in Jude 14-15. Enoch is said to have "prophesied" about certain men— so, too, has Epimenides. Enoch's testimony is assumed to be true— so is that of Epimenides. We know that the quote by Epimenides was not inspired prior to its inclusion in Paul's letter. Nor was it considered to be part of divine oral

tradition— nor even authoritative— prior to its inscripturation. What basis then is there for Hahn's conclusion that the
quote from Enoch must have been a part of divine oral tradition?
Obviously, such a conclusion does not follow; otherwise we must
assume the very same divine origin for the quotes from Greek
poets given above!

To illustrate the point using a contemporary example, I might
quote C. S. Lewis during a presentation that I am giving. The
statement that I quote, while not inspired or necessarily authoritative— nor indeed forming part of divine oral tradition!— may
nevertheless be true. Now, if in the unlikely event that God ever
uses me to write a new book of Scripture, and in it I happen
to quote C. S. Lewis, I can recognize the truthfulness of the
quote without thinking it somehow inspired or having inherent authority. Yet, the instant I include it as truth in this new
book of Scripture, the quote itself becomes Scripture. However,
*the rest of the body of literature written by C. S. Lewis does not
thereby become inspired or authoritative, or a part of divine
oral tradition.* Nor does C. S. Lewis become infallible. Hahn has
not made the necessary distinction between *truth, inspiration
and authority.* Inspired words (when affirmed by Scripture) are
always true; truthful words are not necessarily inspired, nor
necessarily authoritative.

Why is it important for Catholic apologists to argue this way?
Because unless they can demonstrate from Scripture that the
New Testament writers viewed certain non-scriptural sources as
authoritative oral tradition, they have no precedent for the belief
that we should give that same consideration to Catholic tradition.
One way they have done this is to contend that Scripture gives
no explicit statement of its own sufficiency. This is a curious
claim, for Scripture does indeed provide such a statement:

> "All Scripture is God-breathed and is useful for teaching,
> rebuking, correcting and training in righteousness, so that
> the man of God may be thoroughly equipped for every good
> work." (1 Tim 3:16-17).

Several observations need to be made about this passage. First, the Scriptures are said to be "God-breathed" ($\theta\epsilon\acute{o}\pi\nu\epsilon\upsilon\sigma\tau o\varsigma$, *theopneustos*). Scripture alone is given this designation— the New Testament writers never apply this term to tradition. The reason Paul mentions this here is to instill in Timothy confidence in the Scriptures. Paul begins this chapter by reminding Timothy of the "difficult" times that are coming upon them, during which all kinds of heresies and disobedience will arise (3:1-9). In the face of all this, Timothy is to stand firm in the things he has "learned" (v. 14), things known from the "Scriptures" (v. 15). Why should he lean on the Scriptures in the face of all this heresy and disobedience? On what basis can he place his confidence in the Scriptures? Paul seems to anticipate these questions as potential points of wavering in Timothy's mind, and gives the answer in vv. 16-17: Because Scripture is God-breathed (inspired and therefore infallible), it is profitable for "teaching, rebuking, correcting, and training in righteousness." The first of these (teaching) acts as a prevention against heresy (perverse belief), while the last one (training in righteousness) is a prevention against immorality (perverse lifestyle). The two in between (rebuking and correcting) are antidotes for perverse beliefs and lifestyles. Paul's point is that Timothy can safely rely on the Scriptures to be useful in teaching true doctrine and right practice, and in rebuking and correcting those who oppose it.

Second, the God-breathed Scriptures are provided to us in order that "the man of God may be thoroughly equipped for every good work." The Greek text literally states: "in order that the man of God may be complete, fully equipped for every good work." The word "complete" is from $\mathring{\alpha}\rho\tau\iota o\varsigma$ (*artios*) and means "adequately equipped for a task."[144] This in itself implies that nothing more is needed in the realm of faith and practice. For if the Scriptures make the man of God "adequately equipped for a task," and that task is to teach correct doctrine and practice as well as to correct and rebuke heresy and immorality, then the Scriptures are sufficient to equip the man of God for all things that pertain to communicating the apostolic deposit.

But Paul does not leave it at that. He hammers home his point that the Scriptures themselves are able to make the man of God sufficient for these things by using the word ἐξηρτισμένος (*exertismenos*, "fully equipped"). This is the participial form of *artios* that is intensified by the preposition *ek*. The man of God is not only "adequately equipped," but "fully equipped" to do "every good work." In context, "every good work" is defined as "teaching, rebuking, correcting, and training in righteousness"— in other words, correct belief and practice.[145]

But if the man of God is fully equipped by the Scriptures to teach correct doctrine and lifestyle, and to combat their heretical counterparts, then the Scriptures need not be supplemented by oral tradition. The Catholic apologist may respond by pointing out that Paul does not say that *only* Scripture is God-breathed and profitable for these things. Logically, tradition is not excluded from the equation. On the other hand, it is significant that while Paul does not say *only* Scripture is sufficient, he does point *only* to Scripture here. If Paul is attempting to instill confidence in Timothy and to give him the necessary tools for teaching, correcting, rebuking, and training in righteousness— and if he subscribed to the Catholic notion that Scripture is insufficient for these things and must therefore be supplemented by extra-biblical tradition— then it is indeed odd that he would omit something that is *needed* to do the job effectively. In the face of preventing and combating heresy, Paul says nothing about extra-biblical tradition, but points to the Scriptures alone.

But even if this passage did not exist, it is one thing to show that Scripture gives no explicit statement of its own sufficiency— it is quite another thing to show that tradition is given an equal footing with Scripture. Even if it could be shown that Scripture does not explicitly say it is sufficient in itself, it simply does not follow that the alternative must therefore be infallible church tradition. There are several steps in between that the Catholic apologist conveniently ignores.

For instance, one must first show that Scripture is *in*sufficient, not simply that Scripture makes no explicit statement of sufficiency. Catholic apologists must at least admit the possibility that Scripture could be sufficient without having any explicit statement to that effect, but being shown from other statements that lead us in that direction. Analogous to this is the doctrine of the Trinity. Catholic apologists do not require Scripture to give an explicit declaration about this doctrine; yet they also do not hesitate to affirm its truthfulness— in this case, basing their belief on implications and inferences found in Scripture. Catholic apologists affirm the doctrine of the Trinity, not because there is an explicit statement to that effect (there is none), but because Scripture leads us in that direction.[146]

Scripture likewise leads us in the direction of sufficiency, not insufficiency of the Scriptures. The burden of proof is upon the Catholic apologists to show the insufficiency of Scripture in light of the obviously high authority ascribed to it by Jesus and the writers of the New Testament, and in light of the conspicuous absence of any appeal or ascribed authority to extra-biblical tradition.[147]

Once the Catholic apologist has established this much, he must next show that it is *Roman Catholic* tradition that fills this gap and not some other church tradition (such as Eastern Orthodoxy).[148] Or, that it is church *tradition* that is authoritative and not the occasional guidance of the Holy Spirit; or, as Montanus held, the prophetic office. Once this has been shown, it must then be shown that Catholic church tradition must be *infallible*. To marshal support from church tradition itself is circular reasoning. It is one thing to hold that church tradition is generally reliable; it is quite another thing to maintain that church tradition is infallible.

The very reason there was a need for the canon of Scripture to begin with is that, because of heretical figures such as Montanus (who denied a closed canon and believed that the prophetic office was an on-going gift given to the church of all ages), there was seen a need to distinguish between inspired, authoritative teaching and mere human opinion. In other words, there was seen a need for a "rule" (hence, canon) to which every other teaching would be subject, and by which every other teaching would be measured for truthfulness. If the church fathers viewed oral tradition as authoritative and the Catholic church as infallible, what need would there have been to establish a "rule" of Scripture? In that case, there would be no need for Scripture at all; it would be quite sufficient simply to continue handing down teachings orally from one infallible ecclesial body to the next.[149]

Is Scripture Sufficient?

The Catholic apologist argues that we cannot use Scripture alone to determine binding spiritual truth. Instead, we must look to the Catholic church for this truth. Is there some other authority besides Scripture that we are to use in determining what is binding on the believer? One passage that is relevant to this question is Acts 17:11. Here Luke records that:

> "...the Bereans were of more noble character than the Thessalonians, for they received the message with great eagerness and examined the Scriptures every day to see if what Paul said was true."

Note that the Bereans are here praised for testing Paul's teaching by known Scripture. It is significant what Luke does *not* say. He does not say that the Bereans looked into Jewish tradition to test Paul's teaching. Instead, Scripture was the standard, and Scripture *alone*.

When Paul debated with the Jews about the Messiah, he "reasoned with them from the *Scriptures*"[150] to prove that Jesus was the promised one. It is significant that Paul did not use Jewish tradition (a potentially persuasive tool) to convince a Jewish audience about Jesus. The only rational explanation for this is that Paul did not consider tradition to be authoritative.

Such was the attitude of the apostolic church. Everything needed to be justified by Scripture, not oral tradition. This high view of Scripture is replete in the New Testament. The question must be asked: If (as Catholic apologists would like the case to be) the Bereans viewed the Scriptures as insufficient and held tradition on an equal par with Scripture, why is there no mention of tradition in this passage? Why doesn't Luke say, "The Bereans were more noble than the Thessalonians, because they searched the *traditions* daily to see if what Paul was saying was true"? This point must not be missed, nor can it be dismissed as insignificant. Here we have an explicit statement by an inspired writer that the way one determines whether this or that teaching is true is to compare it, not to established tradition, but to the written word. This passage also reveals the basic assumption of the early church that, when there is a question of ecclesial legitimacy (as there most certainly is with the Roman Catholic church), the Scriptures must stand *alone* in evaluating any convention or institution that claims to be of divine origin.

Bill Marshner confuses the issue when he points out that the Bereans searched the Old Testament Scriptures, not the New Testament Scriptures.[151] He concludes, on this basis, that if this passage teaches the sufficiency of Scripture, then the Old Testament must be viewed as sufficient without the New Testament. We can, of course, agree with Marshner that Luke has in mind only the Old Testament when he penned these words; but that, too, misses the point. The Bereans had Jewish traditions available to them, and perhaps they searched even these as well— but they are not *praised* for such an activity. Indeed, they probably did not even search *all* the Old Testament Scriptures, but only those passages that Paul cited in support of the death and Resurrection of Jesus. Does that make the rest of the Old Testament insufficient? Of course not. Rather, the passages that Paul cited in support of his message were sufficient to make *this* point (about the death and resurrection of Christ), but would not be cited in support of *other* theological points where different passages would be more appropriately cited. The Old Testament as a whole is sufficient to affirm or deny religious movements that claim to be based in Old Testament prophecy. This is what Luke is here affirming.

In the same way, the New Testament is sufficient to affirm or deny religious movements that claim to be based on the New Testament. The Scriptures must be taken categorically in regard to their sufficiency. The fact that not every passage of the Old Testament is equally sufficient to prove or disprove this or that particular point does not thereby exclude those passages from the sufficiency of the Old Testament as a whole; for they would be sufficient to prove or disprove other particular points. Likewise, we do not exclude the New Testament from being categorically sufficient with the Old Testament simply because the Old Testament addresses some issues more effectively than does the New Testament (such as proving that the Messiah was prophesied to die and then be raised). Luke clearly did not intend to pit the sufficiency of Old Testament Scripture against New Testament Scripture. His point is that Scripture *as a category* is sufficient to test the validity of any religious teaching that claims divine origin, whether Christianity (as here with the Bereans), Jewish tradition (as with Jesus in Mark 7), or indeed, Catholic tradition. The very fact that the Catholic church consistently shies away from such an examination based entirely on Scripture makes it especially suspect.

Paul gave this same status to his own message, which was sometimes written and sometimes word of mouth. Yet, it was, in any case, the *same* message. No appeal can legitimately be made to 2 Thess 2:15 ("hold to the teachings we passed on to you, whether by word of mouth or by letter") to controvert Luke's statement in Acts 17:11 about the sufficiency of Scripture, as though Paul intended to contradict his traveling companion by introducing an on-going oral tradition that was to be held on par with (yet was distinct from) his written instructions to the churches. Paul's statement was made during a time when there were single copies of his letters circulating throughout the churches. Since sending letters across the Roman empire was a slow process (sometimes taking many months), the churches would naturally need to know the content of these letters before the physical letters actually arrived. The only way this was possible was by "word of mouth" from one church to the next. The content of the verbal message was not different than that of the letters, as is evident from Paul's grouping of them in this passage. Paul does not say "by word of mouth *and* by letter" (which would be expected if each one were a different tradition and both were necessary); instead, Paul says "by word of mouth *or* by letter" (Greek, *eite* [εἴτε]), implying that one *or* the other is equally sufficient to convey Paul's message, and that both are essentially the same. Paul certainly did not intend to convey the Catholic notion of two corpuses of tradition— one written, the other oral— which would be perpetuated by the church throughout its lifetime.

Indeed, when a "tradition" of dubious origin that nevertheless purported to be apostolic made its way into the church, what was Paul's counsel to his churches?

> "Concerning the coming of our Lord Jesus Christ and our being gathered to him, we ask you, brothers, not to become easily unsettled or alarmed by some prophecy, report or letter supposed to have come from us, saying that the day of the Lord has already come. *Don't let anyone deceive you in any way."* (2 Thess 2:1-3) [Italics mine]

Far from advising us to *hold* to such a "tradition," Paul expects us to jettison it. He gives us the same advice again:

> "But even if we or an angel from heaven should preach a gospel other than the one we preached to you, let him be eternally condemned! As we have already said, so now I say again: If anybody is preaching to you a gospel other than what you accepted, let him be eternally condemned!" (Gal 1:8-9)

The implications of Paul's words both here and in the preceding passage are devastating for the Roman Catholic position. What are we to do when someone (pope, ecclesial institution, or even *an angel*) offers us a teaching that is at odds with the apostolic message? The Catholic church would have us humbly submit to such a teaching and ignore the fact that there is a blatant contradiction, proposing that in this case our reasoning faculties have failed us.

But is this what Paul is telling us? How could Paul have instructed his churches to compare pseudo-apostolic teaching to the apostolic message if he assumed his readers did not have the reasoning faculties to do so? "But," the Catholic apologist may rebut, "this is the pope who is telling us these things, and he is the head of the Catholic church which has a pedigree all the way back to the apostles!" Note well Paul's words: "even if *we* or an *angel from heaven* should preach a gospel other than the one we preached to you, let him be eternally condemned!" Paul has covered all the bases here. We are not to believe *any-one*— including an angel from heaven and even the *apostles themselves* ("we")— if the message proffered is inconsistent with the *original* apostolic deposit. How much less are we to believe the pope and a historically corrupt institution under the same circumstances? Catholic apologists are fond of ascribing to Evangelicals the epithet of "the magisterium of one" (by which they mean that Evangelicals deem their individual reasoning faculties to be more authoritative that that of the Catholic magisterium) for rejecting Catholic teachings that conflict with Scripture; but that is precisely what Paul *commands* us to do.

What is Roman Catholic Tradition?

Thus far we have avoided inquiry into the exact content of Roman Catholic Tradition— and for good reason; such an inquiry is virtually impossible to make. Aside from "infallible" dogmas about Mary (her Immaculate Conception and Assumption) there does not seem to be any consensus within Catholicism on the content of this "Tradition" supposedly handed down from the apostles.[152] Some Catholic apologists believe that it is Scripture *and its interpretation* that forms the nucleus of the Tradition.[153] Others, recognizing that at least one Catholic dogma regarding Mary (her Assumption)— and perhaps the other as well (her Immaculate Conception)— finds no support at all from the Scriptures, postulate that Tradition is a broad category that includes Scripture itself, as well as binding ecclesial statements from popes, councils and synods.[154] The disagreement within Catholicism about the nature of Tradition, as well as the absence of concrete examples, leaves Catholic Tradition open to legitimate questions about its validity.[155]

Some Catholic apologists have sought support for the Catholic concept of tradition from the New Testament itself, specifically in the use of the Greek noun παράδοσις (*paradosis*, "tradition"), or its cognitive verb παραδίδωμι (*paradidōmi*, "to hand down").[156] Without going into excessive detail, it is helpful to note that when this word refers to the handing down of a teaching, it can alternatively carry with it negative or positive connotations. It is used negatively of the Jewish or human traditions that contradict the Scriptures (Mark 7; Matt 15; Col 2:8).[157] In a positive sense, the New Testament writers speak of the apostolic deposit as "tradition" in such passages as Luke 1:2, 1 Cor 11:2, 1 Cor 11:23, 1 Cor 15:3 ff., 2 Thess 2:15, 2 Thess 3:6, 2 Pet 2:21, and Jude 3. Catholic apologists often argue that the content of these traditions *differs* from the content of the apostolic teachings found in Scripture.[158]

Yet in each one of the cases above the tradition is defined for us. In Luke 1:2 the things that were "handed down" to Luke are elucidated in the next twenty-four chapters of his gospel. In 1 Cor 11:2 Paul identifies the "tradition" as the use of head coverings for women, and then devotes the next fourteen verses to the subject. In 1 Cor 11:23 Paul provides us with his Lord's Supper tradition, and devotes a major portion of this chapter to explaining this tradition.[159] In 1 Cor 15:3 Paul introduces the tradition he received about the resurrection, and then gives explicit detail about this tradition over the course of the remaining chapter. In 2 Thess 2:15 Paul ends his section on eschatology ("the day of our Lord") by exhorting us to hold fast to his traditions (in context, the specific tradition he has in mind refers to his teaching about end-time events).[160] In 2 Thess 3:6 and following, Paul identifies the tradition as his work ethic: "If a man will not work, he shall not eat" (v. 10). In 2 Pet 2:21 Peter refers to the "sacred command" that was "passed down" to all Christians and rejected by apostates. This, in context, can only be the gospel message itself. Finally, Jude alludes to the apostolic deposit (the "Faith") that was delivered once for all time to the saints (v. 3). Again, this is clearly the gospel message itself, found over and over again in the pages of Scripture.

Ironically, Rome cannot claim a corner on any of these traditions just mentioned; for they are either so explicitly laid out for us in Scripture that no further explanation is needed (such as is the case with the life of Jesus and the gospel message itself), or they are traditions that are not anywhere found in the Roman Tradition. For instance, in the case of the life of Jesus, the Apostle John records for us: "Jesus did many other miraculous signs in the presence of his disciples, which are not recorded in this book" (John 20:30). Catholic apologists often cite this passage as proof of oral tradition not written in Scripture. But if this constitutes proof for non-inscripturated, apostolic oral tradition, then it also provides proof that Rome has not held to that apostolic tradition; for Rome has not preserved any deeds or sayings of Jesus outside of the Scriptures that are considered authoritative and binding on the Catholic. But if Catholic apologists cannot point to concrete examples of non-inscripturated, apostolic traditions of the life of Jesus that have nevertheless been preserved through oral tradition, then the point is moot and they have spent a lot of time and energy arguing what amounts to no support for the Tradition of Rome.

Another apostolic tradition that we have seen in the New

Testament is that of Paul's work ethic (2 Thess 3:6 ff.). But here again, this specific tradition is nowhere to be found in Rome's Tradition. Indeed, Paul's words here reflect what is popularly known as the *Protestant* work ethic. Similarly, Paul's tradition on head coverings (1 Cor 11:2 ff.) is no longer practiced by Rome, and hence no longer part of Rome's Tradition.[161]

Some Catholic apologists argue that Paul's appeal to the "other churches" constitutes more oral tradition that was never inscripturated. Yet while it is true that Paul does appeal to this,[162] it is gratuitous to suggest that these are things that cannot be found either in Paul's explicit teaching or in the narrative form in the New Testament itself. Indeed, in each of the passages where Paul appeals to the universal practice of the church, the "tradition" of Paul is explained to us.

What it comes down to is that Catholic apologists want to use Paul's tradition as a basis for Rome's Tradition— even calling it "authoritative" and pointing out Paul's desire for his churches to "hold to" it. Yet, in each case the tradition is identified for us in the passage itself. Moreover, in many instances these traditions are found to be excluded from Rome's Tradition. So then, those traditions that we can concretely identify as apostolic in the canonical Scriptures are either not unique to Catholic Tradition, or not binding on the Catholic; but those of dubious origin that we find in subsequent church history but *not* in Scripture *are* binding. It is therefore precarious for the Catholic apologist to appeal to the tradition (*paradosis*) found in the New Testament, for nothing could be further removed from the Tradition of the Roman Catholic church.[163]

Whose Scripture is Sufficient?

It is no secret that the Catholic canon of the Old Testament includes many more books than the Evangelical canon recognizes. What is commonly referred to as the Apocrypha by Evangelicals is included as the deuterocanonical Scriptures by Catholics.[164] How does one go about deciding which canon is the right canon? Aside from pointing out the historical, chronological and geographical errors of some of the apocryphal books,[165] and the insistence of many early fathers (including Jerome) that the Apocrypha was not to be regarded as Scripture,[166] one might also ask, Which canon was accepted by the Jews, Jesus, and the New Testament writers?

Jesus gives us an idea of the canon to which he subscribed in one of his many condemnations of the Jewish leaders:

> "Therefore this generation will be held responsible for the blood of all the prophets that has been shed since the beginning of the world, from the blood of Abel to the blood of Zechariah, who was killed between the altar and the sanctuary." (Luke 11:50-51)

Jesus is here referring to the Hebrew canon which began with the book of Genesis and ended with the book of 2 Chronicles. He cites the first murder (Abel) and the last murder (Zechariah)[167] recorded in the Hebrew canon.[168] Josephus provides us with a list of the books of this canon and then comments on them:

> Our books, those which are justly accredited, are but two and twenty, and contain the record of all time. Of these, five are the books of Moses. . . . The prophets subsequent to Moses wrote the history of the events of their own times in thirteen books [Joshua, Judges-Ruth, Samuel, Kings, Isaiah, Jeremiah-Lamentations, Ezekiel, the twelve minor prophets considered as one, Job, Daniel, Ezra-Nehemiah [considered as one], Chronicles, Esther]. The remaining four books contain hymns to God and precepts for the conduct of human life [Psalm, Proverbs, Ecclesiastes, Song of Songs]. [As for the apocryphal books] From Artaxerxes to our own time the complete history has been written but has not been deemed worthy of equal credit with the earlier records, because of the failure of the exact succession of the prophets. We have given practical proof of our reverence for our own Scriptures. For, although such long ages have now passed, no one has ventured either to add, or to remove, or to alter a syllable. And it is the instinct with every Jew, from the day of his birth, to regard them as the decrees of God.[169]

Josephus gives clear testimony to the precise contents of the Hebrew canon, as well as to the fact that the apocryphal books are expressly excluded from that canon. Josephus' canon, although arranged differently, is otherwise identical to the Evangelical Old Testament canon. By indicating the first and last books of the Hebrew canon in Luke 11:50-51, Jesus also defines the limits of the Old Testament canon for us— a canon identical to the Hebrew canon, and one with which the Catholic church differs.

That the apocryphal books do not belong in the canon is further evidenced by the fact that it was Israel, not the church, who was entrusted with the Old Testament oracles of God. Paul tells us in his letter to the Romans:

> Now you, if you call yourself a Jew. . . . an instructor of the foolish . . . because you have in the law the embodiment of knowledge and truth (2:17-20). . . . What advantage, then, is there in being a Jew, or what value is there in circumcision? Much in every way! First of all, they have been entrusted with the very words of God (3:1-2) . . . Theirs is the adoption as sons; theirs the divine glory, the covenants, the receiving of the law, the temple worship and the promises (9:4).

Paul's belief is that Israel was the recipient and guardian of the deposit of Old Testament Scripture. They had received *the embodiment of knowledge and truth* and had been *entrusted with the words of God* (i.e., the Old Testament Scriptures). Since the divinely appointed custodian of the Old Testament (i.e., Israel) excluded the Apocrypha from sacred status, none of the Apocrypha can therefore be considered Scripture.

As we have noted in a previous chapter, Scott Hahn contends that the Pharisees, being in Moses' seat, held ecclesial authority; and that, because of this authority, they were to be regarded as authoritative in what they taught.[170] Yet Hahn does not accept the canon that was used by the Pharisees. The Hebrew Scriptures in Jesus' day did not include the apocryphal books that are included in the Catholic Bible. Hahn is therefore in a precarious position. He cannot concede that the Pharisees (being successors of Moses) may have been wrong in their understanding of the Hebrew canon, for that would mean that the Catholic church (whose pope is the supposed successor of Peter) may be wrong in its understanding of the Catholic canon. Yet, if he agrees with the canon accepted by the Pharisees, then he must acknowledge that the Catholic reckoning of the Old Testament canon is wrong. Hahn cannot have it both ways. If he wants to argue that the Pharisees were to be obeyed because of their divine appointment, and that this is to be seen as a precursor to the divinely appointed authority of the Catholic church, then Hahn must also allow that the Pharisees' reckoning of the canon was correct. Otherwise, the "seat of Moses" is no basis at all for the claims of the ecclesial authority of the Catholic church.

Moreover, it needs to be clarified here that the apocryphal books included in the post-Tridentine Catholic Bible are not exactly those recognized by the pre-Tridentine church: Hippo and Carthage omitted Baruch and included 1 Esdras.[171] What this means is that for more than a millennium Catholics were confused on the precise contents of the Old Testament canon. Indeed, a survey of the views of the contents of the canon from Carthage to Trent reveals that a significant number of Roman Catholic scholars during this time subscribed to a decidedly more Evangelical version of the Old Testament canon than Roman.[172] Ironically, while Roman Catholic apologists accuse Evangelicals of picking and choosing which beliefs of the fathers are to be adhered to, they seem oblivious to the fact that this is exactly what Rome has done with regard to the patristic views of the contents of the Old Testament canon.

The Historicity of Sola Scriptura

Another objection to sola scriptura posited by Hahn is that it is unhistorical. He insists that since no one explicitly pointed to the Scriptures as the sole source of authority for 1400 years, this constitutes proof that its authenticity is improbable. Simply to preface our response, we might ask whether Hahn would like to apply this same criterion to Catholic doctrines such as the Assumption of Mary,[173] Papal Infallibility,[174] the Immaculate Conception,[175] and other recent doctrines of the Catholic church. Would Hahn consider these beliefs invalid because they are unhistorical?

Moreover, Hahn's assumption (namely, that just because no one explicitly affirmed sola scriptura in the words of the Reformers before the sixteenth century then it must be the case that no one believed in it) is itself faulty. There have been many beliefs held by the church for hundreds of years before some controversy forced it into the open and an official statement was made. Very little was said about a belief in the Trinity before the council of Nicaea and the Athanasian creed. Are we to assume that the church did not widely hold to a belief in the Trinity before Nicaea? Of course not, as even Hahn would agree. The reason little was said about the Trinity before Nicaea is that *it was not an issue until Nicaea*. Arius could well have argued that belief in the Trinity was unhistorical in his day (after all, there were no explicit statements about the Trinity for three-hundred years)— and in fact this is just what modern Arians, such as Jehovah's Witnesses, argue today!

The same can be argued about the concept of sola scriptura. The early church held certain assumptions which they felt no need to elaborate upon. Those assumptions, however, are not completely silent. They are the very principles upon which the fathers' words are based. Indeed, there are in fact many statements by the early church fathers that contradict Hahn's assumption. We will here quote at length one such father, Cyril of Jerusalem:

> But if the Lord permit, I will set it forth, according to my powers, with demonstration from the Scriptures. For when we are dealing with the divine and holy mysteries of the faith, we must not deliver anything whatsoever, without the sacred Scriptures, nor let ourselves be misled by mere probability, or by marshalling of arguments. And do not simply credit me, when I tell you these things, unless you get

proof from the Holy Scriptures of the things set forth by me. For this salvation of ours by faith is not by sophistical use of words, but by proof from the sacred Scriptures[176]. . . . For these articles of our faith were not composed out of human opinion, but are the principle points collected out of the whole of Scripture to complete a single doctrinal formulation of the faith[177]

Far from Hahn's contention that the early church did not believe in the sufficiency of Scripture for determining binding spiritual truth, we have just the opposite. Cyril is here instructing his catechumen that Scripture alone is the final authority, and that there is no oral tradition involved in the collection of the articles of faith— all are taken directly from Scripture. But what about those points on which Scripture is silent? Are we then to defer to the teaching magisterium of the church? Again, Cyril of Jerusalem:

> Let us be content with this knowledge [taken from Scripture] and not busy ourselves with questions about the divine nature or hypostasis. I would have spoken of that had it been contained in Scripture. Let us not venture where Scripture does not lead, for it suffices for our salvation to know that there is Father, and Son, and Holy Spirit[178]. . . .
>
> But the Holy Spirit himself has not spoken in the Scriptures about the Son's generation from the Father. Why then busy yourself over something that the Holy Spirit has not expressed in the Scriptures? You do not know all the Scriptures, and yet must get to know what is not in the Scriptures?![179]

What is Cyril's view of Scripture's sole authority? Is it that of the Catholic church? Hardly. Cyril sounds much more like a Evangelical in his view of Scripture than a Catholic. But what about Hahn's contention that we must have an infallible interpreter to understand the Scriptures? Cyril's view is as follows:

> For seeing that not everyone can read the Scriptures, some because they lack the learning and others because, for one reason or another, they find no opportunity to get to know them.[180]

Why, according to Cyril, might someone misinterpret the Scriptures? Not because there is no infallible interpreter, but because someone might not take the time to get to know them well. Cyril clearly saw little need for extra-biblical tradition and an infallible interpreter of Scripture.

Hahn contends that the idea of a self-retiring apostolic tradition (i.e., an oral tradition that ceases upon the death of the last apostle) is untenable. But this is exactly the principle upon which Cyril bases his teachings. It is also the basis upon which Irenaeus was able to write the following:

> We have learned from none others the plan of our salvation, than from those through whom the gospel has come down to us, which they did at one time proclaim in public, and, at a later period, by the will of God, handed them down to us in the Scriptures, to be the ground and pillar of our faith.[181]

Irenaeus here clearly believes in the Evangelical principle of a self-retiring apostolic oral tradition. As Irenaeus notes, whereas at one time the apostles *orally* proclaimed their message, later they committed their message to writing in the Scriptures. And it is from this source, and *none other* (in the words of Irenaeus), that the early church derived its belief. It is in Scripture that their continued legacy is to be found, and it is there that the church is to find the "ground and pillar" of its faith— *not* in oral tradition.

In addition to these fathers we may add Jerome who, after listing the books of the canon, entreats: "I beg of you . . . to live among these books, to meditate upon them, to know nothing else, to seek nothing else."[182] We may also add Rufinus, who likewise after listing the books of the canon, writes: "These are the books which the Fathers have comprised within the canon, and from which they would have us deduce the proofs of our faith."[183] In both cases, the Scriptures are understood to be sufficient as a rule of life and "proofs of our faith."

Statements from the fathers such as these could of course be multiplied; but we will limit our inquiry to just one more father— Athanasius. In his letter to the Bishops of Egypt, Athanasius goes to great lengths to demonstrate that the Arians are heretics. He points out that all heresies, including Arianism, have one thing in common— they all contradict the Scriptures.

> Thus each of these heresies, in respect of the peculiar impiety of its invention, has nothing in common with the Scriptures. And their advocates are aware of this, that the Scriptures are very much, or rather altogether, opposed to the doctrines of every one of them; but [they pretend to study them] for the sake of deceiving the more simple sort (such as are those of whom it is written in the Proverbs, 'The simple believes every word'), . . . and so may persuade their wretched followers to believe what is contrary to the Scriptures.[184]

Athanasius, like Cyril of Jerusalem, believes that the reason one might be swayed by heresy is because he is of the "more simple sort"; not that he cannot know the truth from Scripture on his own, but rather because he "believes every word" and is undiscerning, refusing to look into the Scriptures to know the truth for himself:

> Wherefore the faithful Christian and true disciple of the Gospel, having grace to discern spiritual things, and having built the house of his faith upon a rock, stands continually firm and secure from their deceits. But the simple person, as I said before, that is not thoroughly grounded in knowledge, such an one, considering only the words that are spoken and not perceiving their meaning, is immediately drawn away by their wiles.[185]

Athanasius concludes this section by re-emphasizing the role of Scripture in discerning the truth:

> Now one might write at great length concerning these things, if one desired to go rate details respecting them; for the impiety and perverseness of heresies will appear to be manifold and various, and the craft of the deceivers to be very terrible. *But since holy Scripture is of all things most sufficient for us*, therefore recommending to those who desire to know more of these matters, *to read the Divine word*, I now hasten to set before you that which most claims attention, and for the sake of which principally I have written these things.[186] [Italics mine]

Athanasius makes it clear that Scripture is *sufficient* to teach us the truth and guard us against heresy— if only we will read the Divine word. He certainly does not suggest here the Catholic notion that the Scriptures must be interpreted only by the church in order to understand them correctly, otherwise one might misinterpret them. Nor does he give any hint that the Arians were wrong simply because they tried to interpret the Scriptures for themselves unaided by oral tradition. On the contrary, the Arians, according to Athanasius, *knew* their teachings contradicted the Scriptures, but espoused them anyway! The *sufficiency* of Scripture alone— which is what Athanasius is here imparting to us— is the essence of sola scriptura. How Hahn can conclude, in light of the preceding statements by the fathers, that the belief that *Scripture alone is sufficient* is unhistorical is really quite baffling.

A Correct View of Sola Scriptura

Catholic apologists seem to think that if they can show the necessity of relying on other sources of truth than Scripture, that the principle of sola scriptura must thereby be abandoned, and that we must then rely upon the infallibility of the Roman Catholic church. Their idea of sola scriptura is typically nothing more than a caricature— all truth must be directly taken from Scripture or else rejected. Since the collection of the canon is not taken directly from Scripture (i.e., the New Testament nowhere lists which twenty-seven books should be included in the canon— in other words, there is no built-in table of contents), Evangelicals have no right to accept this collection as truth. This is posited as a prime example of the inadequacy of the principle of sola scriptura. The Evangelical relies on the Scriptures as the sole source of spiritual truth, yet must rely on other sources of truth to tell him what books comprise Scripture, tacitly affirming the Catholic position that more than just the Scriptures are needed to guide any believer.

Catholic apologists have set up an easy-to-knock-down straw man version of sola scriptura. Sola scriptura does not mean that truth can be found only in Scripture. Obviously, we can safely assume the *truth* of the existence of George Washington, even though he is nowhere mentioned in Scripture! Rather, sola scriptura means that all those truths that are binding on the believer are found in Scripture, and that no belief can be binding on the believer if it is not clearly presented in Scripture. We can accept the general reliability of those who collected the canon, thank them for their contribution, and even acknowledge that the Holy Spirit gave infallible guidance to them.[187] But we do not accept their spiritual authority in matters of apostolic truth— especially where *their* beliefs and practices differ so drastically from those of the apostles.

In reality, the Evangelical approach for determining the veracity and authority of Scripture is only slightly different than that which Keating suggests the Catholic approach is.[188] The proper approach begins by treating the Bible as any other historical document, with no presumption of inspiration. Next, we apply principles of textual criticism to the extant biblical documents to determine what the original autographs likely were. As it turns out, there is much more evidence for the accuracy of biblical documents than for any other documents of classical antiquity.[189] We are faced, not with uncertain conjecture, but rather with an abashment of riches when it comes to the number of manuscripts with which we have to work, and the high degree of accuracy of knowing what the original manuscripts actually said.[190]

Next, having determined the historical accuracy of the text of the biblical documents, we examine the accuracy of the writers of these documents. No matter how far historically we push any writer of a biblical book, the outcome is always that the writer is accurate in the recording of history. Even when there has been some question as to the accuracy of this or that writer, later archaeological digs have always vindicated these writers. So now what we have is not only a document that is accurate from the standpoint of what it originally said, but also accurate in every place we can check it against historical fact. We then can safely assume that if the writers of the biblical documents are completely accurate in every area that can be verified from other sources, likely they are just as accurate in those areas that cannot be verified from other sources. In other words, we can have complete confidence in the accuracy of *all* that they record.

Next, we examine the type of testimony that the writers are giving and we find that it is *eye-witness* testimony. The writers are recording things they have actually seen— and this in the face of much opposition. The Jews, for instance, could have written their own documents countering these claims— or better yet, produced the dead body of Jesus, whom the New Testament writers claim rose from the dead— but they didn't. We also find that most of the significant eye-witnesses willingly died for their belief in the truthfulness of their testimony. If this were a hoax, one might expect *one* very deluded eye-witness to die for his belief, but not many.[191]

Finally, we find that these writers record the very words of Jesus, in some cases after much careful research.[192] Jesus claimed over and over again to be God. His claim can be taken in only one of three ways: He was either a liar, a lunatic (either of which would immediately disqualify him from any further consideration as a "good" and "moral" teacher), or God himself. Because of the previous evidence of the willingness on the part of the eye-witnesses to die for their belief that Jesus rose from the dead, we must conclude that Jesus did indeed rise from the dead. And since Jesus is the only person in history who ever accomplished his own resurrection, we must conclude that he was neither a liar nor a lunatic, but that he was just whom he claimed to be; namely, God. And if he is God, then whatever he says must be unfailingly true and authoritative. One of the things he says is that Scripture is completely authoritative and infallible.[193] Another thing he says is that his apostles have been vested with unique authority.

Here is where the Evangelical approach departs from the Catholic approach. The Catholic would agree with every point thus far, but then would postulate that Christ established an infallible church, "with the rudiments of all we see in the Catholic church today— papacy, hierarchy, priesthood, sacraments, teaching authority, and, as a consequence of the last, infallibility."[194] In fact, with the exception of "teaching authority" none of the other things Keating mentions are anywhere found in the New Testament. It is also important to note (contra Keating) that subsequent ecclesial infallibility is not a *logical* consequence of teaching authority. There can be no objection to the notion that God sovereignly prevents his elect from being duped by false teaching,[195] without postulating that a man-made institution must be infallible.[196] It is quite sufficient to hold that the apostles and the other writers of the New Testament themselves are infallible in their writings, without taking the further, unwarranted step of postulating an on-going ecclesial infallibility. We are obliged to recognize the infallible teaching authority granted to the apostles *only*, and their teachings are found in the New Testament documents. Therefore, the teachings found in the New Testament documents, along with those found in the Old Testament documents (also verified on the same grounds), are *alone* binding on the church.

But how do we know that we have not inadvertently included some spurious writings as Scripture, or excluded some inspired books that should have been included? The Evangelical approach would continue along the following lines. We have already seen that Jesus accepted the same Old Testament canon that the Jews accepted, and this without the decision of an ecclesial council. Jesus viewed Scripture as having final authority and used it extensively to silence his opponents. There was never a question on the part of Jesus or the New Testament writers as to whether this or that book should have been included in or excluded from the canon that the Jews had already recognized. This sets a precedent (as argued earlier) that Scripture is self-preserving and would always eventually be recognized as Scripture; i.e. the canon is *self-defining*. Once we have determined this, there no longer remains any teeth to the Catholic apologists' argument against relying on Scripture as the sole source of binding authority for the believer. The Evangelical, it turns out, is simply holding to the same principles and assumptions as did our Lord.

Predictions For the Inscripturation of the New Testament Documents

In some respects we have presented our argument in reverse. We have first shown how the widely accepted, general recognition of the Old Testament canon by Jesus, the apostles, and the Jews set a precedent for determining what is to be included in the New Testament canon. From there we took a step backward to demonstrate the historical reliability and, subsequently, the inspiration of the biblical documents. We now need to take one more step backward to demonstrate from these inspired writings whether there would even be such a thing as the New Testament.

Hahn has argued against the Evangelical notion that Jesus commanded the eventual inscripturation of his words. Evangelicals often turn to standard passages to support this notion:

> "But the Counselor, the Holy Spirit, whom the Father will send in my name, *will teach you all things and will remind you of everything I have said to you* (John 14:26). . . . I have much more to say to you, more than you can now bear. But when he, the Spirit of truth, comes, *he will guide you into all truth.* He will not speak on his own; he will speak only what he hears, and *he will tell you what is yet to come.*" (John 16:12-13) [Italics mine]

John informs us here of three duties of the Holy Spirit: (1) to teach and remind the apostles of the things spoken by Jesus; (2) to guide the apostles into all truth; and (3) to give further revelation that Jesus (due to certain constraints) could not give to the apostles before his departure. Most Evangelicals understand this to be an indication that the apostles would be entrusted eventually to commit Jesus' words to writing.

Hahn, however, objects to using these passages to support

the inscripturation of the New Testament documents. He notes (correctly) that nowhere in these passages is there a command to write Scripture. Therefore, the writing of the New Testament, he argues, is never anticipated in the New Testament itself. Rather, Jesus' intention here is to grant the apostles infallibility in their *oral* proclamation.

A number of things may be said in response to this. First, while it is by no means certain that Jesus has in mind here the inscripturation of the New Testament, neither can that possibility be ruled out of hand. For, although we cannot start with this passage, if we can first determine elsewhere that the apostles understood Jesus to want a written record of certain teachings and events, there can then be no objection to the notion that John understood Jesus' words here in precisely the same way. In fact, this seems to be just what is intended, and we will return to this point momentarily.

Second, Hahn's alternative (namely, oral proclamation) can no more be found in this passage than can the inscripturation of the New Testament. To use Hahn's own argument, Where is there a command in these passages to pass down traditions orally? The answer is, there is none. The most we can determine from these passages is that the apostles would receive divine revelation and help to remember certain events— nothing more. Whether Jesus here meant oral proclamation or the writing of Scripture must be determined elsewhere.

Third, although the two logical alternatives for the meaning of these passages (oral proclamation or inscripturation) have been juxtaposed by Hahn, there really is no need to introduce such a disjunction. In all likelihood, Jesus meant to include *both* apostolic proclamation *and* Scripture. The apostles both orally proclaimed the revelation they received and wrote it down. No thoughtful Evangelical would argue any differently. What Hahn *really* wants us to see in these passages is a third option; namely, an *on-going, infallible church tradition*, not merely an oral proclamation by the apostles. But this is too much weight for these passages to bear. We cannot be certain even of the anteced-ent (oral proclamation) let alone Hahn's proposed consequent (on-going, infallible church tradition). In any case, we need to look elsewhere for both.

Did Jesus Anticipate the Inscripturation of the New Testament?

Mark records an interesting incident for us in the fourteenth chapter of his book:

> "While [Jesus] was in Bethany, reclining at the table in the home of a man known as Simon the Leper, a woman came with an alabaster jar of very expensive perfume, made of pure nard. She broke the jar and poured the perfume on his head. Some of those present were saying indignantly to one another, "Why this waste of perfume? It could have been sold for more than a year's wages and the money given to the poor." And they rebuked her harshly. "Leave her alone," said Jesus. "Why are you bothering her? She has done a beautiful thing to me. The poor you will always have with you, and you can help them any time you want. But you will not always have me. She did what she could. She poured perfume on my body beforehand to prepare for my burial. I tell you the truth, *wherever the gospel is preached throughout the world, what she has done will also be told, in memory of her.*" (Mark 14:3-9) [Italics mine]

In this episode Jesus makes a prediction that makes little sense unless viewed as an anticipation of inscripturation. This woman's deed, we are told, will be recounted wherever the gospel is preached. It is obvious that Jesus is here predicting some future event. Equally obvious is the fact that Jesus cannot be mistaken about anything he predicts. Yet, by what means has the story about this woman been told "wherever the gospel is preached"? Through oral tradition? I know of no one who makes a point of telling this story whenever and wherever he/she preaches the gospel. Through Catholic church tradition? I am unaware of any official Catholic teaching that requires this story to be told— nor anyone in the Catholic church whose job it is to make certain this tradition is faithfully handed down. In fact, this story is nowhere found in church tradition apart from the Scriptures. How then is Jesus' prediction validated? *Only by means of its inclusion in the New Testament.* But if this is the case, then Jesus must necessarily have been anticipating (albeit, cryptically) inscripturation of his words.

Another passage that is relevant to this discussion is found in Matthew. After a lengthy prediction about end-time events, Jesus concludes: "Heaven and earth will pass away, but my words will never pass away."[197] Jesus' words here are reminiscent of what he says elsewhere about the Old Testament Scriptures:

> "Do not think that I have come to abolish the Law or the Prophets; I have not come to abolish them but to fulfill them. I tell you the truth, until heaven and earth disappear, not the smallest letter, not the least stroke of a pen, will by any means disappear from the Law until everything is accomplished."(Matt 5:17-18)

In each case, the meaning is that the word of God will endure longer than heaven and earth. The only way that this can reasonably be accomplished is through inscripturation. It is clear that Jesus is referring to preservation through inscripturation (via the Old Testament) in the second passage cited. Since obviously he is familiar with the concept of preservation through inscripturation with regard to the Old Testament, and since he uses similar terminology with regard to his own words, it is likely that he has inscripturation in mind in the first passage as well.

The Catholic apologist might argue that Jesus' words can be preserved just as well through infallible oral tradition. Yet one must ask, Where are Jesus' words in oral tradition? The most we have through this channel are bits and pieces of Jesus' words— nothing significant in comparison to his written word. If church tradition is the preserving force that Jesus had in mind when he said these words, it must be admitted that he chose a channel that is at best only second-rate, not to mention one that is woefully inadequate in preserving his very words.

Did the Apostles Know Their Writings Were Scripture?

Earlier we made the point that if we can first determine elsewhere that the apostles understood Jesus to want a written record of certain teachings and events, there can then be no objection to the notion that John understood Jesus' words the same way in the passages of his book previously cited.[198] Were the writers of the New Testament aware that they were writing Scripture when (or shortly after) they wrote it?

There are several key passages that will be helpful in determining this. The first of these is found in Paul's first letter to Timothy:

> "The elders who direct the affairs of the church well are worthy of double honor, especially those whose work is preaching and teaching. For the Scripture says, 'Do not muzzle the ox while it is treading out the grain,' and 'The worker deserves his wages.' " (1 Tim 5:17-18)

Paul here is giving directions for how the church should honor her elders. To support his instructions he quotes two passages of Scripture; the first is found in Deut 25:4, while the second is a direct quote from the New Testament book of Luke. Here Luke records Jesus' instructions to the seventy-two he commissioned to preach the gospel:

> "Stay in that house, eating and drinking whatever they give you, for the worker deserves his wages. Do not move around from house to house." (Luke 10:7)

Each one of these quotations (both Deuteronomy and Luke) is called "Scripture" by Paul. Clearly then, Paul regarded Luke's gospel as Scripture, and that as early as 63 AD![199] If Luke, who was not an apostle, wrote a book eventually recognized as Scripture by an apostle, then that opens the possibility for other writers of New Testament Scripture who are not apostles but who nevertheless are apostolic— not to mention that there would most certainly be writings from those who are apostles that would be included in this genre. We will examine the latter first.

Luke is not the only book in the New Testament that is called Scripture by an apostle. Peter also recognized the entire corpus of Paul's writings as Scripture. In his second letter, Peter writes:

> "Bear in mind that our Lord's patience means salvation, just as our dear brother Paul also wrote you with the wisdom that God gave him. He writes the same way in *all his letters*, speaking in them of these matters. His letters contain some things that are hard to understand, which ignorant and unstable people distort, as they do *the other Scriptures*, to their own destruction." (2 Pet 3:15-16)

Two points may be made about this passage: (1) Peter places Paul's letters in the same category as "the other Scriptures," calling Paul's writings "Scripture."; and (2) He includes "all [Paul's] letters" in this category, so that the entire extant corpus of Paul's writings must be viewed as Scripture. Peter recognized Paul's letters as Scripture at approximately the same time Paul recognized Luke's writings as Scripture. It is inconceivable that Peter and Paul, knowing that certain apostolic writings were to be regarded as Scripture, would have failed to convey this fact clearly to the churches. In fact, there was probably a wide acceptance of the New Testament writings as Scripture early on in the life of the first-century church. Indeed, this is borne out by Peter's mention of the "other Scriptures," stated without reference to any specific writings as though his readers were already familiar with what constitutes "Scripture"— both Old Testament and New.

Peter gives us indications that apostolic writings would eventually be included as Scripture, not only in this passage but also in another one. We have already discussed this passage of Peter's second letter in an earlier chapter of this book; however, it will be useful to examine it again:

> "Above all, you must understand that no prophecy of Scripture came about by the prophet's own interpretation. For prophecy never had its origin in the will of man, but men spoke from God as they were carried along by the Holy Spirit." (2 Pet 1:20-21)

No matter which interpretation one adopts about this passage (Catholic or Evangelical), one thing is clear: Peter assumes that oral prophetic truth eventually and inevitably becomes Scripture. He recognizes that "men *spoke*" prophecies in ancient times which were eventually written down and included in the corpus of "Scripture." It would be natural for Peter to expect prophetic truth of his own day to be recorded in writing, and to be included in this corpus. And, indeed, this expectation is exactly what Peter demonstrates when he calls Paul's writings "Scripture" only two chapters later!

One more point that needs to be made is that at least one writer of the New Testament who is not an apostle seems to direct our attention back to the teaching of those who are apostles. Jude, in his short epistle, writes to the church to exhort them to "contend for the faith that was once for all delivered to the saints" (Jude 3). Jude's words are revealing, for they assume a deposit of teaching that would be delivered in its entirety to the church. Moreover, this deposit was delivered *hapax* ($\H{\alpha}\pi\alpha\xi$), literally, "once for all time." In other words, there would be no more additions to this deposit after the apostolic writers laid down their pens. Jude's words must not be taken as excluding other apostolic writings penned after Jude's letter (such as Revelation); this is not Jude's point. His point, rather, is that the apostolic deposit would be given "once" (i.e., during one period of time recognized later as the apostolic age) "for *all* time" (i.e., as opposed to continuing revelation throughout the church age). This flies in the face of an on-going, developing church tradition, such as that to which Catholicism lays claim.[200] While admittedly this does not offer *direct* support to the inscripturation of the New Testament writings, it does eliminate all other rival options.

Concluding Thoughts

What have we gleaned from all of this? Simply that the New Testament writers did indeed recognize each other's writings as Scripture, and that inscripturation of the New Testament writings was not only predicted by Jesus, but anticipated by his followers. Other examples could be added,[201] but these should be sufficient to make the point. The Catholic apologists' argument against an anticipation of New Testament Scripture is simply unwarranted and cannot be substantiated.

Chapter Six

Old Testament Israel—
A Story of the Catholic Church

As we have seen, Jesus and the apostles did not view the Jewish ecclesial authorities as infallible— indeed, even as correct— and yet had complete confidence in the collection of the canon which was compiled by these same authorities. What does this tell us about God's overall dealings with ecclesial authorities of any age? The Old Testament is quite revealing in this regard (1 Cor 10:11), and it will be profitable to learn the answer by examining the history of Israel, God's established ecclesial body in the Old Testament.

God appointed Moses to be a leader over Israel and it was through him that God established his covenant with them. After entering the promised land with Joshua leading the way, Israel was very diligent to keep the terms of the covenant of their God. This lasted approximately until the death of Joshua and his contemporaries (Judg 2:6-12). Judges 2:13-23 gives a brief overview of the spiraling degeneration of Israel from that point on. The text records how "they quickly turned from the way in which their fathers had walked, the way of obedience to the Lord's commands" (2:17).[202] During their downfall, God periodically raised up leaders to save them from their enemies. But whenever that leader died, "the people returned to ways even more corrupt than those of their fathers, following other gods and serving and worshipping them. They refused to give up their evil practices and stubborn ways" (2:19). Indeed, this is the path

Israel took (barring brief periods of revival under such men as David, Asa, Jehu, Hezekiah, Josiah) for the rest of the Old Testament period, all the way down to the time of Jesus.

During this period, Israel took it upon herself to institute extra-Mosaic traditions. One such tradition, worshipping at the so-called "high places," had become so entrenched in the Israelite practice that they were not even aware that God disapproved. The "high places" were shrines and altars set up by Canaanites who worshipped their god, Baal, and that had been taken over by the Israelites for worship of the true God, Yahweh. The law of Moses had earlier prescribed that altars were to be built only at divinely sanctioned places (Exod 20:24; Deut 12:5,8,13-14), and the use of pagan-built altars was strictly forbidden (Num 33:52; Deut 7:5, 12:3). Violation of these commands had occurred almost immediately upon entering the promised land. Apparently, by king Asa's time use of the "high places" was such a common practice that it was no longer seen as a violation of Scripture.[203] This is evident by the Scripture's high praise for king Asa for doing "what was right in the eyes of the Lord, as his father David had done" (1 Kings 15:11). The Scripture continues in its praise of Asa for expelling the male shrine prostitutes, getting rid of all idols, and cutting down and burning the Asherah pole (15:12-13). In fact, the only qualification to this praise is found in v 14: "*although he did not remove the high places*, Asa's heart was fully committed to the Lord all his life."

The practice of worshipping at the high places continued until the time of king Josiah. In addition to the same kind of house-cleaning that Asa conducted, Josiah destroyed all of the high places (2 Kings 23:5,8,13,15,19). What was Josiah's motivation for putting an end to such a long-standing tradition of the religious authorities? The answer is revealing:

> "He went up to the temple of the LORD with the men of Judah, the people of Jerusalem, the priests and the prophets—

all the people from the least to the greatest. He read in their hearing all the words of the Book of the Covenant, which had been found in the temple of the LORD. The king stood by the pillar and renewed the covenant in the presence of the LORD— to follow the LORD and keep his commands, regulations and decrees with all his heart and all his soul, thus confirming the words of the covenant written in this book. Then all the people pledged themselves to the covenant." (2 Kings 23:2-3)

According to this passage, it was not infallible ecclesial tradition that was Josiah's standard of truth. Nor was it to the religious leaders that Josiah turned when he wanted to know what God's will was for Israel. Josiah did not believe that the current ecclesial practices were only *seeming* contradictions which merely needed an infallible interpreter to explain how they aligned with Scripture. Nor did he have any problem with interpreting the plain meaning of Scripture apart from— indeed, in opposition to— the ecclesial authority of his day. It was, rather, the *Book of the Covenant* that sparked Josiah's reformation, with no regard for the current religious authorities. Josiah did indeed include the priests and prophets in this reformation, but only to the extent that they followed him in this renewal— he did not first await their approval. What was God's assessment of Josiah's activity? Was God displeased that Josiah disrupted a tradition of a divinely established ecclesial institution; or, that Josiah took the initiative in this action without prior action on the part of the religious leaders? Again, Scripture is very revealing:

"Neither before nor after Josiah was there a king like him who turned to the LORD as he did— with all his heart and with all his soul and with all his strength, *in accordance with all the Law of Moses.*" (2 Kings 23:25) [Italics mine]

God was pleased with Josiah for judging the current religious practice of the Jews by the original source— the Book of the

Covenant. The standard can be no different under the New Covenant. If we are to be approved by God, we must test all things by the standard found in the canon of Scripture, apart from any ecclesial tradition.

Examples such as these can be multiplied in the Old Testament. The story is always the same: Israel strays, she is called back to the Scriptures, and then she strays again. If the Scriptures acted as the standard for measuring the relative standing of Israel, God's established ecclesial authority under the Old Covenant, then we must hold out that same standard to the Catholic church, which claims to be God's established ecclesial authority under the New Covenant. Can the Catholic church claim to possess divine authority when it strays from the Scriptures in so many places? Is it exempt from the scrutiny of the word of God? Is the Catholic church and its explanations of its violations of Scripture the standard of truth upon which we may place our faith and trust? If we are to avoid the error of Israel and learn the lesson that she never seems to have learned, then the answer to all these must be a resounding *no*. The standard has been and always will be the Scriptures. No other standard is worthy of further consideration.

Catholic apologists often counter this point by noting that God has promised indestructibility and infallibility for his church in passages such as Matt 16:18 and 28:20— promises never granted to Israel.[204] But such an assertion is incorrect. The people of Israel were given many promises that they would never cease to be God's chosen people, as in the following passage:

> "This is what the LORD says, he who appoints the sun to shine by day, who decrees the moon and stars to shine by night, who stirs up the sea so that its waves roar— the LORD Almighty is his name: "Only if these decrees vanish from my sight," declares the LORD, "will the descendants of Israel ever cease to be a nation before me." This is what the LORD says: "Only if the heavens above can be measured and the foundations of the earth below be searched out will I reject all the descendants

of Israel because of all they have done," declares the LORD."
(Jer 31:35-37)

Moreover, Paul insists that it was to the Jews that God entrusted his word (Rom 3:1-2; 9:3-5). He further asserts of "the people of Israel" that:

> "Theirs is the adoption as sons; theirs the divine glory, the covenants, the receiving of the law, the temple worship and the promises. Theirs are the patriarchs, and from them is traced the human ancestry of Christ, who is God over all, forever praised!" (Rom 9:4-5)

According to these passages Israel was promised at least as much as the church was promised. Based on these promises the Pharisees might have made a similar argument for their own authority as Catholic apologists make today regarding the authority of Rome. The Pharisees alone, it could have been argued, were capable of interpreting the Old Testament and the "Fathers" (since they alone were entrusted with God's word, and were promised the Law, the Covenants, and the Patriarchs). Similarly, they might have staked a claim to sole ownership of the tradition of the liturgy (since Paul includes "temple worship" in his list). And, of course, how could anyone deny that they possessed eternal life since they were granted "adoption as sons" and the Messiah himself? Indeed, these statements by Paul and Jeremiah are decidedly at least as strong as (if not much stronger than) those made in reference to the church.

As much as Catholic apologists are reluctant to do so, they must face the fact that their claims to indestructibility (based on the promises of Jesus to his church) are virtually indistinguishable from those made by Israel (based on Jeremiah, and later, Paul). More importantly, they must come to terms with the fact that Israel was dead wrong in just how those promises were to be understood! Israel was promised at least as much as the church was promised. The problem is, they thought they were invincible by virtue of their association with Moses (1 Cor 10:1-5) and their pedigree to Abraham (Matt 3:9)— and they wrongly defined "true Israel" as an institution. These are the same errors made by the Roman Catholic church. Sadly, those who ignore history are destined to repeat it.

In the end, because of her long history of disobedience and moral corruption, Israel as an institution was rejected by God; God then turned to the Gentiles who accepted his word with gladness. Is it such a surprise then that God, after tolerating centuries of abuse and moral corruption, would finally say "enough!," reject the Catholic church and entrust his sacred deposit to Evangelicals who have accepted his word with gladness?

Institution or Remnant?

How then are we to understand the promises of God to both Israel and the church? Paul explains in Rom 9:6-7: "It is not as though God's word had failed. For not all who are descended from Israel are Israel. Nor because they are his descendants are they all Abraham's children." Paul's message (and ultimately Jesus' message) was always an affront to the Jewish institution. Israel's leaders took strong exception to the notion that they would be excluded from the kingdom of heaven in favor of the Gentiles. They vehemently denied that those Jews who had received the gospel message and converted to Christianity comprised true Israel. After all, *they themselves* were descendants of Abraham. *They* had a pedigree. *They* could trace their heritage all the way back to the beginning. They alone could claim to be "true" Israel.

Unfortunately for these leaders, God is not impressed by such things. John the Baptist echoed this same sentiment when he said: "Do not think you can say to yourselves, 'We have Abraham as our father.' I tell you that out of these stones God can raise up children for Abraham" (Mark 3:9). Obviously, even here pedigrees did not define "true" Israel. *True* Israel was the remnant who worshipped God in spirit and in truth (John 4:21-24). It was not defined by geography, visibility, or pedigree— nor are the "true worshippers" of God defined that way today. Indeed, the church has never been defined that way biblically. Sadly, Catholic apologists make the same mistake today when they point to the pedigree of the Catholic church as evidence that it is the "true" church of God.

In the case of Israel, God worked through her instituted religious authorities *only when those authorities sought to align themselves with his written word.* During the bulk of the history of Israel, God used the prophets (veritable "enemies" of the religious authorities) to convey God's displeasure toward Israel. God worked through a small remnant of faithful renegades and outcasts who not only rejected the Jewish leaders' extra-biblical tradition, but exposed it as illegitimate, while at the same time boldly enumerating Israel's violations of, and deviations from the covenant. They were disdained, disregarded, persecuted, and many were put to death. Their standard of appeal was never to tradition— in fact, that is what they condemned— but rather to the terms of the covenant *as originally given.*

God has always worked through his remnant— rarely through an institution, and certainly never through an institution who added its own extra-biblical tradition that contradicted the Scriptures. Apart from the clear examples that we find in the Old Testament, Paul gives us explicit instruction about this. In Rom 9:27, Paul echoes Isaiah's concern that "though the number of the Israelites be like the sand by the sea, only the remnant will be saved." This is followed later by Paul's explanation:

> "God did not reject his people, whom he foreknew. Don't you know what the Scripture says in the passage about Elijah— how he appealed to God against Israel: "Lord, they have killed your prophets and torn down your altars; I am the only one left, and they are trying to kill me"? And what was God's answer to him? "I have reserved for myself seven thousand who have not bowed the knee to Baal." So too, at the present time there is a remnant chosen by grace. (Rom 11:2-5)

Clearly, Paul believed that if the ecclesial body established by God strays from the Scriptures, God works through a remnant of believers who are zealous to obey his word. What implications are there in this for the Catholic church? During the time from the second century to the Reformation, the church underwent a massive falling away from apostolic teaching, which is, in effect, the terms of the New Covenant. Church teaching became so embellished that by the time of the Reformation the link between Scripture and tradition was unrecognizable. Traditions which developed ranged from a magisterial priesthood, to prayer to the saints, to papal authority, to veneration (in reality, adoration) of Mary. Indulgences became a way of paying for sin so that one could "indulge" in the lusts of the flesh without having to incur guilt or penalty, and without losing favor with God. Mary, who is referred to only a few times in the New Testament, became the Mother of the Church and exalted to a level reminiscent of deity. The Reformation day equivalent of Rom 11:4 might well have read, "I have reserved 7000 that have not bowed the knee to Mary!"

Perhaps just as revolting was the Catholic Inquisition, a systematic holocaust of Evangelicals and others who opposed Catholic teaching, during which thousands were murdered. Again, this is strangely reminiscent of Israel who, according to Jesus, "killed the prophets" (Luke 11:48). Interestingly, Jesus declares that even though their forefathers were directly responsible for these murders, first-century Israel would be held accountable:

> "Therefore *this generation will be held responsible* for the blood of all the prophets that has been shed since the beginning of the world, from the blood of Abel to the blood of Zechariah, who was killed between the altar and the sanctuary. Yes, I tell you, *this generation will be held responsible for it all."* (Luke 11:50-51) [Italics mine]

The reason for this seems to be that Israel claimed to be the descendants of Old Testament Israel, and that without qualification. Their forefathers persecuted and put to death the prophets (i.e., those who held to Scripture alone in determining truth, and demanded that Israel return to the terms of the covenant as originally given). So, too, the Catholic church has a bloody history of torture and murder in the Inquisition. Like first-century Israel, the Catholic church of today claims inextricable ties with its forefathers who killed those committed to the Scriptures alone. History has an ironic way of repeating itself. Like Israel, the current Catholic church still bears the guilt for the unrepentant atrocities of its forefathers.[205]

These atrocities are by no means confined to moral issues alone— they also encompass doctrinal issues. Arianism, officially condemned at Nicaea, subsequently became prevalent, so that Athanasius and other major defenders of Nicaea were sent into exile by Arians who, by 340, populated most of the Eastern sees.[206] Athanasius was subsequently restored in 346, and exiled again in 351.[207] He was condemned twice by Western synods: Arles in 353, and Milan in 355. The Arians had complete victory by 356 when Athanasius fled into the desert, and his followers were sent to the mines.[208] By this time, seemingly the only orthodox Christians, Athanasius and Marcellus of Ancyra, were effectively deposed from the scene.[209]

The only thing that saved orthodoxy at this point was not the influence of an infallible decision made by a pope— nor even the decision of a college of bishops— rather, the force that finally put down Arianism was the refusal of the common layperson to accept a diminished view of the deity of Christ. God was, once again, working sovereignly through the common people, in spite of the bungled efforts of the Catholic leadership.

Before Arianism was to end, however, the Western bishops met at Sirmium to produce a pro-Arian statement that forbid the use of any terms that implied Christ was of the same substance as the Father. This was eventually rejected by the common masses, and Nicaea once again won out over Arianism by 361.[210]

The lesson of this historical event should be clear to all: God works through a remnant, not an institution. Indeed, if we are to go along with whatever party has institutional power (and it needs to be said here that the Arians considered themselves the Catholic church— in fact, the sheer number of different views of the relationship between Jesus, the Father, and the Holy Spirit before the Council of Nicaea is staggering!), then why are Catholic apologists unwilling to accept the decisions made by the Arians during this period? They were the ones that held ecclesial authority. Why do Catholic apologists reject the Evangelical Reformers as mavericks who strayed from magisterial authority, and not apply that same standard to Athanasius who, like Luther, stood virtually alone in his defense of the truth? The double standard is glaring. If the standard the Catholic apologist uses to measure orthodoxy cannot be applied to Athanasius, then neither can it be applied to Luther and the Reformers.

Chapter Seven

The Myth of Catholic Unity

Catholic apologists regularly argue that sola scriptura produces a Protestantism that is highly splintered, with very little consensus on anything, often citing a dubious figure of 25,000 Protestant denominations in existence today.[211] Quite often, Protestants are caricatured by Catholic apologists in such a way as to be at virtual war with one another.[212] Hahn's solution is to submit to the Catholic church, and in this way fulfill Jesus' prayer for unity in John 17. What are we to make of this contention?

If the question were merely one of unity, no Evangelical would have a problem with unifying under the auspices of the Catholic church. Unfortunately, Hahn's assessment of the problem is overly simplistic and a bit naive. Are we to assume that, if everyone else agreed to do so, Hahn would submit himself to the authority of, say, the Southern Baptist Convention, all for the sake of unity? It is doubtful that this would be a sufficient reason for Hahn to convert! Evangelicals have fundamental doctrinal differences with Catholics. Unity at the expense of truth is no virtue at all! If Hahn believes that unity of belief is the authenticating mark of Christianity, then he must grapple with groups such as the Jehovah's Witnesses and the Mormons, both of which use the same argument to prove that *they* are God's divinely appointed organization on earth. In fact, they would be able to stake an even greater claim to unity than Rome, for no matter how unified Rome might be, she still has her share of theologians, scholars and laity who dissent from this or that decision of the magisterium. One would be hard-pressed to find a dissenting Jehovah's Witness!

Hahn seems to enjoy pointing to the Reformation as the source of disunity— in his words, anarchy— among Christians. The plethora of denominations which currently exists within Protestantism is, in his view, proof of that disunity. Although he denies that this is "proof" that Protestantism is unbiblical, he comes just short of explicitly saying so; indeed, the very fact that he includes this in his presentation against Protestantism makes it difficult to believe that Hahn thinks otherwise. The question is, does the existence of so many Protestant denominations constitute "proof" that Protestantism is unbiblical?[213] Is Protestantism in violation of Jesus' prayer for unity in John 17?

The answers to these two questions depend on one's definition of unity— a definition we will get to momentarily. The more important question that needs to be addressed first is, Does Hahn apply this same standard to the Catholic church? What kind of unity does the Catholic church really have?

Current Unity Within the Catholic Church

The Catholic apologists' constant appeal to doctrinal disagreements within Protestantism as a sign of its illegitimacy is at odds with the official Catholic teaching that Protestants are "separated brethren" and a "means of salvation."[214] What that means so far as the Catholic is concerned is that Protestants are really part of the Catholic church that has broken away from Rome. Roman apologists cannot therefore speak of Protestant disunity without also speaking of Roman disunity; for if they do, they are contradicting the very authority that they claim is infallible.

Beyond this, Roman Catholic scholars are quite candid about the doctrinal disagreements within Catholicism between the far-right position (the position of most Catholic apologists) and the centrist position (the position of most Catholic scholars). The core of disagreement is not only one of biblical interpretation, but one of the interpretation of Roman documents. One such disagreement revolves around the precise meaning of Vatican II in regard to the teaching on the inerrancy of Scripture. The text of the *Dogmatic Constitution on Divine Revelation (Dei Verbum)* states:

> Since therefore all that the inspired authors or sacred writers affirm should be regarded as affirmed by the Holy Spirit, we must acknowledge that the books of Scripture firmly, faithfully, and without error teach that truth which God, *for the sake of our salvation,* wished to see confined to the Sacred Scriptures.[215] [Italics mine]

R. A. F. MacKenzie points to the italicized phrase as meaning that God ensured inerrancy only to those words in Scripture that are related to salvation (no others have this safeguard).[216] Raymond Brown goes farther when he refers to "religious limitations and even errors" in the Scriptures.[217] Hahn (along with most Catholic apologists) no doubt would take a more conservative stance than either of these scholars. The point is, there is just as much diversity of belief within Catholicism, *even in regard to official statements of the Catholic church,* as there is in the Evangelical church in regard to biblical interpretation.[218]

Another belief worth mentioning here is the *partim/partim* theory of divine revelation advanced by some ultra-conservatives within Catholicism. This belief, which has its basis in the Council of Trent, holds that divine revelation is to be found partly in Scripture and partly in Tradition: "these truths and rules are contained in the written books and in the unwritten traditions."[219] Catholic scholar John McHugh observes that "during the first half of the twentieth century, the most commonly accepted interpretation of [these words of the Council] was that the 'unwritten traditions' mentioned in the decrees differed *in content* from the Holy Scriptures"[220] (Italics mine). The majority of Catholics today believe in the material sufficiency of Scripture, and that unwritten traditions *do not* differ in content from Scripture and that there is no Catholic tradition that does not find its basis in Scripture.[221] But this belief is not binding on the Catholic; the words of Trent lend themselves equally well to either position, and the Catholic is free to choose one belief over the other— resulting, of course, in Roman Catholics holding contradictory beliefs about divine revelation.[222]

Among the smorgasbord of beliefs from which to choose in Roman Catholicism are: (1) whether the creation account in Genesis 1 and 2 should be interpreted literally or mythically,[223] (2) whether or not we should believe that Jonah was really swallowed by a fish, (3) which brand of predestination we should subscribe to (there are as many as four[224]), (4) whether or not we should believe that the Bible contains errors, (5) whether or not Mary is to be seen as Mediatrix of all graces, and if so (6) whether she should be viewed next to Christ facing the church or next to the church facing Christ, (7) whether or not Vatican II is to be considered an infallible council (which invites modern exegesis,[225] embraces the Protestant and Orthodox churches as Christian churches,[226] and displaces the use of force in the propagation of the faith[227]), *or* (8) whether we should instead believe Pius X's *Pascendi Dominici Gregis* (which condemned modern exegesis), Boniface VIII's *Unam Sanctam* (which excluded all non-Catholics from salvation), and the *Fourth Lateran Council* (which ordered Catholics to exterminate non-Catholics unless they recanted), (9) whether we should now believe in evolution (as does the pope), or special creation, (10) whether divine revelation comes partly from Scripture and partly from oral tradition, or whether all tradition has its basis in Scripture, (11) whether infallibility extends only to *ex cathedra* papal statements and ecumenical councils, or whether synods such as Hippo and Carthage are also infallible, (12) which Greek text type (Byzantine or Eclectic) is the correct Greek manuscript behind the New Testament documents,[228] and (13) whether or not the current pope is a legitimate pope!

Add to this the deep rifts between the different sects within Catholicism, such as one finds between Karl Keating's *Catholic Answers* and the *Saint Benedict Center*— the latter has repeatedly issued a debate challenge to Keating on the issue of *Extra Ecclesiam Nulla Salus* ("outside the church there is no salvation").[229] Similar differences of opinion on Catholic teaching may be found between Keating and one-time associate Gerry Matatics,[230] and between Fr. Peter Stravinskas and almost everyone who writes to his publication with a question![231] The Catholic apologetics organization *St. Joseph Communications* points to the profound differences among Catholics on the understanding of the New Order of the Mass defined at *Vatican II*, and openly admits that Catholics are having a difficult time "figuring out what Vatican II really taught about liturgical reform . . . since the documents are vague and are used by all sides to justify their own agendas."[232] These are just some of the differences of belief one finds within Roman Catholicism today, and it is abundantly clear that the "infallible interpreter" in Rome is for all practical purposes functionally useless; for although he could make an infallible decision on every one of these disputes, he chooses not to do so.[233]

In light of all this, one is left scratching one's head as to just what Hahn means by "Catholic unity." Does he mean agreement of belief? If so, belief in what? Agreement on the interpretation of every passage of Scripture? Clearly this cannot be the case, since even within Catholicism there are a number of conflicting interpretations among scholars regarding many passages of Scripture. Does he mean unity in essential doctrines; that is to say, doctrines which the magisterium has declared essential for salvation? If so, then Catholic unity can hardly be distinguished from Evangelical Protestant unity, for historic Evangelicalism also recognizes and holds to essential beliefs of the faith. Liberal Protestant scholars who reject these essentials can no more be held up as an argument against historic Evangelical unity than can their liberal Catholic counterparts be held up against Catholic unity.

What then can Hahn mean? Does he mean by unity that Catholics are united in their submission to the authority of the pope? If so, then Evangelicals can hardly be accused of disunity in their submission to the Scriptures, an authority to which even the pope must submit. If this is what Hahn is referring to when speaking of Catholic unity, then a few comments about that kind of "unity" are in order.

First, Hahn seems confused on just what unity is. To insist to your followers that they must obey you or risk eternal damnation is not unity, but uni*formity* (or, indeed, *con*formity— perhaps even *coercion*). To argue under these circumstances that unity of belief equals biblical unity is really quite silly. In that case, Mormons and Jehovah's Witnesses have even more right to claim this kind of "biblical" unity— and, indeed, this is just what they *do* claim! If Hahn argues that every Catholic agrees on the meaning of every passage of Scripture for which there is official church teaching (which we have already seen is *not* the case— even if there *were* an official teaching on the literal meaning of any passage of Scripture), then the unity to which Hahn refers is self-defined. Evangelicals could just as easily point to Scripture passages, the interpretation of which all Evangelicals would hold. Does this then "prove" Evangelical unity? The fact that so many Evangelicals can subscribe to so many similar beliefs *of their own volition* is of infinitely more value as "proof" of unity than any coerced Catholic unity could ever hope for.[34]

If this is the kind of unity that Hahn means, then Hahn has more in common with the nominal Catholic— who attends church every Sunday, mentally assents to the teachings of the Catholic church, but is engaged in gross immorality during the rest of the week— than he does with the Evangelical who has committed his life to Christ. Is this really the unity intended by Jesus in John 17? Hardly. Rather, it is a *spiritual* unity among Christians that Jesus has in mind. This unity has to do with a fervent love for each other, a common lifestyle and philosophy of life, an eternal citizenship and a common eternal goal. Many who mentally assent to these things will be excluded for not embracing them from the heart (Matt 7:21-23). On the other hand, differing beliefs in nonessential issues excludes no one. Institutional unity could not be further from Jesus' point in any case.[235]

There is one last point that needs to be mentioned to place things in proper perspective. For all of the subtle, secondary differences in Evangelicalism, it must be insisted that none of these compares to the deep rifts within Christianity for which the Catholic church is responsible. Arguably, it is the stubborn arrogance of a Catholic church who historically has refused correction and placed herself as judge over all that has been the cause of all major schisms to the present day— from the Great Schism between East and West, to the schism of the Reformation (which was really caused by an immoral Catholic magisterium that refused biblical correction), to (more recently) the schism that led to the formation of the Old Catholic church as a result of the definition of papal infallibility in 1870. It is therefore the actions of the Catholic church— not Protestantism, not Eastern Orthodoxy, and not the Old Catholic church— that most need to be accounted for. It is sad that the Catholic church seems to be blind to this fact; that *all* of Christianity, with one voice, stands against the notion of Catholic primacy, except for the Catholic church itself. It is ironic that the Catholic church can speak of disunity within Evangelicalism when, in reality, it is the unbiblical tenets of Rome (such as infallibility of the pope and magisterium, the primacy of Rome, and many Marian beliefs) that continue to prevent reunion with Eastern Orthodoxy, Protestantism, and Old Catholics— in short, the world of Christendom as a whole. It is Rome who is separated, not the rest of us.

Chapter Eight

Beliefs About Mary

One of the hallmarks of the Catholic faith is a belief in Mary—not just that historically she existed, but a belief that Mary is much more than an ordinary human being who just happened to be used by God in an extraordinary way. The Scriptures tell us little about Mary beyond the fact that she was the mother of Jesus and that she conceived while still a virgin. In spite of this, Catholic tradition has embellished the role of Mary to the point that she no longer resembles the Mary of the New Testament.

One of the Catholic church's most dearly held embellished beliefs is that Mary is the Mother of God. This seems to be the belief that serves as the catalyst for all other unscriptural beliefs about Mary. As such, we would be well-served to examine this doctrine to see if it holds up under close scrutiny.

Mother of God

The origin of the title "Mother of God" is uncertain, but it was in use by the fifth century during the time of the controversies over the nature of Christ which gave rise to the councils of Chalcedon and Ephesus. Many heresies abounded during this period, including the belief that Jesus was God in a human suit, the belief that Jesus was a divinized human, and the belief that Jesus was two persons in one body. The title "Mother of God" served as a functional term for many during the time of the controversies, the purpose of which was to confirm the deity of Christ *even in the womb*. Interestingly, the title used by the framers of both councils was *Theotokos* (θεοτοκος), which means literally, "God-bearer," and not "Mother of God." They could have used *mêtêr theou* (μήτηρ θεοῦ), which is literally "Mother of God," and which was in use at that time by Cyril; but, significantly, they chose not to.

The use of this title by modern day Catholics to venerate Mary has caused Evangelicals to re-evaluate its significance— indeed, its very legitimacy and accuracy. Several questions need to be raised as to the use of the title "Mother of God." First, is it a legitimate title since the original intent for the title changed from one that upheld the deity of Christ to one that honors Mary? Second, is the title based on sound logic? Third, does the title leave the distinction between the natures of Christ intact? And fourth, does the title imply an ongoing relationship? Each one of these points is dealt with in turn below.

The fifth-century fathers' use of this title, as we have already seen, was an attempt to uphold the deity of Christ. Only later did it develop into an honorific title for Mary. It was used during a time when it was extremely important to show which side of the controversy one was on. Since the focus has changed from a title which upholds the deity of Christ to one that magnifies Mary, the original intent of the title has fallen into obsolescence, and for that reason should be discarded.

If the term itself is not discarded, then one must deal with the problems associated with the next point— namely, that of logical soundness. The belief that Mary is the Mother of God may be placed in the following syllogistic form:

Major Premise:	Jesus is God
Minor Premise:	Mary is the mother of Jesus
Conclusion:	Mary is the mother of God

But, if we are to accept this argument, then we must also accept its logical extension:

Major Premise:	God is a Trinity
Minor Premise:	Mary is the mother of God
Conclusion:	Mary is the mother of the Trinity

And if we are to accept this, we must then accept the next syllogism:

Major Premise:	God the Father subsists within the Trinity
Minor Premise:	Mary is the mother of the Trinity
Conclusion:	Mary is the mother of God the Father

This presents a real problem for the Roman Catholic, for the second and third conclusions are heretical. Yet, they are nothing more than logical extensions of the first argument. All of the syllogisms above seem to have valid form. The only charge one might make against them concerns whether each premise is true or false. If any premise within an argument is not based in reality, the argument becomes "unsound." Therefore, each argument needs to be examined as to its soundness. We will begin with the minor premise of the last argument and work backward. Is Mary the Mother of the Trinity? Obviously not. So we now need to examine the argument that arrived at this conclusion; namely:

Major Premise:	God is a Trinity
Minor Premise:	Mary is the mother of God
Conclusion:	Mary is the mother of the Trinity

To check the soundness of this argument one must ask: Is God a Trinity? And then: Is Mary the Mother of God? Both Evangelicals and Catholics agree that the first premise is true. However, if one is able to confirm *both* premises, then no charge of unsoundness can prevail against the conclusion. If, on the other hand, we were to call into question the truth of the minor premise, then the conclusion (namely, Mary is the mother of the Trinity) cannot follow. Because the Evangelical is free to question the truth of the minor premise, he is also free to examine the soundness of the argument that leads to the conclusion "Mary is the mother of God."

Finally, once we examine the premises of *that* argument (namely, [1] Jesus is God, and [2] Mary is the mother of Jesus) we see where the fallacy occurs. The major premise is presented as a categorical statement affirming something about Jesus. Although always awkward when referring to singular propositions, the major premise is more accurately rendered: *All* of Jesus is God.[236] While this works well for other singular propositions (e.g., "all of Socrates is human"), it does not work well for the present proposition. Why not? Because it is not the case that *all* of Jesus is God, for nothing in Jesus' humanity can be considered divine— otherwise, Monophysitism[237] is orthodox! Jesus is both God and man; therefore, we must use the proposition *some* of Jesus is God.[238] Once we have recognized this, we see that the syllogism in its present form suffers from the fallacy of the undistributed middle. The proposition (some of Jesus is God) is affirmative and particular, and the middle term (Jesus) cannot therefore be distributed. Likewise, Mary cannot be said to be the mother of all of Jesus, but only of his humanity.

Those unfamiliar with the tenets of logic may find it helpful to compare the previous syllogism with another one that suffers from the same fallacy: [Premise 1] some kittens are black animals; [Premise 2] Boots is the mother of some kittens; therefore [Conclusion], Boots is the mother of some black animals. The middle term (kitten) is undistributed; that is to say, there are some kittens that are *not* black animals. This syllogism, like our theological syllogism, has invalid form. It does not follow that Boots is the mother of some black kittens, since this conclusion does not follow necessarily from the premises. In the same way, the conclusion that Mary is the mother of God does not follow from our two premises: (1) some of Jesus is God, and (2) Mary is the mother of some of Jesus; for Mary could very well be (and indeed is) mother of only the non-God part of Jesus.[239]

Catholic apologists often counter that Mary is not the mother of a *nature* (i.e., humanity or divinity), but of a person. True enough. But the instant one says that Mary is the mother of *God*, one has violated that distinction; for then one is affirming that Mary is the mother of deity but not of humanity![240] In other words, "God" is merely descriptive of one of Jesus' natures.[241] The *person* of Jesus isn't merely God, any more than the person of Jesus is merely man. Put another way, Mary gave birth to a person who is *both* God and man. She did not give birth to the pre-incarnate form of the *Logos*. It is proper to call Mary "the mother of Jesus," but not "the mother of God." This leads us to the next objection.

The third objection to the title "Mother of God" is that it does not properly distinguish between the natures of Christ. By calling Mary "mother of God" and not "mother of man" there is an implicit denial of the humanity of Christ; or a divinization of his humanity— both of which are heresies. In other words, it affirms that Mary gave birth to *one* nature— namely, deity— stripped of all true humanity.[242] The framers of the Council of Chalcedon recognized this danger. They did use the term *Theotokos* ("God-bearing one"), but that is as far as any reference to Mary goes. They did not include Cyril's supplementation *mêtêr theou* (μήτηρ θεοῦ), literally "Mother of God," hence confirming that Jesus is one person bearing two natures. The text of Chalcedon called Mary "God-bearer," but not without qualification. The text of the document states, ". . . as regards [Jesus'] *manhood*, begotten . . . of Mary the virgin, the Theotokos. . . ," hence being very careful not to ascribe birth to Christ's deity. Paul took this same view in Rom 1:3 where he says of Jesus, "son of David, *according to the flesh*." Therefore, Chalcedon simply reaffirmed what Scripture had already made clear.

This is what Chalcedon taught— it is also what Nestorius apparently taught. In fact, Nestorius felt quite vindicated with the conclusions of Chalcedon.[243] His opponents mistakenly thought he was teaching only an apparent unity between the two natures of Christ (based on a misunderstanding of his use of *prosôpon* [πρόσωπον], literally, "face").[244] Evangelicals, along with Chalcedon and Nestorius, believe that God and man are indissolubly united in the person of Jesus from the moment of conception; but, that there is no transformation or mixture of the natures.

We must maintain a proper distinction between the natures, or risk falling into heresy.

We may well ask in this regard, What part did Mary play in the incarnation? Clearly, she had a part to play in producing humanity. Was she in any way responsible for producing deity? If not, then is it not more accurate (if one wants to give her credit for one or the other of the two natures) to call her "mother of man"? And is it not even more accurate (if one wants to maintain the proper unity of natures that Chalcedon demands) to call her "mother of Christ" (a blanket term encompassing both natures)? This is exactly what Nestorius attempted to do by introducing the term *Christotokos* (Χριστοτοκος), literally, "Christ-bearing one."

The fourth and final objection to the title "Mother of God" is that such a title implies an ongoing relationship. Let us assume for the moment that we agree on the title "Mother of God." It is one thing to affirm that Mary gave birth to Jesus, and hence *was* the mother of God. It is another thing entirely to postulate that there is an on-going relationship intact, and to say that Mary *is* the mother of God. In other words, even if the Catholic apologist were to prove his point about Mary's role in the hypostatic union, it does not thereby follow that she retains title or status as the "Mother of God."

It is evident from many New Testament passages that Jesus effectively severed all biological ties with Mary before he went to the cross. Matthew records one such instance:

> "While Jesus was still talking to the crowd, his mother and brothers stood outside, wanting to speak to him. Someone told him, "Your mother and brothers are standing outside, wanting to speak to you." He replied to him, 'Who is my mother, and who are my brothers?" Pointing to his disciples, he said, "Here are my mother and my brothers. For whoever does the will of my Father in heaven is my brother and sister and mother.'" (Matt 12:46-50)[245]

Here was Jesus' mother, the "Mother of God" herself, Queen

of the Universe, Co-Redemptress of mankind, "preeminent and wholly unique member of the church,"[246] "Mediatrix of all graces,"[247] who enjoys the "splendor of an entirely unique holiness,"[248] searching for her Son. And how does Jesus respond? Does he single her out, make his way over to her, and point to her as Co-Redemptress, who is worthy of honor, praise and veneration? Does he say anything that would lead us to believe that she is to be exalted over all mankind?[249] Quite the contrary. In essence, Jesus says that no one has special relations with him by virtue of biological ties— *not even his own mother*! His true "mother" and "brothers" and "sisters" are those who do God's will— *not* those who bore him and grew up with him.[250]

Also significant in this regard is John 2:1-4. Here John recounts the events at the wedding in Cana:

> "On the third day a wedding took place at Cana in Galilee. Jesus' mother was there, and Jesus and his disciples had also been invited to the wedding. When the wine was gone, Jesus' mother said to him, "They have no more wine." "Dear woman, why do you involve me?" Jesus replied. 'My time has not yet come.'"

The Greek text of Jesus' response to his mother's request reads "*ti emoi kai soi, gunai*" (τι ἐμοὶ καὶ σοί, γύναι), literally "what to me and to you, woman," and means "what do we have in common with each other." Interestingly, this phrase is always used in the New Testament as a rebuke. There are several New Testament passages where the same Greek construction appears, and in every one of them the idea of distancing and/or rebuff is involved[251] — in fact, all but John 2:4 record demons trying to distance themselves from Jesus.[252] A suitable translation of this phrase would be, "leave me alone!" or "why are you bothering me?" The Septuagint, the Greek version of the Old Testament Scriptures, is replete with such examples using the identical construction.[253] In each case, the meaning is roughly "why are you bothering me?"

Catholic apologists do not like the idea that the Son of God is here rebuking his mother. In fact, some Catholics have attempted to soften the meaning by interpreting Jesus' words as something such as "What has changed between us?,"[254] or "What would you have me do?"[255] Yet, they are unable to show even *one* example where the Greek construction is used with this meaning

Others have attempted to interpret Jesus' title for Mary, "woman," in more endearing terms than the Greek allows, including "dear woman," or "mother."[256] But this is without justification. Even Catholic scholars acknowledge that the title "woman" (Gr., *gunai*, [γύναι]) is "unattested in reference to one's mother."[257] Yet, Jesus *never* calls Mary by the title "mother." In fact, the entire phrase that Jesus uses ("what to me and to you") is a "Hebrew expression of either hostility . . . or denial of common interest."[258]

What it finally comes down to is that Jesus is rebuking Mary in this passage. This is not something subject to interpretation— rather it is a matter of Greek construction. The Greek *demands* this meaning. Jesus was indeed distancing himself from Mary, effectively severing normal biological ties and obligations. Any other view is, in effect, groundless, since it does not adequately grapple with the use of the Greek phrase elsewhere. But if Jesus is here (and everywhere else that he addresses Mary) severing biological ties, then Mary no longer retains title and status as "Mother of God."

Evangelicals have no objection to viewing Mary as a model for believers, on par with any other believer in the New Testament era (though, so little is actually known of Mary, it seems that someone else might be a better model). As to viewing her as the Mother of the church, or to exalt her in any other unwarranted way, perhaps we should take a lesson from the Scriptures. A woman in the New Testament once tried to exalt Mary by saying to Jesus, "Blessed is the mother who gave you birth and nursed you" (Luke 11:27). Here we have someone who intended to give honor to Jesus by virtue of giving honor to his mother. This is exactly what Catholics say they are doing when they honor Mary.

It is important to note here that this woman's honor of Mary is much less blatant than would be the case if she were Catholic. A Roman Catholic might be expected to say something such as "Blessed is the Holy, Virgin Mother of God, who gave you birth and nursed you." The reason I point this out is that since this woman gives only *minimal* honor to Mary in comparison to the honor accorded to her by Catholics, we might expect Jesus to take this opportunity to correct a minimalistic view of Mary and to set the record straight— to give Mary a much higher honor (on par with the honor accorded to her by Catholic teaching), so as to set a precedent for how the church ought to honor her.

It would be difficult to imagine a better opportunity— indeed, we might even view this as the *perfect* opportunity— for Jesus to say, "Ah yes, blessed and exalted is my mother the Virgin Mary, the Holy Mother of God, who is full of grace; amen, let her be the blessed object of mankind's devotion for eternity!" Instead, he says, "Blessed *rather* are those who hear the Word of God and obey it." So far from echoing the honor accorded to Mary by the Catholic church, Jesus takes this opportunity to *lessen the already minimalistic* honor given to her by this woman. Jesus saw Mary as a model for believers *only by virtue of her obedience.* And even then, according to Jesus' own words, *anyone* who is obedient has this same status with Jesus.

But what about the Catholic understanding of John 19:25-27? Does Jesus not confer a high honor on Mary in this passage? Here John records:

> "Near the cross of Jesus stood his mother, his mother's sister, Mary the wife of Clopas, and Mary Magdalene. When Jesus saw his mother there, and the disciple whom he loved standing nearby, he said to his mother, 'Woman,[259] here is your son,'and to the disciple, 'Here is your mother.'" From that time on, this disciple took her into his home.' "

Catholic apologists will argue that the words of Jesus— "behold, your mother" were intended to introduce Mary as the mother of the church. John, they will argue, here represents the church as a whole. Mary is thereby given status as "Mother of the church."[260]

The Catholic understanding of this passage is flawed on several counts. First, the plain sense of the passage is that Jesus is here providing Mary with a means of continued support (financial, spiritual and emotional) so as not to leave her a helpless and lonely widow.[261] This much is obvious from the last clause: "From that time on, this disciple took her into his home." Clearly, John understood Jesus to be saying "provide for her." This is a far cry from the Catholic view that Jesus is here providing the church with a mother!

Second, within the Christian community itself, believers are to view each other as family members who take care of one another.[262] Jesus would have been remiss not to have made arrangements for the care of his mother after his death. Yes, technically, Jesus' brothers were responsible for her primary care. But at this early date they were still unbelievers (John 7:5). It was not until later that they became believers.[263] Jesus' provision for his mother was not merely of a physical kind— he also provided spiritual care by entrusting her to an apostle.

Third, the giving of Mary and John is completely reciprocal. If one wants to argue that Mary is here given to the church as its mother, then one could just as forcefully argue that John is here given to the church as a son! Viewing Mary as a singular person, and John as a corporate personality representing the church, is completely arbitrary and tendentious.

Fourth, as S. Lewis Johnson[264] points out, it is odd, if Jesus' intent here is to introduce Mary as the mother of the church, that Mary is never mentioned in any significant sense after this event in the entire New Testament! It is obvious from this point, as well as the others listed above, that the Catholic understanding of this passage is deficient at best.

The Perpetual Virginity of Mary

One of the cornerstones of the Catholic understanding of

Mary is that she is perpetually a virgin; that is to say, she never had sexual relations with Joseph even after the birth of Christ. The Bible nowhere teaches this, of course— nor did the earliest church fathers— and it is unclear just why this doctrine was conceived in the first place. The Catholic emphasis on preserving Mary from any impurity[265] seems to be the engine that drives this idea.

The New Testament mentions several times that Jesus had biological brothers and sisters. A rundown of the relevant passages follows:

> While Jesus was still talking to the crowd, his mother and brothers stood outside, wanting to speak to him. Someone told him, "Your mother and brothers are standing outside, wanting to speak to you" (Matt 12:46-47).[266] "Isn't this the carpenter's son? Isn't his mother's name Mary, and aren't his brothers James, Joseph, Simon and Judas? Aren't all his sisters with us?" (Matt 13:55-56).[267] After this he went down to Capernaum with his mother and brothers and his disciples. There they stayed for a few days (John 2:12). Jesus' brothers said to him, "You ought to leave here and go to Judea, so that your disciples may see the miracles you do. No one who wants to become a public figure acts in secret. Since you are doing these things, show yourself to the world." For even his own brothers did not believe in him (John 7:3-5). [The apostles] all joined together constantly in prayer, along with the women and Mary the mother of Jesus, and with his brothers (Acts 1:14). Don't we have the right to take a believing wife along with us, as do the other apostles and the Lord's brothers and Cephas? (1 Cor 9:5). I saw none of the other apostles— only James, the Lord's brother (Gal 1:19).

Catholic apologists do not deny that these passages exist; they simply deal with them in a unique way. Keating, for instance, argues that when the New Testament makes reference to the "brothers of Jesus" it really means "cousins" or "relatives."[268] He adduces his evidence from the Septuagint, where the Greek word used in these passages, *adelphos* (ἀδελφὸς), can mean "relative." But to transfer the Septuagint meaning of this word into the New Testament without any clear first-century examples betrays a misinformed, if not irresponsible approach. The fact is, *adelphos never* means "cousin" in the New Testament. Keating is guilty of the exegetical fallacy of semantic obsolescence;[269] that is to say, he is guilty of foisting a meaning on the New Testament usage of *adelphos* that it had 200 odd years prior to the penning of the New Testament, but that it did not have at the time of that penning.[270] Many Greek words change meaning after a period of time. For instance, the word *martus* (μάρτυς), from whence we derive our word "martyr," changed from meaning "one who gives evidence, in or out of court," to meaning "one who dies for a cause," with three other meanings intervening— all within the span of a few hundred years![271]

The same fate happened in the case of the word *adelphos*. Whereas it used to mean "relative" along with the simple meaning "brother," that meaning changed by the time the New Testament was written. It does sometimes mean "spiritual brother,"[272] or is used as a term of endearment in a personal address,[273] but these meanings can hardly be applied to those who "didn't believe him" (John 7:5).

It simply will not do to argue (as Keating does) that the New Testament writers were influenced by the Aramaic language, which had no precise word for "cousin." In fact, in every case where "cousin" is meant (as opposed to "brother"), *adelphos* is not used. There are two other words that were in use by the New Testament writers when they wanted to convey the meaning "cousin" or "relative." One of these words, *anepsios* (ἀνεψιὸς), occurs in Col 4:10 to refer to Mark, the "cousin" of Barnabas. The other, *sungeneis* (συγγενίς), occurs in Luke 1:36 and is used to refer to Elizabeth, the "cousin" of Mary. The New Testament writers could have used either one of these words when referring to the "brothers of Jesus," but, significantly, they did not. That they knew of the distinction between these words and *adelphos* is evident from Luke 21:16 which uses both *adelphos* and *sungeneis*, but in reference to different groups ("You will be betrayed even by parents, *brothers*, *relatives* and friends").

Keating objects to viewing the "brothers" of Jesus as real brothers on the basis that it would result in "insuperable" problems.[274] One of the so-called problems Keating offers us is that, in his estimation, Mary made a vow of lifelong virginity, *even in marriage!*[275] He bases this on Mary's response to the angel in Luke 1:34: "How can this be, since I do not know a man?" According to Keating, Mary's response would make no sense if she had not taken such a vow, for why would Mary ask "how" she would be pregnant if she knew she would be having sexual relations upon marrying Joseph?

Keating's other major points include: (1) Jesus is referred to as "*the* son" of Mary (implying one) and not "*a* son" (implying many);[276] (2) these "brothers" could not have been younger than Jesus since they seem to give him advice (John 7:3-4)— something Keating deems an impossibility given the oriental practice of showing respect for one's elders. Since Mary was clearly a virgin at Jesus birth, these could not have been older (and hence, *real*) brothers. Finally, (3) Jesus, upon his death, entrusts his mother's welfare to John instead of to one of his brothers— an action inconceivable if Mary had other sons to take her in.

Is Keating correct when he characterizes these objections as "insuperable problems"? Let us begin with his first objection; namely, that of Mary's response to the angel. Keating cannot understand how Mary's response could make sense in light of the angel's announcement that she would bear a child. But Keating's objection assumes that Mary does not understand the conception to be immediate. In fact, Mary *does* understand the angel to mean that she would conceive immediately. Notice that Mary does not say, "How can this be, since *I will never* know a man," which is what we might expect if Mary had taken a vow of lifelong virginity. Instead, she says, "How can this be, since *I am not now* knowing a man." The present tense, not the future, is used in this statement. Mary could not fathom how she was going to become pregnant *right now* since she was not currently having sexual relations with any man.

Aside from this issue, Keating has introduced an historical implausibility; namely, that there was such a thing as a *married virgin*. Such a notion cannot be supported either biblically or historically. Indeed, the very notion of a woman making a vow of lifelong chastity while at the same time planning a wedding is the stuff of which myths are made.[277]

Keating does not state explicitly, but implies, that it was a common practice for men and women who had vowed life-long chastity to marry for financial expediency (i.e., so that the woman would have a means of financial support).[278] Yet, Keating's suggested practice is grossly impractical at best. If this were an acceptable practice of Jewish virgins (and of Mary and Joseph), then why are priests and nuns not allowed to marry for this same reason? The answer, I suspect, is that the Catholic church recognizes that the last thing two avowed virgins (male and female) would want to do is to subject each other to unnecessary temptation by living together without supervision in the same house!

Moreover, a married virgin is biblically untenable. There is never any indication from the Old or New Testaments that it is acceptable to be married and at the same time to be a virgin. Paul, in fact, gives us just the opposite directive in the seventh chapter of 1 Corinthians. He tells us that, while it is ideal to remain unmarried (agamos [$\dot{\alpha}\gamma\alpha\mu o\varsigma$]) so that one can better serve the Lord (7:32-35), this would be impractical for those not having the "gift" of celibacy (vv. 7-9). However, if one does marry, that person has a marital debt (v. 3)[279] that is owed to his or her spouse; namely, not to deprive the spouse of his or her body— which, by virtue of marriage, no longer belongs to him or her, but to the spouse (vv. 4-5). He would like unmarried widows and virgins to remain unmarried, but if their passions flare up they too should marry (vv. 8-9, 25-28).

Several points need to made about Paul's words here. First, it is clear by these passages that Paul assumes that if one is married, he or she is also sexually active. Second, Paul maintains that if one is not sexually active within a marriage, that person is depriving his or her spouse of what is *owed*. Moreover, if one wants to live a life of sexual inactivity and undistracted devotion to the Lord, that person is to remain *unmarried*, not to marry for financial expediency. Marriage between two avowed virgins violates the divinely instituted intent of marriage, which is to demonstrate the intimate relationship between Christ and his church (Eph 5:22-32). To marry for any other reason is to pervert that original intent, and shamefully cheapen the marriage relationship. Unconsummated marriage, therefore, is not only *un*biblical, it is in fact *anti*biblical. If this was Mary's practice, then Mary is open to these charges.

Keating's next objection, namely that Jesus is referred to as "*the* son" of Mary and not "*a* son," falters on linguistic grounds. Keating misunderstands the use of the Greek article. The presence of the article does not necessarily imply absolute singularity, any more than the absence of the article necessarily implies plurality. Should we likewise conclude that since Jesus is referred to as "a son" of Mary in Luke 1:31 she must have had other sons as well? Or, since in John 4:5 the patriarch Joseph is called "the son" of Jacob, do we conclude that Jacob had no other sons? One wonders how Jesus ever had time for his ministry since Mark 6:3 calls him "the carpenter." If we follow Keating's logic, we would have to conclude that Jesus must have been the only carpenter in Nazareth— quite a feat indeed for Jesus to have built all the houses and furniture in the entire city, and still have had time to minister to the crowds! It would not be at all odd if Jesus, the focal point of the entire New Testament, is singled out and called *the* son of Mary, even though Mary had other sons. Likewise, Jesus' birth by a virgin distinguishes him sufficiently from his half-brothers to justify calling him *the* son of Mary by the writers of the gospels.[280] Moreover, Jesus could be called *the* son of Mary because he is her most notable son— mainly by virtue of his first-born status. The Greek article is often used to single out a special member of a class[281] — not that that object is the *only* member in the class.

Keating also objects to the notion that the "brothers" of Jesus could have been real brothers since there are instances where these brothers give advice to Jesus. Keating cites a passage in John to support this:

> "Jesus' brothers said to him, 'You ought to leave here and go to Judea, so that your disciples may see the miracles you do. No one who wants to become a public figure acts in secret. Since you are doing these things, show yourself to the world.'" (John 7:3-4)

Since in the first-century Palestinian culture it would have been disrespectful for younger men to give advice to older siblings, and since we know that Jesus was the first-born son of Mary, these brothers must not be have been immediate brothers but rather older cousins.

Incredibly, Keating misses the point of the passage. Yes, it is true that to give advice to an older sibling was considered disrespectful (although Keating over-simplifies this custom), but that is just what John wanted to show. Keating fails to cite the entire passage, which really is incomplete without v. 5: "For even his own brothers did not believe in him." The reason his brothers said this to him was certainly not to give advice— they could not care less if Jesus' popularity was at stake. Rather, they were mocking him! Older sibling or not, if one believes that his brother is "insane" (Mark 3:21) one is certainly not going to offer the usual respect afforded to older siblings.[282]

Keating's final objection— namely, that Jesus, upon his death, entrusts his mother's welfare to John instead of to one of Mary's other sons, thereby demonstrating that Mary had no other sons— has already been dealt with in depth. Suffice it now to say that Jesus was also providing his mother with a means of spiritual (not merely financial) support.

No discussion about Mary's virginity would be complete, of course, without addressing Matt 1:25. Matthew informs us that Joseph "had no union with [Mary] until she gave birth to a son. And he gave him the name Jesus." At issue is the meaning of the word "until" (*heôs hou* [ἕως οὗ]). If we take this word at face value, then the clear meaning is that, whereas Mary and Joseph had no sexual relations before the birth of Christ, they did afterward.

Keating argues that the word "until" here does not necessarily imply that sexual relations ensued after the birth of Jesus, but only that they did not occur before that point. He cites a few passages from the Old Testament (2 Sam 6:23, Gen 8:7, Deut 34:6) and Apocrypha (1 Mac 5:54) where "until" has this meaning. He concludes on this basis that Matt 1:25 lends no support to those who deny the perpetual virginity of Mary.[283]

Keating's major flaw here is that he does not take into account the differences of the Greek constructions used. In each of the passages he cites in support of his thesis *heôs* alone is used. Yet in the passage under consideration the construction *heôs hou* is used. This Greek construction (*heôs hou* or *heôs hotou*) has only two major connotations in the New Testament. In a few instances it has the temporal meaning "while" (a meaning that can hardly be applied to the passage in question). The other meaning is "until," and, without exception, implies a discontinuation of the action of the main clause. In the case of Matt 1:25, it would mean that Joseph "had no union with [Mary] until she gave birth to a son [but then *did* have union with her]." There are a handful of instances in the Septuagint where this construction has the meaning Keating wants to assign to Matt 1:25 (although Keating has not mentioned any); but even here this usage is extremely rare. Moreover, the Septuagint was completed in the second century B.C., approximately two-hundred years before Matthew wrote his gospel. Between the completion of the Septuagint and the writing of Matthew there is not even one unambiguous instance of *heôs hou*, in the available literature of the two centuries immediately surrounding the birth of Christ, where the construction has the meaning Keating assigns to Matt 1:25.[284] Keating's argument is thereby rendered groundless.

One other passage that deserves mention in this regard is Matt 1:18:

> "This is how the birth of Jesus Christ came about: His mother Mary was pledged to be married to Joseph, but before they came together, she was found to be with child through the Holy Spirit."

The phrase "before they came together" makes sense here only if Mary *did not* make a vow of lifelong virginity. Matthew is making a point of letting his readers know that the child was conceived before any sexual union took place. Even if we understand this phrase to mean "before marriage," sexual union is implied; for that is what occurred when two Palestinian Jews came together on their wedding day. What sense would it make for Matthew to point out that Mary was with child *before* her wedding if he believed that Mary had taken a vow of lifelong virginity? In that case, it would be no more remarkable (or significant) that she was pregnant *before* her wedding than it would if she became pregnant *after* her wedding.

Overall, Keating's arguments are without merit. Jesus did indeed have brothers and sisters, and Mary did indeed have other children.[285] She was not, in any case, a perpetual virgin.

Veneration of Mary

While we have dealt generally with this subject in some depth above, it will be helpful to take a closer look at some of the claims made by the Catholic church in regard to the person of Mary. It is admitted by Catholic apologists that many of the beliefs about Mary lack explicit Scriptural support and/or have been explicitly defined by the Catholic church only recently.[285a] Other beliefs came about as a gradual process, the antecedents of which can be found in some of the writings of the church fathers[286] (although not to the extent that they are practiced and believed today).[287] While we cannot here repeat information covered elsewhere in this book, it will be beneficial to examine beliefs concerned specifically with Marian devotion. Three such beliefs about Mary— the worship of Mary, the Immaculate Conception, and Mary as Mediatrix/Co-Redemptress— will suffice to address the issue as a whole.

Worship of Mary

Although Catholics deny that they worship and adore Mary, they generally contradict that denial by their practice. There seems to be some confusion on the part of Catholics as to what worship is. They insist in their writings that Mary is to receive honor, not worship;[288] but their explicit practice more resembles worship than honor— bowing to, praying to, and singing praises to anyone must be considered worship, not mere honor.[289] Keating confuses the issue when he notes that we call certain civil magistrates "your honor" and that we are to "honor" our spouses, and then postulates that there is no difference between this kind of honor and the honor given to Mary and the other saints. If this were the kind of honor given to Mary and the saints then no Evangelical would have any problem with it. In fact, most Evangelicals give this kind of honor to Paul.

Of course, the honor given to civil magistrates and spouses (and, for that matter, Paul) is not at all like the honor given by Catholics to Mary and the saints. We do not bow down to statues of Lincoln and Washington.[290] We do not sing praises of thanks for spiritual salvation, or pray to Paul. Those kinds of actions go well beyond the boundaries of mere honor; they are, in fact, acts of worship— acts reserved for deity alone.

Exodus 20:4-5 expressly forbids us, not only to bow down before religious statues, but also to make them:

> "You shall not make for yourself an idol in the form of anything in heaven above or on the earth beneath or in the waters below. You shall not bow down to them or worship them; for I, the LORD your God, am a jealous God."

Clearly, the Scriptures consider *bowing* before images an act of worship. All of Keating's objections to the contrary could also have been raised by Israel when this command was originally given— "it's not really worship, it's honor; it's no different than honoring a civil magistrate; statues simply recall to mind the person depicted"— but God made no exception to the rule. Any time one bows down before— or prays to— a statue or other created thing, it is nothing short of idolatry.

Catholic apologists are, of course, bound to uphold the official position of Rome on the veneration of saints and their images. The official Roman position defined at Trent is represented by the following excerpt:

> The holy Synod enjoins . . . that, agreeably to the usage of the Catholic and Apostolic Church, received from the primitive times of the Christian religion, and agreeably to the unanimous teaching of the holy Fathers, and to the decrees of sacred Councils, they especially instruct the faithful diligently concerning the intercession and invocation of saints; the honor (paid) to relics; and the legitimate use of images: teaching them . . . that it is good and useful to invoke them. . . . But that they . . . who deny that the saints . . . are to be invoked . . . or, that it is foolish to supplicate, vocally, or mentally, those who reign in heaven. . . . are wholly to be condemned.[291]

The council of Trent makes it clear that to venerate images is not only permissible but spiritually beneficial; this is, according to Trent, the "unanimous" view of the fathers. A statement such as this begs investigation. Is it really the case that the fathers speak with one voice on this issue?

Many of the fathers expressly deny that the use of visible images for religious purposes (not to mention, veneration of them) is or even can be a Christian practice. Clement of Alexandria is one such father: "The Law itself exhibits justice. It teaches wisdom by abstinence from visible images and by inviting us to the Maker and Father of the universe."[292] Clement appeals to the Law of Moses and its expression of God's unchanging character. The reason that "Moses expressly commanded that neither a carved, nor molten, nor molded, nor painted likeness should be made" was, in Clement's view, because God did not want us to "cling to things of sense. . . . For familiarity with the sense of sight disparages the reverence of what is divine."[293]

Although Tertullian does not usually carry much weight with Roman Catholics, his thoughts on this echo Clement's above. Battling the charge of atheism, Tertullian asks rhetorically: "if we refuse our homage to statues and frigid images . . . does it not merit praise instead of penalty that we have rejected what we have come to see is error?"[294]

Origen is yet another father who rejected the use of images for religious purposes. In Origen's judgment, those "who address themselves to inanimate objects as to God" must be "intoxicated." Moreover, anyone who imagines that images, "fashioned by men of worthless and sometimes most wicked character, confer any honour upon genuine divinities" is equally "insane."[295] While it is true that Origen is specifically referring to images of "gods," and not specifically the saints, no one who makes such statements can at the same time assume that images may legitimately be used in the religious practice of venerating the saints.

Origen is very clear that venerating and praying to images is quite inconsonant with Christianity when he later writes:

> The Scythians, the nomadic Libyans, the godless Seres, and the Persians agree in this [rejection of images] with the Christians and Jews. However, they are actuated by very different principles. For none of these other groups abhor altars and images on the ground

that they are afraid of degrading the worship of God and reducing it to the worship of material things. . . . *It is not possible at the same time to know God and to address prayers to images.*[296] [italics mine]

Origen's words speak for themselves. Trent has mistakenly— and quite carelessly— asserted that the legitimacy of venerating images was the unanimous view of the fathers. On the contrary, Origen went to great lengths to defend the "conduct of the Christians in refusing homage to *any object* except the Most High God, and the First-Born of all creation."[297] Their refusal to venerate images was solely because they had "learned from Jesus Christ the true way of serving God. And we shrink from [images which], under a pretense of piety, leads to utter impiety."[298]

Origen's views were certainly not unique to him. This was the view of the all of apostolic Christianity. The early Christians were convinced that "that which is incorporeal must be offered to God, for He accepts this. . . . For, if God is not seen, he should be worshipped with things that are not seen."[299]

Also revealing is Trent's insistence that the Catholic believer is not venerating the image but rather what the image is a representation of:

> . . . [not] that trust is to be reposed in images, as was of old done by the Gentiles who placed their hope in idols; but because the honor which is shown them is referred to the prototypes which those images represent; in such wise that by the images which we kiss, and before which we uncover the head, and prostrate ourselves, we adore Christ; and we venerate the saints, whose similitude they bear.[300]

Yet, according to several of the early fathers, this was the same line of reasoning used by the pagans, and one which the fathers categorically rejected. This is well illustrated by a statement from Athenagoras:

> It is asserted by some [pagans] that, although these are only images, yet there exist gods in honor of whom they are made. They say that the prayers and sacrifices presented to the images are to be referred to the gods, and are in fact made to the gods.[301]

Athenagoras later tells us that he is not raising this point to indict the pagans but rather to provide justification for the Christian rejection of images:

> And I would beseech you, greatest of emperors, before I enter on this discussion, to be indulgent to me while I bring forward true considerations; for it is not my design to show the fallacy of idols, but, by disproving the calumnies vented against us, to offer a reason for the course of life we follow.[302]

Athenagoras writes to defend the course of life "we" follow (as distinct from the pagans), and to refute the accusations against "us." Clearly, Athenagoras is speaking categorically for all Christians in his day, and he tells us that the singular Christian practice is to reject visible images. Similarly, Arnobius, quoting his opponents, reiterates and then rejects the argument used by the pagans to justify the use of images:

> Here also the advocates of images are wont to say this also, that the ancients knew well that images have no divine nature, and that there is no sense in them, but that they formed them profitably and wisely, for the sake of the unmanageable and ignorant mob.[303] . . . "But you err," says my opponent, "and are mistaken. For we do not consider either copper, gold, silver, or those other materials of which statues are made to be in themselves gods and sacred deities. Rather, in them we worship and venerate those beings whom their dedication as sacred items cause to dwell in those statues made by workmen."[304]

The arguments used by Arnobius' opponents are strikingly similar to those used by Trent and Catholic apologists as a whole. Both attempt to justify their practice by claiming that to venerate the image is in reality to venerate the person represented by the image. Arnobius flatly denies that this is possible. Lactantius also provides us with similar testimony:

> What madness is it, then, either to form those objects that they themselves may afterwards fear, or to fear the things that they have formed? However, they say, "We do not fear the images themselves, but those beings after whose likeness they were formed, and to whose names they are dedicated." No doubt you fear them for this reason: because you think that they are in heaven.[305]

Once again, the rationale of the pagans in regard to images is precisely that proffered by Trent. They were not really venerating images, but rather what those images represented. As with Origen, Lactantius is thinking here about images of gods and not specifically saints; but this is not surprising when we consider that the invocation of saints was completely unheard of in the primitive church. Yet the rationale that he gives here applies equally to images of saints:

> So why, then [since you think that they are in heaven], do you not raise your eyes to heaven? Why do you not invoke their names and offer sacrifices in the open air? Why do you look to walls, wood, and stone— rather than to the place where you believe them to be? What is the meaning of temples and altars? What, in short, is the meaning of the images themselves, which are memorials either of the dead or of the absent?[306]

These statements from the fathers condemning the practice of venerating (or even creating) images are by no means confined to images of pagan gods. Irenaeus relates an early attempt by the Gnostics to set up Christian images for veneration:

> [They] call themselves Gnostics. They also possess images, some of them painted, and others formed from different kinds of material. They maintain that a likeness of Christ was made by Pilate at that time when Jesus lived among them. They crown these images, and set them up along with the images of the philosophers of the world. That is to say, they place them with the images of Pythagoras, Plato, Aristotle, and the rest. They have also other modes of honoring these images, after the same manner of the Gentiles.[307]

As with the other fathers cited above, Irenaeus' statement betrays a categorical rejection of the use of images for religious purposes. He observes the Gnostics from a distance and notes that "they" possess images, and that "they" maintain a legend about an image of Christ made by Pilate. "They" honor these images the same way the Gentiles honor their pagan images. No one who speaks this way can at the same time entertain a legitimate Christian use of images. Indeed, it was the heretical

Gnostics (not Irenaeus and orthodoxy) that set up and venerated the image of Christ— a decidedly Christian image. It would require very little imagination to conjecture what Irenaeus' response would be to the Catholic crucifix!

Such was the view of the earliest fathers. There was no such thing as a Christian image made after the likeness of a saint in the earliest years of Christianity. Such things were frowned upon, even if the images were created merely for artistic merit. As Clement of Alexandria once noted: "It is with a different kind of spell that art deludes you. . . . It leads you to pay religious honor and worship to images and pictures."[308] For this reason, "works of art cannot be sacred and divine."[309] Clement was so opposed to the use of images that he would not even allow that the images of the cherubim on top of the ark should be taken literally:

> Those golden figures, each of them with six wings, signify either the two bears (as some would have it) or rather the two hemispheres. For the name cherubim meant "much knowledge." . . . For He who prohibited the making of a graven image would never Himself have made an image in the likeness of holy things.[310]

Similarly, Tertullian goes so far as to ascribe demonic activity to the veneration of images:

> We know that the names of the dead are nothing, as are their images. But when images are set up, we know well enough, too, who carry on their wicked work under these names. We know who exult in the homage rendered to the images. We know who pretend to be divine. It is none other than accursed spirits.[311] . . . for idolatry, in fact, is a sort of homage to the departed; the one as well as the other is a service to dead men. Moreover, demons have abode in the images of the dead.[312] . . . "Not that an idol is anything," as the apostle says, but that the homage they render to it is to demons. These are the real occupants of these consecrated images— whether of dead men or (as they think) of gods.[313]

Whatever view one takes on the decisions of the later fathers regarding the veneration of images (namely, those at Nicaea II), one thing is absolutely clear; the acceptance of images for religious purposes was by no means the "unanimous teaching" of the fathers as Trent so erroneously claimed. Indeed, as we have shown, it was roundly rejected by the earliest fathers, and can therefore have no basis even in a supposed oral tradition of the apostles.

The Immaculate Conception

The Catholic basis for the Immaculate Conception (i.e., the belief that Mary was conceived without original sin) is found in Luke 1:28, where the angel says to Mary: "Hail, favored one, the Lord is with you." The word translated "favored one" is from the Greek word *charitoô* ($\chi\alpha\rho\iota\tau\delta\omega$). Keating takes this word to mean "a perfection of grace,"[314] and concludes from this that Mary was "full of grace" from conception to her life's end. He bases this (presumably, though he does not say) on the fact that Luke uses the perfect tense of this word (popularly understood as "you who have been and currently are favored").[315]

But Keating misunderstands the Greek here. First, this same word is used in Eph 1:6 where it refers to *all* believers. Does Keating want to argue that all believers are without original sin? Keating might attempt to distinguish these two words on the basis that Eph 1:6 does not use the perfect tense whereas Luke 1:28 does. But this does not help Keating either since the perfect tense speaks only of the *current state* of the subject without reference to *how long* the subject has been in that state, or *will be* in that state.[316]

Keating, either by being misinformed about the Greek language or by his desire to justify his beliefs from Scripture (or both!), attempts to make the Greek say something that it does not really say. In any case, no informed Greek scholar would dare push the Greek perfect tense to the extent that Keating pushes it here. The standard Greek lexicon used by scholars everywhere, BAGD,[317] defines the word *charito* as "to bestow favor upon, favor highly, [or] bless." It is an action on the part of God extrinsic to the receiver and unconditioned on the anteced-ent state of the receiver. There is no sense in which this word means what Keating and the Catholic church want it to mean; namely, an intrinsic and permanent quality of grace within Mary. Mary was considered "favored," not because of some intrinsic quality she possessed, but because she was the one chosen to give birth to the Christ. Put another way, Mary was not (as the Catholic church teaches) chosen because she was considered "highly favored"; rather she became highly favored because God chose her for this task.

One must also ask the question, What need is there to postulate that Mary lived in a permanent state of grace and without original sin? There does not seem to be any explicit, official Catholic statement as to why this would be necessary. Speculations range from a desire to provide a "clean" vessel through which our Lord was born, to viewing Mary as the second Eve (who was originally sinless) in order to parallel her with Christ (the second Adam). In any case, there is absolutely no scriptural evidence— either through implication or mere inference— that Mary was without original sin.

Mary as Co-Redemptress and Mediatrix

One last belief about Mary that we shall address is her alleged role as Co-Redemptress and Mediatrix. According to Keating, Mary "freely cooperated with God's plan" to provide the world a Redeemer (hence, Co-Redemptress), and currently "intercedes for us in heaven" so that "grace is not conferred on anyone without Mary's cooperation" (hence, Mediatrix).[318]

Evangelicals object to this role for Mary on several counts. First, as even Keating admits, there is no Scriptural evidence to suggest that Mary mediates on our behalf.[319] On the contrary, the Scriptures tell us in no uncertain terms that there is only one mediator between man and God— Christ alone: "For there is one God and one mediator between God and men, the man Christ Jesus" (1 Tim 2:5).

Catholic apologists, recognizing this to be true, have countered by pointing out that we all mediate for each other every time we pray for one another. And if this mediation for one another does not destroy the sole mediatorship of Christ, then neither can it be said that Mary's mediation destroys it.

While it is true that we all intercede on behalf of one another, the Catholic claim for Mary's mediation goes well beyond the kind of mediation of which all believers partake. Otherwise (if just anyone could mediate in the way Mary does), what sense would it make for Catholics to point to Mary alone as Mediatrix? The very title suggests that Mary intercedes in a way that no one else can. It is in this sense of mediation that the Scriptures so clearly point to Christ alone, and deny that any other person occupies this place. In 1 Tim 2:5, Paul parallels the uniqueness of Christ's role as Mediator with the uniqueness of God himself; in the very same way that there is only "one God," so also there is only "one Mediator" between God and men. Calling Mary Mediatrix is just another Catholic-made obstacle (in a long series of obstacles) that prevents us from approaching God, with confidence, through his Son alone.[320]

A second objection is that Mary is said to mediate through prayer to her. Scripture explicitly condemns contacting the dead for any reason:

> "When men tell you to consult mediums and spiritists, who whisper and mutter, should not a people inquire of their God? Why consult the dead on behalf of the living?" (Isa 8:19); "Let no one be found among you . . . who consults the dead." (Deut 18:10-11); "The Egyptians . . . will consult the idols and the spirits of the dead, the mediums and the spiritists."(Isa 19:3).

Clearly, to contact the dead is explicitly prohibited by God. Since Mary is among the dead,[321] to pray to her is to violate clear biblical mandates.[322]

Madrid attempts to distinguish between the Roman Catholic practice of praying to the saints, and the practice of contacting the dead condemned in Scripture. He defines the latter as:

... an attempt to harness diabolical powers in order to ... communicate with 'familiar spirits.' ... But this has nothing to do with our
asking saints to pray for us. ... [Catholics] should take the opportunity
to explain that aside from the method of communication, asking our
fellow Christians in heaven to intercede on our behalf is no different
from asking a fellow Christian here on earth to pray for us.[323]

Madrid continues his defense by insisting that Catholics who
pray to the saints are not attempting to "conjure up" their spirits,
that the saints are not really dead anyway, and that the practice
condemned in the Old Testament had to do with Satan, death,
and the underworld— not saints, who are in heaven.[324]

But, Madrid again makes some unfortunate blunders. First,
while we may agree with Madrid that the practice of contacting the dead does indeed have to do with Satan, death and the
underworld, he has not thereby distinguished the Catholic practice from the practice of contacting the dead in the Old Testament. Does he really think that the Israelites who were practicing
such things *thought* they were dabbling in satanic powers? All
they wanted to do was contact their "familiar" loved ones who
had passed away.

Second, Madrid throws out a red herring by asserting that
the saints "aren't really dead." He thinks that by pointing this
out he has somehow escaped the charge of contacting the dead.
But what can be said of the saints of the New Testament applies
with equal force to the saints of the Old Testament. Neither were
they "really dead" as Jesus so clearly points out to the Sadducees
who denied the resurrection:

> "Have you not read in the book of Moses, in the account of
> the bush, how God said to him, 'I am the God of Abraham,
> the God of Isaac, and the God of Jacob'? He is not the God of
> the dead, but of the living. You are badly mistaken!" (Mark
> 12:26-27).

Madrid equivocates on the meaning of the word "dead." In
the Old Testament passages under discussion "dead" refers to
physical death with no thought of where they might have gone

afterwards (heaven or hell). But Madrid changes the meaning of "death," in the case of praying to the saints, to *eternal* death. The problem is, the most explicit example of necromancy that we have in the Old Testament is that of Saul contacting Samuel— who no doubt possesses eternal life. In this episode (1 Sam 28:7-20), Saul seeks out a medium who contacts Samuel. The biblical writer affirms that this is indeed Samuel and not just a demon disguised as Samuel. Yet, even when we know that the contact made is legitimately with someone who is in heaven, *the practice is still condemned.*

The point is, the Israelites probably had the best of intentions in wanting to contact the dead. They did not wish to dabble with Satan, to harness diabolical powers, or to conjure up spirits from the underworld. They just wanted assistance from their dead loved ones whom they knew had closer access to God. The practice was condemned nevertheless. But is this not precisely what Catholics are doing? Most Catholics have the best of intentions in this practice and have no idea that what they are really doing is "harnessing diabolical powers." Yet ignorance of these things does not thereby make them any less dangerous— and wrong!

Madrid's polemical advice to his Catholic readers is equally remarkable. There he counsels his readers to explain to their Evangelical inquisitors that, "aside from the method of communication, asking our fellow Christians in heaven to intercede on our behalf is no different from asking a fellow Christian here on earth to pray for us."[325] But the "method of communication" is just what is at issue here— neither is contacting the dead any different than contacting a person here on earth *aside from the method of communication!*[326]

Another objection to the Catholic practice of praying to the saints is that it *implies* the saints possess attributes of deity. Suppose someone in the United States were to pray to Mary at a certain time during the day. Suppose further that, at exactly that same moment, someone in Europe begins also to pray to Mary. Which one does she hear? Or, does she hear both at once? To offer a more realistic scenario, suppose at that same moment hundreds of thousands of devoted Catholics from all over the world begin praying the rosary. Who does Mary single out to listen to? In order for Mary to hear all of those prayers at once she would have to be either *omniscient* ("all-knowing") or omnipresent ("everywhere present")— attributes that are the property of God *alone*.

Madrid disputes this point by arguing that in eternity we are not limited by space and time, and so factors in this dimension which might limit our ability to hear many prayers at once do not apply to Mary and the saints in eternity. Madrid further argues that since omniscience and omnipresence "refer to God's *infinite* knowledge and presence," neither one is needed since no matter how many prayers are said at one time, it is still a *finite* number.[327]

Madrid's suggestion creates so many consequent theological difficulties that it is difficult to believe he could be satisfied with it. One may as well argue that omniscience is not needed even by God himself since all things that can be known, no matter how many— are nevertheless finite in number.

In spite of Madrid's assertions to the contrary, one must indeed be omniscient or omnipresent (or both) before he can hear more than one prayer at a time. Madrid engages in special pleading when he counters: "Our inability to understand *how* the saints can hear so many prayers is hardly a reason to deny that they *can* hear them."[328] While this is certainly sound logic when applied to biblical teachings such as the predestination of the elect to salvation vis-à-vis human responsibility, this cannot be applied to the ability of Mary and the saints to hear our prayers. For in the former case there is *explicit* biblical teaching; so much so that not only do we have both teachings presented in unambiguous terms (sometimes in the very same sentence!—

cf. Acts 2:23 and 4:27-28), but we also have the biblical writers admitting they cannot understand it (Rom 11:32-36).

In the case of Mary and the saints, not only do we have absolutely no shred of explicit biblical support, but we do not even have implicit biblical support[329] — indeed, what we *do* have by way of biblical teaching on this matter are explicit prohibitions against the practice! Clearly Madrid would disallow the very form of argumentation that he himself has engaged in if, say, the Mormon used it to advance his belief that we will one day be gods ourselves. Yes (the Mormon could argue), it is true that the Scriptures do not explicitly assert this, and one may even find biblical passages that seem to deny this— but, in the words of Madrid, just because we do not understand *how* this could be done is hardly a reason for denying that it *could* be done! Such argumentation would have to allow for the possible legitimacy of any and every heretical belief imaginable.

To complicate matters even further, some prayers to Mary are silent prayers. Mary would then need the ability to read the minds of her petitioners. Anyone who holds that Mary (or *any* saint for that matter) can be prayed to places himself in the precarious position of having to grapple with the biblical and theological conundrum this position creates. It will not do to argue that nothing in the Scriptures prevents Mary from being able to hear our prayers— whether verbal or silent prayers. This is a convenient line of argument, and one that Keating, Madrid, and others fall back on quite often to support their points. Keating, for instance, argues that Mary can indeed hear our prayers because God has granted to her a limited omniscience. Yet the Scriptures insist that God *alone* enjoys this prerogative:

> "Deal with each man according to all he does, since you know his heart (for you alone know the hearts of all men)." (1 Kings 8:39; 2 Chron 6:30); "I the Lord search the heart and examine the mind." (Jer 17:10.); "And he who searches our hearts knows the mind of the Spirit." (Rom 8:27); Then all the churches will know that I am he who searches the hearts and minds (Rev 2:23).

All of these passages assert or imply that God alone knows the private thoughts of a person. Neither Mary nor any other saint, no matter how exalted, can be considered anything more than a creature with all the attendant limitations.

These passages notwithstanding, Madrid insists that by denying Mary the ability to hear our private thoughts we are "confusing two categories: kind and degree."[330] Madrid goes on to explain that God imparts to us lesser degrees of his infinite attributes. For instance, he is all loving, all merciful and all knowing; but he has also given us the capacity to love, show mercy, and know— only to a lesser degree. Madrid then applies this principle to the ability to read the minds and hearts of men. Mary and the saints, Madrid contends, are able to read our thoughts *only when we ask them to*; they are not, however, able to read our thoughts "unbidden."[331] Madrid sees no difference between this practice and the Evangelical practice of asking other Christians to pray for us:

> Svendsen's argument crumbles here because he would have to admit that if he were to ask his pastor to pray for him, his pastor would know his private thoughts (i.e., wanting prayer). Is that unbiblical? Of course not. The very nature of human discourse involves the communication of private thoughts by one person to another.[332]

What are we to make of Madrid's comments here? First, as Madrid has correctly pointed out, God does indeed communicate certain of his attributes to us. But Madrid has confused communicable and incommunicable attributes of God. Although "knowledge" is a communicable attribute of God (i.e., one that God imparts to man), the ability to know the thoughts and hearts of men is incommunicable; for God at times defines himself by his unique ability to do this: "Then all the churches will know that *I am he who searches the hearts and minds*" (Rev 2:23). We have already seen (above) the other passages that make the same point. It would be quite senseless for Jesus to have defined himself by an ability to which he has no unique claim. Imagine if instead he had said: "I am he who is able to disappear and reappear, and to walk through walls"— hardly something we should be impressed by since even angels can do this! But the very language itself suggests that this ability is unique to God. He does not say, "I am *one* who is able," but rather, "I am *he* who is able" (lit., "I am *the one* searching the minds and hearts"). Indeed, this is the very reason why God alone must judge mankind— he alone can see the heart.

Second, while Madrid insists that none of the passages to this effect "conflicts with the Catholic teaching that we can invoke the intercession of the saints,"[333] he has not explained how this is so in the case of 1 Kings 8:39 and 2 Chron 6:30, both of which unequivocally assert that God *alone* knows the hearts of men. Again we have a direct biblical statement that contradicts Roman Catholic belief. If Mary and the saints (including Old Testament saints[334]) can know our private thoughts then it is certainly not true that God *alone* can do this. The biblical writers obviously knew nothing of the Roman Catholic practice of praying to saints.

Third, Madrid equivocates here on the meaning of "private thoughts" in order to make the Catholic practice of praying mentally to Mary more biblically palatable. He wants us to believe that Mary can know the "private thoughts" of her petitioners in the same way that a pastor can know the "private thoughts" of a church member who asks him for prayer. It is exceedingly difficult to believe that Madrid has thought this through very carefully. Of course the pastor cannot know the "private thoughts" of someone who asks him for prayer, for the instant that person verbally communicates those thoughts to him they are, by definition, no longer *private* thoughts.

In any case, the differences between this practice and the Catholic practice are immense. In the former, the person is vocalizing his request; in the latter, Mary reads his thoughts. In the former, the pastor is in the same dimension as the petitioner; in the latter, Mary is in a different dimension. In the former, the petitioner is not only in the same dimension as the pastor, but also has some legitimate method of communication (in person, telephone, etc.); in the latter, not only is the petitioner in a different dimension than Mary, but also communicates to her in a way that is expressly prohibited by the Scriptures. In spite of Madrid's assertions to the contrary, there are indeed major differences between the Evangelical practice and that of Rome.

Keating cites Jer 15:1 as an example of Moses and Samuel interceding (after death) in behalf of the Jews: "And Jeremiah himself wrote that Moses and Samuel made intercession for the Jews."[335] Madrid, likewise, cites the apocryphal book of 2 Maccabees; namely 15:12-14 where Onias and Jeremiah are said to pray for Israel and the holy city. But Keating and Madrid draw all the wrong conclusions from these texts. In the case of Jer 15:1, the text says: "Then the Lord said to me, 'Even if Moses and Samuel were to stand before me, my heart would not go out to this people." This passage does not teach that Moses and Samuel were interceding on behalf of Israel; God simply says that even if they *were* to do that, he would not listen to them.

Similarly, Madrid has introduced the apocryphal passage as a response against what he perceives to be an Evangelical argument: Writing as an Evangelical interlocutor, Madrid asks, "The Bible nowhere mentions . . . the idea that saints can pray for us. So how does the Catholic Church justify its claim that we should ask Mary and the saints for their prayers?"[336] The careful observer will note here two incongruities. First, Evangelicals do not believe that the saints cannot pray for us. Madrid has simply created a straw man. Second, Madrid has *sneaked* in his conclusion (*asking* Mary and the saints for prayer) on the coat-tails of his premise (the saints' *ability* to pray for us). If Madrid can demonstrate the latter, he thinks he has also demonstrated the former.[337]

But it is just these kinds of logical fallacies that plague both Madrid and Keating's books. Both seem completely unaware that there is a marked difference between the saints praying *for* us, and our praying *to* the saints— they simply assume that the second is somehow a logical extension of the first. No one denies that those in heaven have the ability to ask for God's favor toward those in his church on earth; but this is a far cry from our asking favor from those in heaven. These are two distinct categories, and the first no more necessitates the second than does the fact that I have the ability to pray for jailed Christians in China necessitate the notion that jailed Chinese Christians are free to contact me and ask for prayer! Being united together in Christ does not *guarantee* the ability to communicate with each other as Madrid and Keating assume, for circumstances such as remote location, imprisonment— or, indeed, death!— may very well prevent it. In their zeal for Rome, both Keating and Madrid completely miss the point of the passages they cite.

While we cannot here address all of the points Madrid and Keating make on this topic, one final passage that deserves mentioning is Luke 16. This is the passage where the rich man who, after death, finds himself in a place of torment, and pleads with Abraham (who can be seen by him across a gulf) to send Lazarus to tell his brothers about this place. Keating asks: "If Dives could pray [*sic*] to Lazarus . . . across the unbridgeable abyss, then why should we not be able to pray to saints?"[338] The answer, of course, is that although the rich man was unable to cross the abyss, he was still able to shout over to Abraham and Lazarus[339]; this is vastly different than contacting someone in a different dimension.

Co-Redemptress

In close connection with her role as Mediatrix, Mary is also called Co-Redemptress.[340] Some (such as Keating[341]) lump both roles together into one. However one wishes to categorizes it, Mary is believed by Catholics to be Co-Redemptress by virtue of her cooperation with God in the plan of salvation. Mary (it is argued) said "yes" to the angel when he announced that she would conceive a son. If not for her willing cooperation, mankind could not have been redeemed.

Several observations need to be made about this claim. First, it needs to be stated that no one asked Mary to cooperate in the virgin birth; she was simply told what was going to happen, she had one or two questions about it, and then the angel went on his way. Certainly she cooperated, but she had no more choice in the matter than did the apostles about being included in the twelve. Jesus told his apostles, "You did not choose me, but I chose you" (John 15:16). One need go no further than to the examples of Moses, Jeremiah, or Jonah to see that God gets what he wants, regardless of the reluctance on the part of the one he chooses. The same must be said of all those chosen to serve God in whatever capacity. Mary, a Palestinian Jewish girl, knew this principle only too well.

Second, even if Mary had a choice in the matter and refused to cooperate, this certainly does not mean all would have been lost. It is absurd to postulate that if Mary had refused to cooperate, God would not have chosen someone else to carry out the task. God is not dependent upon the decision of any creature; otherwise God would not be sovereign.

Third, if cooperation in the plan of salvation qualifies one to be Co-Redeemer, then other Co-Redeemers would have to include Joseph (who also gave his consent to live with Mary so that she would not have been stoned to death as an adulteress), John the Baptist (who consented to "prepare the way for the Lord"), Judas (who cooperated in fulfilling the Scriptures to betray Jesus, without which betrayal Christ would not have been put to death and the sins of the world would not have been paid for), Pilate (who cooperated with the divine plan by ordering Jesus' crucifixion), and the mob of people who shouted "crucify him!" All of these were just as necessary as Mary in the divine plan in order to fulfill all that the Scriptures prophesied about Christ.[342] Should we also honor Pilate as a Co-Redeemer?

It is clear from all this that the role of Mary in Catholicism is a contrived one, unsupported by (indeed, contradicted by) Scripture, theology and sound logic. She is neither Co-Redemptress, nor Mediatrix of *any* graces. Her position is no higher in honor than that of anyone else who has faithfully carried out divine orders.

Chapter Nine

The Catholic Priesthood

Three issues that figure prominently in the Catholic faith include that of the Priesthood, the Mass, and the Eucharist. The three issues, while not normally addressed together, are indeed directly related. The Catholic Mass is viewed as a re-presenting of the sacrifice of Christ on the cross; the Eucharist is viewed as the actual transubstantiated body of Christ presented at that sacrifice; and the priest is viewed as the instrument of that sacrifice.

One of the most obvious observations that can be made about the Catholic understanding of the priesthood is that it is nowhere to be found in the pages of the New Testament.[343] The term "priest" does appear in the writings of the early fathers, but is not mentioned (in the Catholic sense of a special order of church leaders) by the apostolic witnesses themselves. The New Testament does speak of a priesthood, but applies that term either to Christ alone, or to all followers of Christ. In fact, there are two priesthoods under the New Covenant: the Melchizedekian priesthood of Christ, and the general priesthood of all believers. Since the former priesthood is more appropriately addressed under the issue of the Mass, we will here address only the latter.[344]

The General Priesthood of all Believers

The Catholic church teaches that there is a specially ordained class of clergy called the ministerial priesthood.[345] While lip service is given to the existence of a "common" priesthood of the laity, it is clear that this is an insignificant priesthood in comparison to the ministerial priesthood.[346] The New Testament, on the other hand, speaks only of a common priesthood of all believers:

> "To him who loves us and has freed us from our sins by his blood, and has made us to be a kingdom and *priests* to serve his God and Father— to him be glory and power for ever and ever! Amen." (Rev 1:5-6); "You have made them to be a kingdom and *priests* to serve our God, and they will reign on the earth." (Rev 5:10); "Blessed and holy are those who have part in the first resurrection. The second death has no power over them, but they will *be priests* of God and of Christ and will reign with him for a thousand years." (Rev 20:6); "... you also, like living stones, are being built into a spiritual house to be a holy priesthood, offering spiritual sacrifices acceptable to God through Jesus Christ." (1 Pet 2:5); "But you are a chosen people, *a royal priesthood*, a holy nation, a people belonging to God, that you may declare the praises of him who called you out of darkness into his wonderful light." (1 Pet 2:9) [Emphasis mine]

Clearly then, the New Testament writers recognize a general priesthood of all believers. More importantly for our purposes, those same writers never give any indication that there is legitimacy to a special priestly class that does not include all believers. There are many titles for leaders given in the New Testament (apostles, prophets, teachers, evangelists, etc.[347]), some of which are used interchangeably of the same person (elders, overseers, and shepherds[348]). Yet never is there any reference to "priest" as a title of a leader of the church. Consequently, the Catholic notion of a priestly class, with all the attendant duties, is nothing more than a later development that was not a part of the apostolic deposit.

The Title "Father"

All priests are given the title "Father." This seems to be in blatant disregard of Jesus' command not to call anyone on earth by that title (Matt 23:9). Surprisingly, Catholic apologists rarely address this issue head-on, opting instead to skirt the issue by pointing out that we call many people "father," including our biological fathers, our grandfathers, the "father" of our country, etc. But, clearly, Jesus had in mind *spiritual* fathers when he made this prohibition, not just any father. Paul, however, does refer to his converts as "children," and makes claims for being a "father" of sorts to the Corinthians: "Even though you have ten thousand guardians in Christ, you do not have many fathers, for in Christ Jesus I became your father through the gospel" (1 Cor 4:15).

Catholic apologists, seeing in this passage support for the Catholic practice, claim that Paul here confers on himself the title "Father." But this is simply not the case. First, just because Paul claims to be a father to the Corinthians, it does not thereby follow that he took on the title "Father" (much the same way that a teacher does not necessarily take on the title "Teacher"). Second, it is important to notice *why* Paul considers himself a father; it is because he was directly responsible for the Corinthians' spiritual birth through the gospel. In contrast, *all* Catholic priests are to be called by the title "Father" by *all* Catholics, regardless of their participation in spiritual birth. Third, Paul denies that anyone else can be regarded as a father to the Corinthians when he states that although they may have many teachers, they "do not have many fathers." The reason for this is precisely because a "father" is someone who is directly responsible for birth. In contrast, the title is void of any significance in the Catholic church,[349] for anyone who is ordained a priest is "father" to all Catholic laity. The difference between the Catholic practice and Paul's practice is, in short, that Paul was a true father without the title while Catholic priests are fathers by title only.

Mandatory Celibacy of the Priesthood

Another aspect of the Catholic priesthood that is in direct violation of Scripture is the forced celibacy of priests. Paul warns us about religious systems that forbid marriage of some or all of its members when he writes:

The Spirit clearly says that in later times—

> "... some will abandon the faith and follow deceiving spirits and things taught by demons. Such teachings come through hypocritical liars, whose consciences have been seared as with a hot iron. They forbid people to marry and order them to abstain from certain foods, which God created to be received with thanksgiving by those who believe and who know the truth." (1 Tim 4:1-3)

Catholic apologists attempt to soften Paul's teaching here, claiming that Paul had in mind only those groups that see marriage as evil.[350] While this category of people is no doubt Paul's primary concern, the passage itself has a much broader application than to combat incipient gnosticism. To forbid marriage for *any* reason is wrong, otherwise Paul's words make little sense; for if forbidding marriage were not inherently wrong, on what basis is Paul condemning these people?

Keating attempts to argue that the Catholic church really does not forbid marriage to anyone, since only priests are forbidden to marry and no one is forced to become a priest.[351] True, but if anyone wishes to aspire to a significant role of spiritual leadership within the Catholic church, that individual must submit to the prohibition of marriage. To the extent that *all* Catholics are denied these leadership roles unless they are celibate, to that extent all Catholics are subject to the same prohibition. It matters little that the Catholic church forbids marriage categorically or particularly, for it forbids marriage nevertheless. To that extent it is in violation of Paul's clear teaching.

Keating cites Paul's words in 1 Coronthians 7 as justification for the Catholic practice of forbidding marriage within the priesthood. Paul does say here that one who is single can serve the Lord with complete devotion, while one who is married has divided interests. Yet, nowhere in this chapter does Paul forbid marriage to those who want to be spiritual leaders within the church. While it may be a good idea to remain single, Paul realizes that every person either has or does not have the gift of celibacy (7:7), irrespective of their qualifications for leadership positions. Paul does not in any way require celibacy for any reason. Indeed, Paul assumes that church leaders will be married, and points to the ability of a man to govern his own household (wife and children) as a test to verify whether that same man is qualified to manage the affairs of the church (1 Tim 3:2, 4-5; Tit 1:5-6). This qualification would certainly be odd if Paul assumed most church leaders would be celibate. It would also be odd if Paul did not see spiritual benefit in the marriage of a church leader. The fact is, almost all of the apostles were married[352]; and Paul assumed that church leaders by and large would be married (1 Tim 3:2, 4; Tit 1:6).

By Keating's own admission, the prohibition against marriage for priests in the Western Rite did not occur until the early Middle Ages.[353] This certainly calls into question its legitimacy as an apostolic church practice; for if the church did not understand the biblical record to imply a celibate leadership for the first five centuries of its existence, then it most certainly cannot be traced to the apostles. Here we have a tradition of men that is in direct conflict with Scripture— but one which we are nevertheless required to believe simply because Rome says we must— providing yet another example of just how far Rome has strayed from the apostolic deposit.

Chapter Ten

The Eucharist and the Mass

In his short book, *This Is My Body*,[354] Mark Shea relates his conversion experience from Evangelicalism to Catholicism. His thesis is that, while examining the Catholic teaching about the Eucharist, all of his prior Evangelical objections were satisfactorily answered, and he was convinced that the Catholic understanding of the Eucharist is in fact biblical. His former objections to the Catholic notion of the Eucharist were fivefold: (1) God forbids human sacrifice; (2) the sacrifice of the Eucharist contradicts Christ's once-for-all sacrifice; (3) God forbids consumption of blood; (4) Eucharistic teaching implies salvation by works, and is a form of idolatry; and (5) Christ's words "this is my body" were clearly intended to be symbolic.[355] It is important to note that only points 2, 4, and 5 are given serious consideration by even-handed Evangelical scholars; points 1 and 3 are likely products of Shea's former Fundamentalism, not Evangelicalism.[356] It is also important to note that Shea omits (or simply does not think through) other equally important objections that will be addressed later in this chapter. In short, Shea seems to have made this journey without doing much research into the biblical data. Had he done so, he may have found the support he claims to have been looking for.

The Eucharist as a Sacrifice

Having noted that not all of Shea's original objections were valid to begin with, we shall address only points 2, 4, and 5, as well as a few other objections that Shea has missed. One of the major objections to the Catholic understanding of the Eucharist is that it is seen as a sacrifice of Christ on the cross. Evangelicals will point out that any kind of re-sacrificing of Christ stands in direct contradiction to several key passages in the book of Hebrews:

> "Unlike the other high priests, [Christ] *does not need to offer sacrifices day after day*, first for his own sins, and then for the sins of the people. *He sacrificed for their sins once for all* when he offered himself." (7:27); "Nor did he enter heaven *to offer himself again and again*, the way the high priest enters the Most Holy Place every year with blood that is not his own. *Then Christ would have had to suffer many times since the creation of the world.* . . . so *Christ was sacrificed once* to take away the sins of many people." (9:25-28); "Day after day every priest stands and performs his religious duties; again and again he offers the same sacrifices, which can never take away sins. *But when this priest had offered for all time one sacrifice for sins, he sat down at the right hand of God.* Since that time he waits for his enemies to be made his footstool, because by *one sacrifice* he has made perfect forever those who are being made holy. . . . Their sins and lawless acts I will remember no more. *And where these have been forgiven, there is no longer any sacrifice for sin.*" (10:11-18) [Italics mine]

According to the writer of Hebrews, the very thing that distinguishes Christ's priesthood from all others is that he does not need to offer himself repeatedly, day after day, or year after year. Rather, he offered *one* sacrifice (himself) *once for all time*. The Greek words for "once" used throughout these passages are *hapax* (ἅπαξ) and *ephapax* (ἐφάπαξ), both of which mean "*once for all time*" (as opposed to any notion of a continuing or repeated sacrifice).

Countering popular misunderstandings that Jesus is being re-sacrificed in the Mass, Catholic apologists insist that the Mass is a re-*presenting* of the original sacrifice, not a re-*sacrificing* of him.[357] But it is difficult to know just what the real difference is between a re-presenting of Christ's sacrifice and a re-sacrificing of him. Does a *re-presenting* mean that Christ is not actually but only symbolically sacrificed at the Mass? This does not seem to be the case.[358] Yet, if Christ is actually being sacrificed at the Mass, it matters not whether this sacrifice is a *continuum* of the original sacrifice, or a repeated sacrifice— both are precluded by the writer of Hebrews. According to the passages above, Christ's sacrifice is *one* in number, *once* in time,[359] and *completed*. This last point is illustrated by the writer of Hebrews when he says that, after his sacrifice, Christ "sat down at the right hand of God." The purpose of this phrase is to show absolute *completion* of the sacrifice— it cannot be repeated, nor can it be continued. Contrary to Catholic belief, Christ is not continuing this one sacrifice, but (in regard to sacrificial work) is now *seated*, waiting for his enemies to be made his footstool.

Two other observations need to be addressed with regard to these passages in Hebrews. First, the author of Hebrews writes with remarkable clarity of the singularity and finality of Christ's once-for-all-time sacrifice for sins; and he does so (again, remarkably) without any qualification. If the writer of Hebrews held the same view of Christ's sacrifice as does the Catholic church, one might expect him to clarify that, although Christ's sacrifice is one in number, it is a *continual, eternal* sacrifice. Significantly, he gives no such qualification. One would be hard-pressed to find *any* Catholic teaching (whether official or unofficial) on the singularity and finality of Christ's sacrifice (as expressed in the book of Hebrews) without the accompanying qualification that it is a *continual* sacrifice through the Mass.

Second, in spite of ample opportunity to do so, not once does the writer of Hebrews connect the sacrifice of Christ to the Eucharist. In a book replete with sacrificial language, it is indeed odd (if the Catholic understanding of the Mass is correct) that our author does not make this connection. The implications of this are revealing; for what Catholic could read the words of the writer of Hebrews without immediately associating them with the Mass? As it stands, the underlying assumptions of the Roman Catholic apologist reading this passage are demonstrably different than those of the writer of the passage.[360]

Transubstantiation

At the heart of the Catholic understanding about the Eucharist is the belief that the elements (bread and wine), while retaining their original appearance,[361] are physically changed (transubstantiated) into the actual body and blood of Jesus. This teaching is based on two distinct passages; one in the synoptic gospels (Matthew, Mark, and Luke), and one in John.

In Matt 26:26, Jesus, referring to the bread in his hand, says "this is my body."[362] Catholics take this, along with the saying about the cup ("this is my blood"), to mean literally that the bread and wine become Jesus' physical body and blood. Catholic apologists make much of the fact that since Evangelicals are known for taking Scripture literally, they are inconsistent for not taking this saying literally.[363] But this misses the point. It is not so much an issue of a literal vs. symbolic interpretation— most Evangelicals do not say that Scripture must be taken literally; rather, Scripture must be taken in its plain, ordinary sense, and interpreted in context. In this case, there are good reasons for believing that Christ did not mean "this is my *actual* body," and "this is my *actual* blood."

First, the lack of confusion on the part of the Apostles to Jesus' words indicates that they took his words to mean that the bread and wine *represent* the body and blood of the Lord, not that the bread and wine *become* his body and blood. Ironically, Shea argues just the opposite; namely, that the lack of confusion on the part of the Apostles shows that they understood Jesus to be referring to his actual body and blood.[364] Yet, Shea's argument assumes that the Apostles are incapable of rightly interpreting

Jesus' words symbolically, and that they would therefore require some kind of clarification from Jesus.

Second, the phrase "this is my body" is paralleled in Matt 26:28 and Mark 14:24 by the phrase "this is my blood of the covenant," but in Luke 22:20 and 1 Cor 11:25 by the phrase "this cup is the new covenant in my blood." If the phrase "this is my body" means that the bread is literally transubstantiated into Christ's body, then what does the cup literally transubstantiate into— Christ's blood (according to Matthew and Mark), or the new covenant (according to Luke and Paul)? The Roman Catholic is obliged to believe the former. Yet, if the Roman Catholic concedes that the cup in Luke 22:20 and 1 Cor 11:25 only represents the new covenant (and does not actually transubstantiate into the new covenant), then his entire thesis, that the first phrase-"this is my body"— must be taken literally, falls to the ground.

Moreover, it must be pointed out that Jesus was physically present at the table. If the Apostles had taken Jesus' words literally, wouldn't their natural response have been one of confusion? Obviously, if the Apostles had understood the bread to *have become* the body of Christ, and they were still seeing something that looked like the body of Jesus sitting and holding what looked like bread, then they most certainly would have wondered just what it was that was holding the bread. Further, if they had understood the bread to be "part" of the body of Christ, then they naturally would have wondered just what part it was. Was it his elbow? His knee? His toe?

The Apostles would more naturally have taken Jesus' words symbolically. To illustrate this point, suppose someone who plays in a symphony were to hold up his violin and proclaim to the audience, "this is my right arm." How would those in the audience take that statement— literally or symbolically? If they took it symbolically, would they be asking questions of clarification? Would they be confused? Would it not be sufficiently clear to them that, since the man's right arm was still intact, he must be speaking symbolically? Would there be any question at all in the minds of those in the audience that this person was not speaking literally? It seems doubtful that there would be any confusion at all among those in the audience.

Let us assume for the sake of argument the unlikely scenario that the audience does take the man literally. Would they not be full of questions as to how the man's arm mysteriously transubstantiated into the violin? Would they not have a question or two as to why, if the violin is the "real" arm of the man, they could still see the man's physical arm. Or, how the violin and the man's arm could be one and the same? As it stands, the very fact that the Apostles had no questions is a strong case for assuming that the Apostles understood Jesus' statement to be symbolic and not literal.

There are, of course, other problems with the understanding of the bread becoming the real, physical body of Jesus. One is that it contradicts the thrust of the Councils of Chalcedon and Ephesus. Both councils opposed three major heresies: (1) Apollinarianism and (2) Monophysitism, both of which taught a single nature of Christ, although with varying emphases; and (3) Nestorianism, which allegedly taught that Jesus Christ is two persons (rather than two natures). The councils affirmed that Christ is one person having two natures (not two persons); a human nature and a divine nature. They condemned any kind of separation of persons, and at the same time condemned any attempt to deify the humanity of Christ.[365] Augustine echoed this same concern:

> Since, then, Christ is God and man ... we must take account of both these natures in Him when He speaks or when Scripture speaks of Him, and we must mark in what sense anything is said. When we say that Christ is the Son of God we do not separate His humanity from Him, nor when we say that the same Christ is the Son of man do we lose sight of His divinity. For, as man He was on earth, not in heaven where He now is ... although in His nature as Son of God He was in heaven, but as Son of man He was still on earth and had not yet ascended into heaven. ... and He will so come, on the testimony of the

angel's voice, as He was seen going into heaven, that is, in the same form and substance of flesh to which, it is true, He gave immortality, but He did not take away its nature. *According to this form, we are not to think that He is everywhere present. We must beware of so building up the divinity of the man that we destroy the reality of His body.* It does not follow that what is in God is in Him so as to be everywhere as God is. . . . God and man in Him are one Person, and both are the one Jesus Christ who is everywhere as God, but in heaven as man.[366] [Italics mine]

The concept of transubstantiation effectively deifies the human nature of Christ by ascribing to it the attribute of omnipresence. The bread becomes the body of Christ in thousands of different locations of local churches at exactly the same moment. This confuses Christ's deity (which is omnipresent) with Christ's humanity (which is not omnipresent). The only way Christ could be in the bread and wine is through his deity; i.e., spiritually. Just as Christ in his physical body cannot be in more than one place at a time, so also if the eucharistic bread becomes the actual body of Christ, then it can be in no more than one particular location at a time.

Closely related to this point is the notion that the Eucharist is to receive adoration.[367] The Catholic church holds that since Christ was worshipped in his human body on earth, it follows that we may worship the body of Christ in the Eucharist. The fallacy again lies in not making the proper distinction between the humanity and deity of Christ. No one in the first century worshipped the *body* of Christ *per se*, but rather the person of Christ who happened to be embodied. It is one thing to worship Christ's person; it is quite another thing to worship Christ's *body*, which is idolatry.

The Eucharist in John

One last passage that Catholics point to for justification of transubstantiation is the sixth chapter of John's gospel, which reads in part:

"I am the bread of life. Your forefathers ate the manna in the desert, yet they died. But here is the bread that comes down from heaven, which a man may eat and not die. I am the living bread that came down from heaven. If anyone eats of this bread, he will live forever. This bread is my flesh, which I will give for the life of the world." Then the Jews began to argue sharply among themselves, "How can this man give us his flesh to eat?" Jesus said to them, "I tell you the truth, unless you eat the flesh of the Son of Man and drink his blood, you have no life in you. Whoever eats my flesh and drinks my blood has eternal life, and I will raise him up at the last day. For my flesh is real food and my blood is real drink. Whoever eats my flesh and drinks my blood remains in me, and I in him. Just as the living Father sent me and I live because of the Father, so the one who feeds on me will live because of me. This is the bread that came down from heaven. Your forefathers ate manna and died, but he who feeds on this bread will live forever." (John 6:48-58)

Catholics see in this passage a direct teaching by Jesus about the Eucharist. They point out that Jesus calls himself the "bread" of life and that the one who "eats" this bread will live forever. They note that in order to have eternal life one must "eat [Jesus'] flesh" and "drink [Jesus'] blood," because Jesus' flesh is "real" food and his blood is "real" drink.

What are we to make of these claims? Is this passage referring to the Eucharist? It must be pointed out at the start that the episode recorded in John 6 happened before the institution of the Eucharist in the other gospels.[368] Therefore, none of the original hearers would have understood Jesus to be referring to the Eucharist. Instead, when Jesus did finally speak the eucharistic words "this is my body" the hearers would naturally have recalled Jesus' words in John 6. The significance of this is that the Eucharist must then be seen as symbolizing Jesus' teaching in John 6, not the other way around.

It must also be insisted that this passage is to be interpreted in light of the surrounding context. Jesus had just fed the five thousand (6:5-14). The very next day these same people, remembering what Jesus had done, compare Jesus' miracle to Moses' miracle of feeding the Israelites manna ("bread from heaven") for *forty years* (vv. 30-31), while Jesus had fed them for only a day. Jesus, playing off of the crowd's comparison, states that he is the *true* bread from heaven (vv. 32-33). The crowd, still dull in understanding, asks to be given this "true" bread, whereupon Jesus says: "I am the bread of life. He who comes to me will never go hungry, and he who believes in me will never be thirsty" (v. 35).

Jesus, of course, is saying nothing new. The same crowd had previously asked him what "work" needed to be done to earn eternal life (v. 28). Jesus, again playing off of their dullness, answers in an ironic fashion: "The work of God is this: to believe in the one he has sent" (v. 29). In other words, Jesus says: "You want works? Okay, here's the work God requires— believe!" Jesus takes this same ironic tone with those in the crowd when answering their question about Moses' provision of bread for forty years. Bread was considered a staple (as it is today), and Moses' provision of "bread from heaven" meant that Moses provided that which was necessary to sustain life. Jesus picks up on that idea and says in essence: "You think Moses provided you with the necessities of life? He provided the sustenance for mere physical life. I will provide you with all the necessities to sustain *eternal* life!" Jesus uses the analogy of bread *only because that is what the crowd was interested in at that moment.*

That this is Jesus' intent is clear from other passages in this same chapter. In the midst of the bread discourse Jesus affirms: "I am the bread of life. He who comes to me will never go hungry, and he who believes in me will never be thirsty" (v. 35) There can be no doubt that what Jesus meant by "eating" and "drinking" him was *to come* to him and *to believe* in him. This is further evident from v. 47: "I tell you the truth, he who believes has everlasting life," which is immediately followed by:

> "I am the bread of life. Your forefathers ate the manna in the desert, yet they died. But here is the bread that comes down from heaven, which a man may eat and not die." (vv. 48-50)

Again, Jesus equates the "eating" of him to believing in him. This belief results in eternal life:

> "For my Father's will is that everyone who looks to the Son and believes in him [notice, this time not "eats" and "drinks" him] shall have eternal life, and I will raise him up at the last day." (v. 40)

Elsewhere in this passage Jesus states the same truth, but uses the analogy of bread— the sustenance of life:

> "I am the living bread that came down from heaven. If anyone eats of this bread, he will live forever." (v. 51); "I tell you the truth, unless you eat the flesh of the Son of Man and drink his blood, you have no life in you. Whoever eats my flesh and drinks my blood has eternal life, and I will raise him up at the last day. For my flesh is real food and my blood is real drink." (vv. 53-55)

Jesus' point is that, just as physical bread sustains physical life by physically eating it, so Jesus is the heavenly bread that sustains spiritual life by spiritually "eating" him (i.e., believing in him). Physical food is no more in view here than is *physical life*. Augustine himself noted this when commenting on this passage:

> If the sentence is one of command, either forbidding a crime or vice, or enjoining an act of prudence or benevolence, it is not figurative. If, however, it seems to enjoin a crime or vice, or to forbid an act of prudence or benevolence, it is figurative. "Except ye eat the flesh of the Son of man," says Christ, "and drink His blood, ye have no life in you." This seems to enjoin a crime or a vice; it is therefore a figure, enjoining that we should have a share in the sufferings of our Lord, and that we should retain a sweet and profitable memory of the fact

that His flesh was wounded and crucified for us.[369]

Augustine's view of this passage parallels the Evangelical view. To interpret it otherwise destroys the physical/spiritual contrast, reduces a life-giving, personal relationship to the mere physical consumption of food, and makes absolutely no sense at all of the text.

Another example of this kind of metaphor is found in John 4, where Jesus is met at the well by a Samaritan woman. After some preliminary conversation Jesus says:

> "If you knew the gift of God and who it is that asks you for a drink, you would have asked him and he would have given you living water." "Sir," the woman said, "you have nothing to draw with and the well is deep. Where can you get this living water? Are you greater than our father Jacob, who gave us the well and drank from it himself, as did also his sons and his flocks and herds?" Jesus answered, "Everyone who drinks this water will be thirsty again, but whoever drinks the water I give him will never thirst. Indeed, the water I give him will become in him a spring of water welling up to eternal life." The woman said to him, "Sir, give me this water so that I won't get thirsty and have to keep coming here to draw water" (John 4:10-15).

This passage has many remarkable similarities to the John 6 passage. In John 6, Jesus picks up on the crowd's interest in bread: in John 4, Jesus picks up on the woman's interest in water. In both cases eternal life is in view. In both cases a metaphor of consumption is used to illustrate belief in Jesus. In both cases Jesus' audience mistakenly takes the metaphor literally. In John 4, Jesus makes no attempt to clear up the woman's confusion (i.e., he did not expressly state that drinking "living water" means to believe in him and have eternal life). In John 6, Jesus makes at least some attempt to explain what his metaphor means.[370] In both cases Jesus' audience compares him to one of the Old Testament patriarchs (John 4—Jacob; John 6—Moses).

Since Jesus is obviously speaking of the same thing in both passages (eternal life), the question must be asked: If the Catholic church insists on viewing Jesus' words in John 6 literally (so that we must literally eat bread to gain eternal life), why does that same Catholic church not teach that we must drink *physical water* to gain eternal life per John 4? Why understand the "eating and drinking" in John 6 as literal, physical eating, and not understand the "drinking" in John 4 as a literal, physical drinking? Conversely, if one understands John 4 symbolically, then one has no basis for rejecting the symbolic understanding of John 6.

Even if one chooses to ignore the above argument, a few other observations must be pointed out. First, there are two Greek words used for "eating" in John 6: *esthiô* (ἐσθίω) and *trôgô* (τρώγω). Catholic apologists point out that the latter (*trôgô*) means to "gnaw" or "munch." Their point for doing so is to suggest that this must be a physical eating, otherwise *esthiô* would have been used throughout.[371] But this is mere conjecture. Jesus obviously uses these terms interchangeably (since he uses each one independently to make the same point). Moreover, *esthiô* is used in all of the Last Supper passages ("take and *eat*, this is my body"), not *trôgô*. For Catholic apologists to make the point that a *different* word is used in John 6 than is used in any of the Last Supper passages seems to be a strike against their position, not for it; for if a different word is used, then it is likely that a different point is being made in each case.

Second, the Greek word used in John 6 to designate that which we are to eat is *sarx* (σάρξ; translated "flesh"), while the Greek word used in the Last Supper texts is always *sôma* (σῶμα; translated "body"). The differences between these words suggests that if a connection between John 6 and the Eucharist is made, it must at best be a loose one. This fits well with the symbolic understanding of John 6.

Third, if one insists that John 6 is a reference to the Eucharist, then the inescapable conclusion according to this passage is that anyone who does not partake of the Eucharist does not have eternal life. Christ states unequivocally that "unless you eat the flesh of the Son of Man and drink his blood, you have no life in you" (John 6:53). Clearly, if this is a reference to the Eucharist, then no Evangelical has eternal life. Catholic apologists do not want to take Jesus' statement to its logical conclusion. They believe that Evangelicals can and do have eternal life without partaking of the Catholic Eucharist. Yet, Jesus' words could not be clearer. Catholic apologists want to have their eucharistic cake and eat it too; but they cannot. Either Jesus is not referring to the Catholic Eucharist in this passage and Evangelicals can have eternal life; or Jesus is referring to the Catholic Eucharist and Evangelicals cannot have eternal life. The latter proposition contradicts the Catholic Catechism, which refers to Protestants as "separated brethren" whose churches are a "means of salvation."[372] The Catholic apologist will have to decide whether he believes Jesus' clear statement in John 6, or the official teaching of Rome. They cannot both be true.

Transubstantiation in the Early Church Fathers

In a debate with James White, Gerry Matatics baldly asserts that there is not even one father who held to the Protestant view of the Eucharist as symbolizing Christ's body.[373] While there is no doubt that Catholic apologists are able to produce writings from the Fathers that seem to support transubstantiation, the fact is there was no consensus or clarification on this issue in the Catholic Church until the Fourth Lateran Council in 1215.[374] While the views of the Fathers are not the standard of truth for the Evangelical (although they are of some value), they *are* an important standard of truth for the Catholic. It will be beneficial therefore to show that some significant Fathers did not believe in transubstantiation.

One such Father, Irenaeus, states his belief about the Eucharist in these words:

> For as the bread of the earth, receiving the invocation of God, is no longer common bread but Eucharist, consisting of two things, an earthly and a heavenly.[375] [italics mine]

Irenaeus' words sound more like *con*substantiation (the elements intermingle with the bread and wine) than *tran*substantiation (the elements replace the bread and wine).[376] In any case, it is clear that this is not Rome's concept of transubstantiation, which holds that there is nothing left of the bread and wine which is not transubstantiated into the body and blood of Christ.

It is equally clear that Augustine did not hold to anything like transubstantiation when he writes:

> To be sure, we often speak in the following way: As Pascha approaches, we say that tomorrow, or the day after, is "the Passion of the Lord," although He suffered so many years before, and His Passion occurred only once. Indeed, on that particular Lord's Day we say "Today the Lord has risen," although many, many years have passed since the time when he arose. Why is it that there is no one so foolish as to accuse us of being liars when we speak in this way? It is because we name these days according to a likeness to the days on which those events took place. Thus a day, which is not the actual day, but like to it in the circle of the year, takes its name from the actual day because of the celebration of the sacrament which occurred, not on the very day of the celebration, but long ago. . . . For if sacraments did not have a certain likeness to the things of which they are the sacraments, they would not be sacraments at all. . . . Therefore . . . in a certain way the sacrament of the body of Christ is the body of Christ.[377] [Italics mine]

In this letter to Boniface of Cataquas, Augustine reveals what his concept of a sacrament is. It is clear that Augustine uses "sacrament" as a virtual synonym for "symbol." Just as the Lord symbolically rises on each Paschal Lord's Day— that is, each Paschal Lord's Day bears a "likeness" to the actual day that the Lord arose— so also "in a certain way" (i.e., in a way that symbolizes the original) "the sacrament of the body of Christ *is* the body of Christ." So, for Augustine, there is a "real" presence of the body of Christ during the Lord's Supper, but it not the "actual" body of Christ that is present. Instead, the eucharistic bread is "like" the original in that it "takes its name from the actual" body of Christ.

That this is Augustine's understanding of the Eucharist is further demonstrated by his explanation of the eucharistic word's of Christ: "You are not going to eat this body which you see, nor are you going to drink the blood which those who will crucify me are going to shed. I have given you a sacrament."[378] Here again Augustine specifically denies that the bread of the Eucharist is the same "body" as that indwelt by Christ— it is, for Augustine, clearly a symbolic body. No one who makes statements such as these can in the same instance hold to the Catholic notion of transubstantiation. Consequently, "obscure though his view of the Eucharist undoubtedly is, it is at any rate certain that [Augustine] did not believe in transubstantiation."[379]

Other fathers may by cited, including Peter Lombard, who believed in the "substantial" presence while rejecting a belief in transubstantiation.[380] In similar vein, the fifth century father, Theodoret of Cyrus, understands the consecration of the Eucharist not to be a complete eradication of the physical bread and wine, but rather a supplementation of them. In his dialogue with the heretical Eranistes, Theodoret (assuming the orthodox side) expressly rejects the notion of transubstantiation. It will be helpful to reproduce the relevant portion of that dialogue here:

> Eran[istes]: "Therefore, just as the symbols of the Lord's body and of his blood are one thing before the priest's invocation, but after the invocation are changed, and become something else, so to was the Lord's body changed, after the ascension, into the divine essence."

> Ortho[dox Theodoret]: "You have been caught in the nets which you have woven, for not even after the consecration do the mystical symbols depart from their own nature! *They*

continue in their former essence, both in shape and appearance, and are visible, and palpable, as they were beforehand."[381] [Italics mine]

Again we have the views of a father that fly in the face of Rome's concept of transubstantiation: Rome does not believe that the bread and wine continue in their former essence as Theodoret does. Indeed, the transubstantiation of modern Roman Catholicism is indistinguishable from the heretical views of Eranistes!

While this list is not exhaustive, it is sufficient to show that the Catholic view of the Eucharist certainly cannot be considered a unanimous teaching of the Fathers. Yes, they did believe in a "real" presence— but then so do most Evangelicals believe in a "real" presence. That is not what is at issue.[382] The question is, Is the "real" presence a *physical* or a *spiritual* presence? Jesus tells us that worship under the New Covenant would not be characterized by locality and materiality— "a time is coming when you will worship the Father neither on this mountain nor in Jerusalem" (John 4:21)— but rather by that which is spiritual:

> "A time is coming and has now come when the true worshipers will worship the Father in spirit and truth, for they are the kind of worshipers the Father seeks. God is spirit, and his worshipers must worship in spirit and in truth." (John 4:23-24)

Catholic apologists make the mistake of equating "spiritual" with that which is not "real." Yet, Jesus makes the exact opposite point— the *true* ("real") worshipers are those who worship in *spirit,* not in the material.

Indeed, when taken to its logical end, even Catholic apologists waver in their belief that the bread and wine are so radically changed that nothing of either remains except in appearance. When confronted with the question of whether it would be safe to consume arsenic-laden bread since, according to Catholic teaching, nothing of the original remains after transubstantiation, Keating states:

> Only the bread, not the poison, could be transubstantiated. Anything mixed with the bread would have remained unaltered. . . . The arsenic would have remained poison. Transubstantiation would not have made the arsenic disappear.[383]

Although "bread" is not a single ingredient but a mixture of many ingredients (composed at least of flour and water), we can agree with Keating that, if transubstantiation is true, these basic ingredients are all that would change in the case of additions not normally contained in bread (such as arsenic). However, while this explanation may very well vindicate the eucharistic bread that is transubstantiated, it does not do the same for the eucharistic wine. Is the alcohol content of the wine transubstantiated into the blood of Christ also? It surely cannot be argued that alcohol is not part of the wine; that it is something that is added to the recipe. Yet, if one were to drink enough of the eucharistic wine, would he become drunk? If not, then how is it that some of the Corinthians were becoming drunk on the "transubstantiated" wine at the Lord's Supper?[384] If so, then the alcohol content cannot be said to have changed during transubstantiation, for it still has the same effect that it had before the change. In that case, the wine has not been changed in all its parts, and there is still an intermingling of the wine and the blood of Christ. Consequently, one cannot hold that the wine becomes nothing more than the blood of Christ, and transubstantiation cannot be true. When put to the test and pressed with hard questions and real biblical examples, the idea of transubstantiation simply does not wash.

Conclusion

We have examined the claims of only a few of the major
Catholic apologists, though these claims are the ones that attract
the most attention of the Catholic layman. It is important to
note that there is much more that could be said about these
issues and others— by no means have these *Evangelical Answers*
been exhaustive. Hopefully, this will be sufficient to prompt the
Catholic apologist to rethink some of the issues, and to take a
more realistic look at the Catholic church— both in its history
and in its theology— rather than to continue to hold to highly
romantic ideas of what the church should be, but is not.

Throughout his tape series, Scott Hahn emphasizes over and
over again that the strength of the Catholic position lies in the
collective weight of all the arguments put together. Yet a chain is
no stronger than its weakest link. If each of the Catholic apologists' arguments will not hold up individually, no amount of
stringing them together can make them any stronger. We have
not found even one argument of these Catholic apologists that
stands on its own. The arguments presented look impressive at
first glance, and the weight of the evidence appears massive—
but only until we discover that the Catholic apologists' arguments are a house of cards. The instant we pull out one card that
does not belong, the entire structure comes tumbling down.

Endnotes

Introduction

1 Many of them seem to label all those who disagree with their beliefs as "anti-Catholic" or "Catholic bashers." In reality, most of us simply have honest differences and difficulties with Catholic doctrine.

2 *Catholicism and Fundamentalism* (San Francisco: Ignatius Press , 1988), 159, 276. There are other such condescending statements in his book as well.

3 Taken from an e-mail note sent to me by Madrid during an informal debate with him.

4 One way the Catholic apologist does this is to argue that Protestantism cannot be legitimate for the simple fact that there are over 20,000 denominations all "bickering" with each other (Bob Sungenis, *Surprised By Truth: 11 Converts Give the Biblical and Historical Reasons for Becoming Catholic* [ed. Patrick Madrid; San Diego: Basilica Press, 1994], 119) (see chap. 7 for details).

5 This is quite evident, for instance, in Patrick Madrid's, *Any Friend of God is a Friend of Mine* (San Diego: Basilica Press, 1996).

6 Jack Chick is the quintessential example of this. His tracts are littered with ad hominem arguments, historical inaccuracies, and questionable exegetical conclusions.

7 Such as is characterized by the ecumenical document, *Evangelicals and Catholics Together*, authored in part by Chuck Colson and Bill Bright.

8 The statements, phrases and tone used by many Catholic apologists very often speak for themselves, and we would be little served by reciprocating them.

Chapter One: Infallibility of the Catholic Church

9 All references to Hahn's position are taken from his tape series titled, *The Bible Alone* (St. Joseph Communication, Inc.).

10 *External evidence* is simply evidence from a source outside the New Testament that would indicate authorship.

11 For instance, the style of writing, the phrases used, the differences between how the writer addresses himself and how he addresses everyone else, etc. One compelling piece of internal evidence is detailed in *An Introduction to the New Testament* (ed. D. A. Carson et al; Grand Rapids: Zondervan, 1992). Carson shows that the titles of the gospels (e.g., κατὰ Ματθαῖον, *According to Matthew*) are actually part of the original text of the gospels: "we have no evidence that these gospels ever circulated without an appropriate designation," 66. This, of course, completely overturns Hahn's contention that we must rely on the tradition of the church for these designations.

12 For a detailed list of this evidence the reader is referred to Carson, *NT Introduction*, passim.

13 Raymond Brown, *Mary in the New Testament* (Philadelphia: Fortress Press, 1978), 17. This change of policy on the part of the Catholic magisterium also calls into question the wisdom of submitting to any belief solely on the basis of a supposed ecclesial authority.

14 Irenaeus, Hippolytus of Rome, and the Muratorian Fragment all insist that Paul is not the author.

15 *Epistle* 129.3.

16 *Forgiveness of Sins* 1.50.

17 F. F. Bruce, The *Book of Hebrews*, NICNT, Revised Edition (Grand Rapids: Wm. B. Eerdmans Publishing Com-

pany, 1990), 17. See also D. A. Carson, *Introduction*, 395. This in spite of the fact that both Hippo (393) and the Third Synod of Carthage (397), regularly cited by Catholic apologists as the councils that determined the canon, attributed non-Pauline authorship to Hebrews: "Of Paul the Apostle, thirteen epistles; of the same to the Hebrews, one."

18 Carson, *Introduction* (395), notes that the last major defense of this view was written in 1939.

19 See chapter 4 of this book for a detailed discussion of the canon.

20 So also, David Palm ("Oral Tradition in the New Testament," *This Rock* [reprinted internet version from the May 1995 issue]): "This verse about Moses' chair illuminates why we say that the successor of Peter, when he gives a solemn teaching for the whole Church, is said to speak ex cathedra or 'from the chair.'"

21 F. F. Bruce, *New Testament History* (New York: Doubleday, 1971), 71 (fn 7).

22 Ibid., 63, 74-75.

23 We are here assuming for the sake of argument that Jesus' words are spoken in earnest. There is compelling reason to believe that Jesus is instead speaking with "biting irony" (cf. D. A. Carson, "Matthew," *The Expositor's Bible Commentary*, Vol. 8 [ed. Frank E. Gaebelein. Grand Rapids: Zondervan, 1976], 473-74).

24 Bruce, 78, "The high priests were regularly selected from the wealthy Sadducean families."

25 See e.g., Isa 6:8-13; Jer 1:4-10, 2:1 ff; 20:1-6; Ezek 2:14, 13:1-8; Joel 1:1-2; Mic 1:1, 3:1; Zech 1:1-6; and Mal 1:1, 6-14, 2:1 ff.

26 Actually the Sadducees were formally in charge, but their authority and teachings were not very popular among the masses. The Pharisees were not professional clergy, but rather laymen who took religious matters into their own hands. This is, of course, devastating to Hahn's

thesis, for the exclusive magisterial priesthood of the Sadducees, as well as their more legitimate claim to unbroken succession from Moses, more nearly conforms to the Roman Catholic notion of ecclesial authority than does the comparatively new and decidedly colloquial leadership of the Pharisees.

27 Keating, 215 ff.

28 Ibid., 215.

29 It is interesting to note that at least one Catholic apologist, Paul J. Glenn (*Apologetics* [Rockford: Tan Books, 1980], 272), admits: "Obviously, we can make no direct demonstrative proof [from Scripture] of the justice of this claim [to infallibility]. . . . [and] . . . Since such demonstration would be a sort of 'begging the question,' we shall not attempt it." Other apologists, such as Keating and Hahn, would do well to concede the same point.

30 Although the Catholic interpretation of this passage as a support for papal primacy was held by no one before the fourth century. Until the eighth century the East held to the personal primacy of Peter without any notion of Roman primacy (Hans Küng, *Infallible? An Unresolved Enquiry*, New Expanded Edition [New York: Continuum, 1994], 91).

31 Carson, "Matthew," 367 ff.

32 Peter is indeed the foundation upon which the church was built, but so are the rest of the apostles (Eph 2:20). The Greek words used in both Matt 16:18 ("I will build") and Eph 2:20 ("built upon") are different forms of the same verb ($οἰκοδομέω$). Matt 16:18 affirms that the church would be built upon Peter, and Eph 2:20 affirms that the church was built upon all the apostles. The singling out of Peter in Matt 16:18 can be no more significant than that Paul in Gal 2:20 singles himself out from among all other Christians to affirm that Christ died for *him*. Both passages are intended to personalize, not exclude.

33 See Phil 2:15-18.

34 Cf. Acts 2:14-41 (Peter's first binding), 3:11-26, 4:8-22

(Peter's first loosing), 16:30-34 (one of Paul's bindings).

35 It should be noted here that Augustine, one of the greatest theologians of the church, did not hold the Catholic interpretation of this passage, nor did such prominent fathers as Chrysostom, Hilary, Origen, Cyril, or Theodoret (William Webster, "Did I Really Leave the Holy Catholic Church?," *Roman Catholicism: Evangelical Evangelicals Analyze What Divides and Unites Us* [Chicago: Moody Press, 1994], 278-282 passim). In light of this, it is dubious just how pivotal this passage could be for the Catholic apologist. Indeed, any Catholic who chooses to use this passage in support of papal primacy will find himself at odds with the vast majority of church fathers. James White (*The Roman Catholic Controversy* [Minneapolis: Bethany House Publishers, 1996], 120) has shown that as many as 80% of the fathers who interpret this passage dissent from Rome's current understanding of it.

36 "What is that to you? You follow me!" (John 21:22).

37 Cf. 1 Pet 5:1-4.

38 Küng, 207.

39 Ironically, Hahn hammers away at the Evangelical understanding of this passage that Jesus here guarantees infallible inscripturation of truth. He asks the question, "where in this passage is there a command to write Scripture?" Yet, the Catholic apologist must face the same reality that there is in this passage no statement that the apostles or the church would be infallible. The most that can be gleaned from this passage is that the apostles would *receive* infallible information, not that they would then proclaim that information infallibly.

40 Later in the New Testament, although we find two methods of transmitting the apostolic deposit (written and oral proclamation), we find that only one of these receives the designation θεόπνευστος (*theopneustos*, "God-breathed"); hence, only one is necessarily infallible.

41 J. Blunch, "Firm, Foundation, Certainty, Confirm," *The New International Dictionary of New Testament Theology*, vol. 1

(ed. Colin Brown; Grand Rapids: Zondervan, 1986), 662. A survey of the major translations seems not to favor one rendition over the other: KJV, "ground"; *ASV*, "ground"; *RSV*, "bulwark"; *NEB*, "bulwark" (Webster defines "bulwark" as a "defensive wall"); *NIV*, "foundation"; *NAB*, "foundation"; *NASB*, "support." Perhaps, though, the Greek construction here is best taken as a hendiadys ("one through two"), which means that the second term is a synonym of the first ("the church, which is the pillar—that is, defensive wall—of the truth").

42 See, e.g., Dave Armstrong's "50 New Testament Proofs for Petrine Primacy and the Papacy" on his *Biblical Evidence for Catholicism* internet web page.

43 Some Catholic apologists even go so far as to see in James' words, "Simon has declared" (v. 14), an acknowledgment by James that Peter has "declarative" power as the pope. But this is simply disingenuous. The word used here (ἐξηγέομαι) simply means "to explain," and is usually used (as it is here) to explain events. Hence, Cornelius "explained" to his servants the vision he had (Acts 10:8); the two who walked with Jesus on the road to Emmaus afterward "explained" to the eleven the events of their journey (Luke 24:35); Paul "explained" to the Jerusalem church what God had done during his missionary journey (Acts 21:19); and Jesus "explained" the Father to us (John 1:18). Indeed, the same word is used of Paul and Barnabas in the very passage under consideration: "The whole assembly became silent as they listened to Barnabas and Paul telling [ἐξηγέομαι] about the miraculous signs and wonders God had done among the Gentiles through them" (Acts 15:12). The fact that the whole assembly became "silent" only when Paul spoke might lead us to believe that perhaps Paul has declarative power!

44 James White illustrates this when he cogently points out that many of the traditions about Mary not only have no support in patristic literature, but were expressly not included as part of the Catholic Tradition even as late

as the nineteenth century ("The Sola Scriptura Debate," available through Alpha and Omega Ministries, Phoenix, AZ).

45 This point is humorously illustrated by the following excerpt from an as yet unpublished novel:

"You know," John said laughing, "it sounds like the pope has older brother syndrome." The others obviously didn't catch the reference. "Well," he began, explaining, "an older brother will tell you that he has a leprechaun in his pocket, and the leprechaun says you have to do the dishes or he'll turn you into a toad. You ask to see the leprechaun, but, of course, the leprechaun doesn't want to be seen. Only your brother can see him, and only he can talk to him. It sounds to me like anybody who has an older brother should know better than to believe Rome's claims to authority." "That's an interesting way of looking at it," Anne said. "Rome says it's subject to Scripture and Tradition, but then it's very clear that only the pope gets to interpret Scripture and Tradition," she laughed. "I guess it's very much like your older brother with the lep- rechaun—the leprechaun will only speak to him. The story just doesn't sound right, and you can't trust somebody who won't lay their cards on the table" (Greg Krehbiel, *The Witch's Promise*).

46 See Küng, 150, where he notes that in the Middle Ages it was the "universally shared basic belief" that the church itself could err. This principle may be illustrated by Vincent of Lerins in his *Commonitorium* (434), in which he gives guidelines for distinguishing the true catholic faith from heresies. Vincent clearly believed in the possi- bility that a "contagion" could "infect the whole church," in which case we are to "cleave to antiquity." And if antiquity itself is found to be infected, we are to hold to the plenary councils (III. 7-8). Vincent makes it clear elsewhere that he subscribes to a correct interpretation of the Scriptures through oral tradition. But the implication of his point here is equally clear: Vincent could not have believed in ecclesial infallibility and at the same time have entertained the possibility that the "whole church"

might some day become infected with heresy. For all his seemingly Roman Catholic beliefs, Vincent is decidedly *non*-Roman Catholic in this belief.

47 *Vatican I, Session IV,* quoted in Bettenson, *Documents of the Christian Church* (Oxford: Oxford University Press, 1963), 273.

48 Callistus spoke against Sabellius "but continued to use rather Sabellian language" (Harold O.J. Brown, *Heresies: The Image of Christ in the Mirror of Heresy and Orthodoxy from the Apostles to the Present* [Grand Rapids: Baker, 1984], 103).

49 Ibid., 190. Keating attempts to soft-peddle this incident by asserting that "Actually, Honorius elected to teach nothing at all" (229). This is not, as Keating suggests, a case where a pope simply did not define a doctrine. Honorius made positive statements in support of the monothelite position ("Wherefore we acknowledge *one* will of our Lord Jesus Christ," *The Catholic Encyclopedia,* Vol VII [New York: Encyclopedia Press, 1913], 453), gave his official support to it in a letter to Sergius ("The letter cannot be called a private one, for it is an official reply to a formal consultation," ibid.), was officially condemned by pope Agatho and the Sixth Ecumenical Council ("We decide that Honorius . . . be anathematized . . . because we have found by his letter to Sergius that he followed his opinion in all things, and confirmed his wicked dogma," ibid., 454), and was specifically called a heretic ("To Honorius, the heretic, anathema!" Session XVI, Sixth Ecumenical Council). Moreover, for several centuries thereafter every new pope was made to repeat the anathema against Honorius as part of his papal oath. Apparently, those who were closest to the actual events (as opposed to modern Catholic apologists, who are more than a dozen centuries removed) were quite clear that Honorius' stance on this issue was heretical, and that he himself was a heretic. Catholic apologists are in a very precarious position here. For if they side with the council and admit that Honorius taught heresy, they

have ipso facto denied papal infallibility. On the other
hand, if they defend Honorius, and even argue that his
position was orthodox, then they have contradicted an
Ecumenical council, pope Agatho, and the testimony of
several centuries of papal oaths that follow. Catholic apologists often accuse Evangelicals of operating as a "magisterium of one" because we make individual judgments on
what is orthodox and what is heretical. But this is exactly
what Catholic apologists are forced to do here. They are,
in essence, trusting their own fallible opinions over those
of several popes, as well as hundreds of bishops meeting
in ecumenical councils (the anathema against Honorius
was repeated in subsequent ecumenical councils as well).

50 Bettenson, 59, 81. Keating, thinking that Zosimus
declared a *person* orthodox and not a doctrine per se,
does not see this as an "attempted exercise of infallibility"
(226). But Keating is misinformed: Zosimus did indeed
declare a heretical teaching orthodox, for he made the
declaration on the basis of the *confession of faith* that he
received from both men! In spite of Keating's optimistic
thinking to the contrary, Zosimus did indeed err. Nor
does it matter (contra Keating) that Zosimus may have
had an incomplete knowledge of all the issues. After all,
Keating has argued that infallibility is a *negative* protection against error (215-217 passim). Yet, Zosimus made
positive declarations about a heretical doctrine. Is this not
the very thing against which infallibility is supposed to
guard him?

51 *The New Schaff-Herzog Encyclopedia of Religious Knowledge*, vol. V; ed. Samuel M. Jackson (Grand Rapids: Baker,
1977), 489.

52 Ibid.

53 *Heresies*, 301.

54 Küng, 56.

55 *The Congregation of the Index*, under the direction of
Pope Paul V, decreed in 1616 that "the Pythagorean doctrine, which is false and contrary to Holy Scripture, . . .

teaches the motion of the earth and the immobility of the sun" (cited in Jerome J. Langford, *Galileo, Science, and the Church*, rev. ed. [Ann Arbor: University of Michigan Press], 98). This decree was fully supported and promulgated in 1633 by Paul V's successor, Urban VIII. The official text of the condemnation accused Galileo of "heresy, namely, having believed and held the doctrine which is false and contrary to the Sacred and Divine Scriptures" (ibid., 152). Galileo's condemnation was finalized in 1664 by Pope Alexander VII in his bull *Speculatores domus Israel* which condemned "all books which affirm the motion of the earth." Although he later attempts to show that this was not an infallible act, Langford (a Catholic priest) candidly admits, "The decree of Sentence was both *doctrinal* and disciplinary" (ibid., 156).

The reason we point this out is because Catholic apologists commonly downplay this case as not falling in the category of infallible statements. Yet, there is no question that all Catholics during this time were *required* to believe, with the Catholic Magisterium, that the Sun revolved around the earth, and that this understanding was based in Scripture. The fact that the Catholic church took an "official" position, and derived that position from Scripture, means (as Langford concedes above) that it considered this a matter of dogma. Yet everyone who submitted themselves to the Catholic Magisterium's belief during this time was *in error*. How then was the Catholic church protected from error in this case? How can we be certain (based on Rome's track record) that 100 years from now archaeologists won't dig up the remains of Mary and that some 21st century Catholic apologist won't make the argument that the Assumption of Mary never met the criteria for infallibility to begin with?

56 This point was made by Pius XII who said, "If the Popes in their official acts deliberately pass judgment on a matter that has been debated up to then, it is clear to all that the matter . . . cannot be considered any longer a question open for discussion among theologians," (quoted

in William G. Most, *Catholic Apologetics Today* [Rockford: Tan Books, 1986], 166). The fact that there was much opposition and debate about the pope's plans to move the see is also well known: "There was protest against this from all sides. Among the loudest was that of Petrarch..., one of the greatest figures of the Italian Renaissance" (*Eerdmans' Handbook to the History of Christianity* [New York: Eerdmans, 1977], 326).

57 *Catechism*, Art. 834.

58 Ibid., Art. 880.

59 Ibid., Art. 882.

60 This in spite of the fact that the headquarters for the church in the New Testament is first Jerusalem and then Antioch—never Rome. Moreover, in Rev 2—3, Jesus addresses seven churches: (1) none of them is the Roman church; (2) none of them is told to submit to the Roman church; (3) Jesus addresses them independently of the others, suggesting independent local churches, not *one* church under Rome. But if Rome has always been supreme "from the incarnate Word's descent to us," why didn't Jesus just tell Rome what he wanted and have Rome in turn tell all the local churches? As it is, Jesus bypasses any supposed primacy of Rome. Moreover, the Eastern church never accepted the primacy of the West, but rather claimed equality with Rome (Bettenson, 82-83).

61 As Küng points out, these historical difficulties "make any attempt to demonstrate a historical succession of the Bishops of Rome in a Petrine primacy a highly question-able enterprise" (79).

62 Aside from the "official" original sources cited by the Catechism, the Catechism itself is an "official" church document, ordered written by the Pope in 1986, and "officially" approved in an Apostolic Constitution entitled *Fidei Depositum* on Oct. 11, 1992, with the words "I today order [the publication of the Catechism] by virtue of my Apostolic Authority" to be a "sure and authentic reference

text for teaching catholic doctrine" (*Catechism*, 5).

63 Keating, 219. Keating's reconstruction misses the point of subsequent papal legitimacy.

64 This same point, of course, can be made of the election of Alexander V, and the deposition of the successors of Urban VI and Clement VII.

65 *Catechism*, Art. 883.

66 Ibid., Art. 884.

67 One might also mention the dual popeship between Eugene IV and Felix V, and that of Alexander III and Victor IV.

68 Included here are the practices of *Reservations* (popes reserving the richest benefices for themselves), *Indulgences* (sold to the laity to secure forgiveness for sins), *Expectancies* (tickets that were sold to bishops who then could bid even more money on an office that would be opening up soon), *Dispensations* (forgiveness from violations of canon Law that could be bought with money), and *Nepotism* (placement in the papacy of the pope's illegitimate children). A classic example of an immoral decree may be found in the Fourth Lateran Council, which commanded that "Catholics . . . shall exterminate the heretics, possess the land without dispute and preserve it in the true faith. . . . Hence if forgers . . . are straightway justly put to death, . . . with much more justice can heretics . . . be not only excommunicated but also put to death" (quoted in Bettenson, 133-34).

69 "They profess to know God, but *by their deeds* they deny him" (Tit 1:16). "Prove yourselves doers of the Word, and not merely hearers who delude themselves," "If anyone thinks himself to be religious . . . . This is pure and undefiled religion in the sight of our God . . . to keep oneself unstained by the world . . . [otherwise] . . . this man's religion is worthless" (Jas 1:22, 26-27). "You tolerate that woman Jezebel, who calls herself a prophetess, who teaches and leads my servants into sexual immorality" (Rev 2:20).

70 Leo V was murdered by his successor, who in turn was murdered and succeeded by Sergius III.

71 Witness the period known as the *Pornocracy*, which began with Sergius III.

72 John XII not only invoked Jupiter and Venus but turned the papal palace into a house of prostitution.

73 The German emperor Ortho called together a synod of bishops who deposed John XII; Henry III deposed Gregory VI; Benedict XIII and Gregory XII were both deposed by the Council of Pisa; Eugenius was deposed by a national French synod.

74 E.g., John XXII, who recanted his heresy on his death-bed. Even Benedict XIII and Gregory XII, two of the rival popes of the Captivity, were condemned as heretics by the Council of Pisa in 1409.

75 Bettenson, 115-16.

76 To this may be added the words of Pope Innocent III at the *Fourth Lateran Council*, "There is but one universal Church of the faithful, outside which no one at all is saved"; and those of Pope Eugene IV in his papal Bull, *Cantate Domino*, "The most Holy Roman Church firmly believes, professes and preaches that none of those existing outside the Catholic Church, not only pagans, but also Jews and heretics and schismatics, can have a share in life eternal. . . . No one, let his almsgiving be as great as it may, no one, even if he pour out his blood for the Name of Christ, can be saved, unless he remain within the bosom and the unity of the Catholic Church."

77 *Ineffabilis Deus.* Clearly both *Ineffabilis Deus* and *Unam Sanctam* are infallible according to the criteria given by Vatican I. An *ex cathedra* statement is a statement issued by the pope that defines a dogma of faith or morals to be held by all Christians everywhere. Does *Ineffabilis Deus* meet this criteria? Its use of the words *declare, pronounce* and *define* suggests that it does, and all Catholics would agree that it is. What about *Unam Sanctam*? Does it fall under the rubric of infallibility? It, too, uses the

words *declare, pronounce* and *define*, but adds to that, *state*, thereby making the statement even stronger. *Ineffabilis Deus* makes the statement that it must be believed by all the faithful. *Unam Sanctam* makes that same claim to mandatory and universal belief when it states: "We are *obliged . . . to believe . . . that it is altogether necessary to salvation* for every human creature to be subject to the Roman pontiff" (emphasis mine). Again, *Unam Sanctam* seems to be much stronger in its assertion that it *must* be believed. Incidentally, both statements are accompanied by anathemas for those refusing to believe.

Some Catholics downplay the significance of *Unam Sanctum* by taking refuge in the historical context of the papal document; that is, the document is a *political* rather than *ecclesial* polemic. Yet, it must be noted that *no* papal statement is ever issued in a vacuum—all of them are in response to some historical context, including *Unam Sanctam* and including *Ineffabilis Deus*. Remember, though, that this is precisely what Catholics say infallibility is supposed to guard popes against, insisting over and over again that infallibility is a *negative* protection against error. We may legitimately ask then, Where is that negative protection operating in the case of *Unam Sanctum* vs. *Vatican II*?

78 *Catechism*, Art. 818-819.

79 Ibid., Art. 838. This (latter) citation was added because it is commonly argued by Catholic apologists who are confronted with these conflicting statements that there were no Protestants in existence when *Unam Sanctum* was penned, so that *Unam Sanctum* has no relevance today. However, the catechetical citation above also includes the Eastern Orthodox church which *was* in existence during that time.

80 *Corporis Juris Canonici*, Vol II, ed. by A. Friedberg (Leipzig, 1881), 287.

81 Cf. Keating's explanation, 215-231. Keating reconstructs the historical evidence in the softest possible way.

82 Granted, but then should we call these immoral popes "holy father"? Should we still acknowledge them as God's representatives? The New Testament writers have much to say about our attitude toward those pretending to represent him while living immorally (1 Cor 5:1-12; 2 Cor 6:14-18; 2 Pet 2:1-2; 1 John 3:7-10; Jude 3-4, 12-13).

83 Some Catholic apologists (e.g., Hahn) attempt to distinguish between those times when a pope might proclaim a doctrine (fallibly?), and other times when a pope proclaims a doctrine while speaking in the capacity of "supreme pastor and teacher" (infallibly). This distinction, however, is artificial. It is extremely doubtful that the official definition of infallibility meant to imply that there are times when the pope proclaims a doctrine outside of his role as supreme pastor and teacher.

84 This is far from merely hypothetical. As we have already seen, this very thing happened in the case of the contradictory teachings between *Unam Sanctam* and *Vatican II.*

85 But then any religious group could claim that same type of infallibility. Any non-Catholic group could say that its doctrine is infallible only if it meets certain criteria (carefully selected, of course, after the fact)—indeed, there are many groups who have done just that, including Jehovah's Witnesses. What is the basis of this criteria? It is simply made up—proclaimed to be so. There is no substantial difference between the pope's proclamation and that of any other group who makes the same claim. If the Catholic church can pull infallibility out of a hat, so too can others.

86 In fact, in the Catechism, these words are nowhere to be found in connection with infallibility.

87 Bettenson, 83.

88 Küng, 167.

89 Ibid., 168.

90 "[The Nicaean Council] speaks the truth because

despite its use of new words it was not saying anything new" (Ibid., 208).

91 Ibid., 168-69.

92 *On Baptism, Against The Donatists*, II, 3.2.

93 This, of course, is not the only standard by which to measure truth. John points out others (1 John 3:10, 4:2, 6), as do the other writers of Scripture.

94 See chapter six of this book.

95 This is not to suggest that the belief of the majority is necessarily correct; nor that unique beliefs of the minority are necessarily wrong—after all, the Arian denial of the deity of Christ was once the majority belief and the orthodox position was the minority. The difference in this case is that the proposed belief is completely without Scriptural support.

96 Hahn pushes this point forcefully. He wants to know what the difference is between Jehovah's Witnesses and Protestants since each has their own interpretation of Scripture. This is a rather odd point to raise, however, since the Watchtower much more resembles the structure and claims of the Roman Catholic church than it does the Protestant church. The Jehovah's Witnesses and the Catholic church alike claim to have a body of infallible interpreters. In fact, every cult (including, among others, the Seventh Day Adventists and the Mormon church) has some kind of infallible interpreter of Scripture to whom everyone else must submit.

97 Hahn, "The Bible Alone?"

98 Indeed, Hahn's proposal is self-refuting. None of the passages he uses to argue in support of the Catholic position have an "official" (and therefore, infallible) interpretation by the Catholic church. Since this is the case, how can Hahn be certain that he is interpreting *any* passage correctly? The fact is, *all* Catholic apologists use unofficial interpretations of Scripture in their writings and debates, and *none* of them seems to feel constrained by that fact. In

every case, what Catholic apologists so forcefully affirm about their belief in the inability to interpret Scripture without an infallible interpreter is implicitly denied by their actual practice.

99 "Of what value is a purely formal official statement of the 'meaning' of the Christian faith without an understanding of what the meaning means?" (Robert Strimple, "Roman Catholic Theology Today," in *Roman Catholicism*, 100).

100 Taken from a taped debate titled, "What Still Divides Us? An Evangelical & Roman Catholic Debate", (produced by Christians United For Reformation, 1995).

101 Although, even in this case, if the pope were to give an understanding that is not consonant with the context, his understanding might legitimately be called into question. As one who travels internationally teaching seminars in communication skills, I can verify the phenomena known as "leveling," "assimilating," and "sharpening" the message—all of which means simply that one hears what one wants or expects to hear. All of us, including the pope, filter information through personal experiences and assumptions.

102 This fact should not alarm the reader; textual critics are in large agreement (1) that we have all the correct readings of the text (the question is simply one of deciding *which* reading is the correct one), (2) that we are certain of the correct reading of 98-99% of the entire New Testament, and (3) that the 1 or 2% that is in question involves non-doctrinal content (most of these are concerned with issues such as whether the text reads "And Jesus said to him" or "And He said to him"—clearly insignificant as far as doctrinal matters are concerned).

103 This type of circular "hindsight" criteria for determining infallible teachings is typical of *all* traditions of Rome for which there is historical support.

104 Carthage omitted Baruch and included 1 Esdras. The modern day Catholic Bible reverses this. See the discus-

sion of the canon in chapter five of this book.

105 There is a crucial point to be made here. While Catholic apologists tend to lump all Protestants together (all liberal brands and all conservative brands) in order to point out the vast differences of belief, it is a fact that Evangelicals do not embrace liberal Protestants as brothers, but view them as heretics. We exclude them from the fold—and indeed, we are quite free to do so. The Catholic apologist, on the other hand, does not have this freedom. He cannot call moderate Catholics (such as Raymond Brown and the majority of Catholic scholars who reject the conservative view of the inerrancy of Scripture) "heretics" for the simple reason that Rome has not done so. At Vatican II Rome embraced modern exegesis and higher criticism, and has not uttered one word against it since that time. Indeed, with the pope's recent endorsement of evolutionary theory, the moderate Catholic scholar has been given even more leverage in his view of Genesis as "historic myth"—and the conservative Catholic apologist is gradually becoming the step-child of Catholicism. There is, therefore, a much greater degree of differences of belief in Catholicism than in Evangelicalism.

106 Cf., e.g., Raymond Brown (*The Critical Meaning of the Bible* [New York: Paulist, 1981], 3), who recognizes the "real struggle . . . between the Catholic center and the Catholic far-right" in reference to the meaning of the doctrine of the inerrancy of the Scriptures. He also points out that "there are sharp differences in the way doctrines are understood" (ibid., 84).

107 Indeed, in *Surprised By Truth*, Steve Wood states that before becoming Catholic he understood the central message of the Bible: "the Scriptures seemed to be opened to my understanding. I felt as though God were speaking to me personally through the pages of Scripture. . . . It didn't take much Bible reading to discover that I was a sinner and needed Christ's forgiveness," (79-80). Wood's experience is not unusual in Evangelicalism. He himself admits that he needed no infallible interpreter—nor at

this point even spiritual life—to understand the plain meaning of the Scriptures.

108 *Responses to 101 Questions on the Bible* (New York: Paulist Press, 1990), 25.

109 Most Catholic apologists would disagree with Brown on this—but that only serves to illustrate the point. On what basis are they deciding that *they* are right in their understanding of papal definitions and Brown is wrong? Obviously, their infallible interpreter has been no help here, since both are appealing to the same papal statements to defend their respective positions. The result is that each Catholic is left to his own reasoning faculties to decide the answer to this, as well as to other important issues. In other words, each individual Catholic must finally become his own magisterium.

110 John is here battling the heresy of incipient gnosticism. He calls the false teachers "antichrists" (v. 18) who "deny that Jesus is the Christ" (v. 22).

111 This certainly does not discount the value and necessity of genuine teachers in the body of Christ. Indeed, Paul places teachers only behind apostles and prophets in his list of gifts in the church (1 Cor 12:28). The "lie-detector" spoken of by John has to do with a negative protection against falling prey to rank heresy, while the teaching office in the church has to do with positive doctrinal reinforcement.

112 *New American Bible.*

113 "The Bible Alone?"

114 "Woman, why are you bothering me?" See discussion of this passage in chapter eight.

115 See chapter seven of this book for details on Brown's view.

116 Michael Green (*2 Peter and Jude,* Tyndale New Testament Commentaries [Grand Rapids: Eerdmans, 1987], 101) comments that "grammatically, this clause goes with what precedes, not what follows." Consequently, "Peter is not

talking about *interpretation* but *authentication*" [emphasis his].

117 This word is used in the ancient papyri for the "discharge" of an account (A. C. Thiselton, "ἐπιλύω," *NIDNTT*, vol. 1, 577).

118 The presence of the word "prophet" (*NIV*), which does not appear in the original Greek, is based on common usage of the word *epilusis* (ἐπίλυσις) in Aquila's Septuagint (Gen 40:8; 41:8, 12) and the early fathers (see, e.g., *Shepherd of Hermas*, Parable 5:6; 7:1; 9:13) where it is the *prophet's* interpretation of the revelation that is in view (the word occurs only here in the NT).

119 Jerome H. Neyrey (*2 Peter, Jude*, The Anchor Bible, vol. 37c [New York: Doubleday, 1993], 184), a Jesuit priest, appeals to Peter's words later in this same epistle (viz., that some of Paul's letters are "hard to understand," 3:16) as an interpretive key to understanding 1:20-21. This, however, seems a bit forced. The passage makes good sense in its immediate context, and appealing to the remote context to overturn the plain sense of the text suggests to us that Neyrey has prior loyalties to uphold.

120 "If interpretation were his subject [in v. 20], then verse 21 would be utterly irrelevant to his argument," Green, 102.

Chapter Two: The Nature of the Church

121 Scott Hahn, "The Bible Alone?" It should be pointed out that many Catholic apologists argue that the longevity of the Catholic church is itself "proof" of its divine appointment. But would these Catholic apologists also want to argue this same point about Hinduism and Buddhism, each of which exceeds the age of Catholicism by hundreds or thousands of years? Longevity is more often the result of institutionalism than divine appointment.

122 Far from retaining ties with an organization of immoral infidels, we are expressly commanded in Scripture "not to associate with any so-called brother who is immoral," (1 Cor 5:11) to "clean out the old leaven that

you may be a new lump," (5:7), to *"come out from them and be separate*, says the Lord. Touch no unclean thing, and I will receive you" (2 Cor 6:17), and not to "be bound together with unbelievers" (6:14). It is difficult, in light of these passages, to understand how Catholic apologists can insist that the Reformation (which came about largely in response to immoralities and corruption in the Catholic magisterium) was somehow outside of God's will.

123 *Catechism*, Art. 823.

124 This point is well illustrated by Paul J. Glenn, *Apologetics*, who writes, "If the Catholic Church is not to endure intact until the end of time, where shall we find a Church of which this must be anticipated? Yet, surely, the *true* Church *will* and *must* exist intact until the end of time" (276). Yet this is true only if the church is an institution. The church, however, is *not* an institution, but rather a collective group of individuals who, in the mind of God, have been foreknown, predestined, called, justified, and glorified before the foundation of the world (Rom 8:28-30).

125 This is evident from the text of the Confession itself, which states the following:

> The visible Church, which is also catholic or universal under the Gospel (not confined to one nation as before under the law), consists of all those throughout the world that profess the true religion; and of their children: and is the kingdom of the Lord Jesus Christ, the house and family of God, out of which there is no ordinary possibility of salvation (25:2). . . . This catholic Church hath been sometimes more, sometimes less visible. And particular Churches, which are members thereof, are more or less pure, according as the doctrine of the Gospel is taught and embraced, ordinances administered, and public worship performed more or less purely in them (25:4).

It is clear that the framers of the Westminster Confession envisioned a church that was both visible *and* invisible. The invisible (spiritual) church has always existed and always will exist—and will always believe in the truth of

the gospel. That same church is visible in local churches
to the extent that those local churches are faithful to the
gospel of Christ.

126 *Catechism*, Art. 818-819.

Chapter Three: Apostolic Succession

127 "The Bible Alone?"

128 Irenaeus, *Against Heresies*, Book III, 3:1-3

129 Ibid., Book II, 22:4-5.

130 Another instance of apostolic tradition that contradicts contemporary Roman Catholic belief is purported
to have been given by Papias: "Papias, who is now mentioned by us, affirms that he received the sayings of the
apostles from those who accompanied them, and he moreover asserts that he heard in person Aristion and the
presbyter John. Accordingly he mentions them frequently
by name, and in his writings gives their traditions. . . .
The same person, moreover, has set down other things as
coming to him from unwritten tradition, amongst these
some strange parables and instructions of the Savior, and
some other things of a more fabulous nature. Amongst
these he says that there will be a millennium after the
resurrection from the dead, when the personal reign
of Christ will be established on this earth" (*Fragments
of Papias: From The Exposition Of The Oracles Of The
Lord*, VI:10-13). The "apostolic tradition" expressed here
is decidedly premillennial—contra the Roman Catholic
church which holds to an amillennial eschatology.

131 See, e.g., Ignatius, *Eph.* 2:5; 4:8; 5:7-9; 20:14-16.
Although even here a pope is not mentioned. Instead,
submission to the local bishop is commanded.

Chapter Four: The Canon

132 Catholic apologists also commit the fallacy of com-
position when they argue that since the Catholic church
was without error in its determination of the books of
the New Testament, it must therefore be without error in

everything it teaches. One might as well argue that if all
the parts of a machine are light in weight, the machine
itself must therefore be light in weight. Or, that since the
Catholic church is in error about some things, it must
therefore be in error about everything it teaches.

133 So Küng, "the binding nature of statements of faith
does not mean necessarily accepting their infallibility,"
123.

134 *Eerdmans' Handbook to the History of Christianity*, 106.
See Athanasius' letter in Philip Schaff, *The Nicene and Post-
Nicene Fathers*, Vol IV (Grand Rapids: Eerdmans, 1953),
551-52. It is also evident from this letter that Athanasius
and the Eastern church did not include the Apocrypha as
part of the Old Testament canon.

135 This borrowing of capital from non-Roman sources
is not an isolated incident. Küng notes that the Catholic
understanding of the inerrancy of Scripture is borrowed
from Evangelical Protestantism: "It was only towards the
end of the nineteenth century that the popes, under the
pressure of destructive critical exegesis, took over the
theory of literal inspiration worked out by Protestant
Orthodoxy," 174. Catholic apologists who make much of a
supposed "Evangelical borrowing" of a "Catholic" canon
are caught in a strange irony.

136 Cf. R. K. Harrison, "Apocrypha," *The Origin of the
Bible* (ed. Philip Comfort, Wheaton: Tyndale House, 1992),
85. See also, R. T. Beckwith, "The Canon of the Old Testament," *Origin*, 61.

137 Bill Marshner ("What Still Divides Us") makes a
similar point when he appeals to Evangelicals not to
fall back on the argument that the inscripturation and
recognition of the New Testament Scriptures "stands to
reason," since an infallible interpreter of Scripture (viz.,
the Catholic church) also stands to reason. The difference
between the two, of course, is that the inscripturation and
recognition of a canon of Scripture for the New Covenant
stands to reason precisely because it is the belief that
Jesus himself held about the inscripturation and recogni-

tion of the canon of Scripture for the Old Covenant. Jesus held no such assumption about an infallible interpreter in Old Testament Israel.

138 The Jews accepted a canon consisting of twenty-two or twenty-four books, but never accepted the apocryphal books found in the Catholic Bible (Beckwith, "Canon," 62). See also the discussion entitled, "*Whose* Scripture is Sufficient," in the following chapter.

139 So Harrison, who states, "Only when they had been circulated, read, and assessed favorably by comparison with the spirituality of the Torah were they accorded general canonicity. Hence the distinction between the canonical and apocryphal writings came as much through usage and general consent on the part of orthodox Judaism as in any other manner" (85).

140 Even the apocryphal books that are currently included in the Catholic Bible were never officially recognized as inspired or authoritative until the Council of Trent. But by that time, the Reformers had already decided that these books should be excluded from the Scriptures. This is just one more example of how God preserves his word against additions, so that no noncanonical book would ever receive wide, general recognition.

141 Barring, of course, heretical groups.

Chapter Five: The Sufficiency of Scripture

142 "The Bible Alone?"

143 The desire to justify non-biblical Catholic traditions causes David Palm ("Oral Tradition") to conclude the following about Jude's citation of the *Assumption of Moses* (which he unfortunately refers to as "oral" tradition):

> In addition, this text relates well to a Catholic dogma that troubles many non-Catholics—the bodily Assumption of Mary. There is no explicit biblical evidence for Mary's Assumption (although see Rev. 12:1-6), but Jude

not only provides us with a third biblical example of the
bodily assumption of one of God's special servants (see
also Gen. 5:24, 2 Kgs. 2:11), he shows that oral Tradition
can be the ground on which belief in such a dogma may
be based.

Aside for the fact that the *Assumption of Moses* is inscripturated (not "oral") tradition, and forms a part of the
Pseudepigrapha, Palm makes theological points about this
text that Jude does not. Palm wants us to glean from
this text support for the bodily assumption of Mary. All
Jude wants us to glean is that we should hesitate to rail
judgments against demons. We cannot even be certain
that Jude wants us to view his quote of the *Assumption
of Moses* as historical fact. A modern day Christian writer
might appeal to this or that action of "Christian" in John
Bunyan's mythical tale *Pilgrim's Progress* in an attempt to
exhort his readers to right behavior. Do we conclude on
that basis that such a writer wants us to view *Pilgrim's
Progress* as historical?

144 BAGD, "able to meet all demands."

145 Catholic apologists often appeal to Jas 1:4 as an
argument against the sufficiency of Scripture in the present passage ("Perseverance must finish its work so that
you may be mature and complete, not lacking anything").
Perseverance (we are told) seems here to be "sufficient" to
make us "mature and complete." But (we are asked) are
not other things needed beside perseverance before we
can be "mature and complete"? Aside from the fact that
the Greek word used here is different than that found in 1
Tim 3:17 ($\tau\acute{\epsilon}\lambda\epsilon\iota o\varsigma$ is used, not $\ddot{\alpha}\rho\tau\iota o\varsigma$), Catholic apologists
miss the point of both passages entirely. Each passage
refers only to those things for which the subject is fitted.
In the case of Jas 1:4, perseverance accomplishes maturity
and completeness *only* in the "testing of your faith" (v. 3).
In 1 Tim 3:16-17, Scripture makes the man of God "fully
equipped" *only* to "teach, rebuke, correct, and train." Of
course, the man of God also needs qualities such as love,
patience, a chaste life, and other such virtues; but as far

as the categories of teaching right doctrine, rebuking and correcting wrong doctrine, and training in righteousness are concerned, the Scriptures alone are said to make the man of God "fully equipped."

146 Catholic apologists may claim that they believe in the Trinity because they have it on the authority of the Catholic church, and not because it is found in Scripture. Yet they will not hesitate to prove this doctrine from Scripture if someone challenges them on it (such as a Jehovah's Witness), revealing their true belief that it *can* be proven from Scripture apart from Catholic tradition. What the Catholic apologists so vehemently profess about the necessity of Catholic tradition (and the insufficiency of Scripture) to "correct" wrong belief is directly contradicted by their actual practice.

147 See comments on 2 Thess 2:15 later in this chapter.

148 Indeed, there is no logical reason for choosing Rome over the Eastern Orthodox church if the criterion is church tradition; for the Eastern Orthodox church appeals to the very same church tradition to justify its own beliefs to the exclusion of Roman beliefs (e.g., the Filioque controversy, the question of Roman and papal authority, and the Easter controversy just to name a few). In these cases the Roman Catholic apologist cannot appeal to the Scriptures, for he has already argued that they are insufficient in these matters. Nor ironically can he appeal to the fathers, for a different "catholic" denomination that traces its existence to those same fathers (the Eastern Orthodox church) has arrived at a different conclusion in these matters. What it comes down to is that the Roman Catholic apologist must ultimately trust that his own fallible reasoning process has chosen the correct church.

149 Catholic apologists often ask where the New Testament indicates that oral tradition would cease after the death of the apostles. The answer is, as with the canon, it is the biblical precedent we have in the New Testament regarding the Old Testament. There was no binding oral tradition after the last Old Testament author laid down

his pen.

150 Acts 17:2-3.

151 "What Still Divides Us?"

152 Ironically, the only dogmas which we may be certain are part of Roman Catholic Tradition are just as certainly later developments that could not have been handed down from the apostles.

153 Yet, as we have already seen, this, too, is problematic; for, according to Raymond Brown, Rome has not yet given an "official" interpretation of any passage of Scripture.

154 Appeal is often made to Basil who on occasion speaks of unwritten traditions (cf. his Canon 92). But these traditions are always either concerned with practices and customs of the church (some of which are not currently held by Rome, such as the ecclesial limitations imposed on one who has committed murder, Canon 56), or with the proper wording of doxologies that were to be sung (*On the Holy Spirit* VII)—yet even here he appeals to Scripture as well.

155 Bill Webster points out the confusion of the early church on the issue of the apostolic origin of tradition when he notes the following (taken from an internet debate on the Sola-L list):

But the problem with the claims that these practices are apostolic in origin is the fact that they are simply claims with no means of verification—they are simply assumptions made by the fathers. Historically there have been contradictory practices embraced by East and West both claiming apostolic authority. One example is the Easter controversy of the 2nd century and another is the conflict between Stephen, the bishop of Rome with Cyprian and Firmilian, along with other Eastern bishops, over the issue of the rebaptizing of heretics. Firmilian, in support of Cyprian, explicitly states that Stephen's claim to apostolic authority for his position is spurious and that his (Firmilian's) is the true teaching handed down from Christ and the Apostles. He complained that the Roman Church had embraced a number of customs which were contrary to apostolic teaching and practice.

156 Gerry Matatics has appealed to this word in a taped debate with James White ("The Sola Scriptura Debate," available through Alpha and Omega Ministries, Phoenix, AZ). I have encountered other Catholic apologists online who have appealed to the same word.

157 The content of these Jewish traditions was, interestingly enough, the Jewish *interpretation* of the Law; the very thing we are told is the content of Catholic Tradition (the NT documents substituting for the Law in the case of the latter).

158 Yet those who argue this way are implicitly subscribing to the *partim/partim* theory of Scripture and Tradition (divine revelation is to be found partly in Scripture and partly in Tradition) and denying the material sufficiency of Scripture (see the discussion in chapter seven of this book).

159 The entire "tradition" itself is contained in vv. 23-25. Everything else in this section is Paul's commentary on that tradition. This same principle (that the tradition is presented in credal form and then given a commentary) is true of almost all the instances of paradosis cited above (cf. esp. 1 Cor 15:3-5 [the tradition], followed by Paul's commentary in vv. 6 ff).

160 Some have taken this to refer to the gospel message since the immediate context speaks of God's predestination. If this is the case, then we have lost nothing since the gospel message is clearly given to us throughout Scripture. Nevertheless, the phrase "by word of mouth or by letter" is more likely to be taken as ending the section begun in vv. 1-2 where the same language is used ("report or letter supposed to have come from us"). Roman Catholic apologists often point out that Paul claims in this passage to have previously explained to them more than he is telling them here (2:5). But while it is true that Paul alludes to the fact that he has told the Thessalonians all

this before, this should not be misconstrued to mean that he has communicated to them something *different* than can be found in the current letter, or indeed in the rest of his writings.

161 Yet even when it was part of the Roman Tradition, its only support was found in Scripture, not oral tradition.

162 "As in all the congregations of the saints" (1 Cor 14:33); "Did the word of God originate with you? Or are you the only people it has reached?" (1 Cor 14:36); "If anyone wants to be contentious about this, we have no other practice, nor do the churches of God" (1 Cor 11:16); "I urge you to imitate me . . . . Timothy . . . will remind you of my way of life . . . which agrees with what I teach everywhere in every church" (1 Cor 4:16-17).

163 The idea of a tradition that is different in content from the New Testament is moot in any case as has been pointed out by Heiko Oberman (*The Harvest of Medieval Theology* [Grand Rapids: Eeerdmans, 1967]): "As regards the pre-Augustinian Church. . . . The Tradition is not understood as an addition to the kergyma contained in Scripture but as the handing down of that same kerygma in living form. . . . The writings of the Apostles which were in the process of being received—not produced by the Church—were understood to contain the original ker-ygma *in toto*." [emphasis in original]

164 Included here are Baruch, Judith, 1&2 Maccabees, Sirach (Ecclesiasticus), Tobit and Wisdom, as well as some additions to Daniel and Esther.

165 Harrison, 86-88.

166 Ibid., 84.

167 Recorded in 2 Chron 24:20-22. Some Catholic apolo-gists dispute the idea that Jesus is referring here to 2 Chronicles based on the parallel in Matt 23:35 where this Zechariah is identified as the son of Berekiah. Since the Zechariah of 2 Chronicles is identified as the son of Jehoiada (24:20), these apologists postulate that the Zecha-riah referred to here is the father of John the Baptist

(Luke 1:5). They base this on the testimony of some apocryphal gospels which embellish the accounts of Matthew and Luke. Aside from the conflicting reasons cited by these early writers for the execution of the father of John the Baptist (which execution is itself highly suspect), we might also point out that there is no evidence that the father of John the Baptist bore the patronym "son of Berekiah." Moreover, it is inconceivable that John the Baptist (whose execution Matthew records nine chapters prior to Jesus' words here; cf. Matthew 14) would not have been listed as the last prophet put to death if Jesus were thinking of all martyrs up to his time (Herod, after all, was a Jew who martyred a prophet sent to him). At the end of the day, it seems best to view this Zechariah as the one whose death is recorded in 2 Chron 24:20-22. It was not uncommon for chronologists to regard a man as the "son of" a grandfather or great grandfather (compare Zech 1:1 where Zechariah is called son of Berekiak with Ezra 6:14 where the same prophet is called son of Iddo). The Berekiak under our consideration may well have been the unnamed son of Jehoiada. See the discussions on this by R. T. Beckwith (*The Old Testament Canon of the New Testament Church* [Grand Rapids: Eerdmans, 1985], 212-222), and D. A. Carson, *Matthew*, 485-86.

168 The last actual murder chronologically is that of Uriah, son of Shemaiah recorded in Jer 26:20-23. This is further evidence that Jesus was referring specifically to the Hebrew canon. After all, what sense would it make to tell the Jews that they were responsible for all biblical murders up to Zechariah but no one after that?

169 Josephus, *Against Apion*, 1:37-42. These same books are listed and counted as twenty-four in the Talmud (Baba Bathra 14-15; cf. 2 Esdr 14:44). Origen, Athanasius, Jerome and others confirm that the Hebrew canon consists of twenty-two books, giving their own lists of its books. It is well known that the Hebrew canon is sometimes reckoned as twenty-two books and sometimes twenty-four books. The shorter list, found in Josephus, is a result of counting Judges-Ruth and Jeremiah-Lamentations as

two rather than four books (David Dunbar, "The Biblical Canon," *Hermeneutics, Authority, and Canon* [ed. by D.A. Carson and John Woodbridge, Grand Rapids: Zondervan, 1986], 303-304).

170 "The Bible Alone?"

171 "Besides the canonical Scriptures, nothing shall be read, in the church, under the title of 'divine writings.' The canonical books are: Genesis, Exodus, Leviticus, Numbers, Deuteronomy, Joshua, Judges, Ruth, the four books of Kings, the two books of Paraleipomena (Chronicles), Job, the Psalms of David, the five books of Solomon, the twelve books of the (Minor) Prophets, Isaiah, Jeremiah, Daniel, Ezekiel, Tobias, Judith, Esther, the two books of Esdras, two books of the Maccabees. The books of the New Testament are: the four Gospels, the Acts of the Apostles, thirteen Epistles of S. Paul, one Epistle of S. Paul to the Hebrews, two Epistles of S. Peter, three Epistles of S. John, the Epistle of S. James, the Epistle of S. Jude, the Revelation of S. John. Concerning the confirmation of this canon, the transmarine Church shall be consulted" (Synod of Hippo, Canon 36). Canon 24 (Greek 27) of Carthage has an identical list.

172 The following is a list of fathers, spanning from the fourth century to the sixteenth century, who adhered to a Hebrew reckoning of the OT canon, either by listing the specific books, enumerating the total count of the books, consigning to a secondary status the apocryphal books, or a combination of two or more of the above. I am indebted to the meticulously detailed work of Bill Webster who has providing this list via the Sola-L list on the internet:

Athanasius, Cyril of Jerusalem, Epiphanius, Basil, Gregory of Nazianzus, Amphilochius. Rufinus, Jerome, John of Damascus, The Council of Trullo (6th Ecumenical Council), Cardinal Cajetan, Walafrid, Nicholas of Lyra, Tostado, Melito of Sardis, Origen, Hilary of Poitiers, Amphilochius, Rufinus, Jerome, Gregory the Great, Junilius, Primaius, Anastasius of Antioch, Leontius, Isidore of Seville, Bede, Alcuin, Nicephorus of Constantinople, Rabanus Maurus,

Agobard of Lyons, Rupert of Tuits, Petrus Mauritius, Hugo of St. Victor, Richard of St. Victor, Peter Comestor, John Beleth, John of Salisbury, The Glossa Ordinaria, Johannes de Columna, Nicholas of Lyra, William Occham, Antoninus, Thomas Aquinas, Nicholas of Lira, Alphonsus Tostatus, Francis Ximenius, Jacobus Faber Stapulensis, and Erasmus.

Bill Webster concludes his list (the details of which have been omitted here for the sake of brevity) by citing the lamentations of B. F. Westcott: "This fatal decree in which the Council [of Trent] . . . gave a new aspect to the whole question of the Canon, was ratified by fifty-three prelates, among whom there was not one German, not one scholar distinguished for historical learning, not one who was fitted by special study for the examination of a subject in which the truth could only be determined by the voice of antiquity. How completely the decision was opposed to the spirit and letter of the original judgments of the Greek and Latin Churches, how far in doctrinal equalization of the disputed and acknowledged books of the Old Testament it was at variance with the traditional opinion of the West, how absolutely unprecedented was the conversion of an ecclesiastical usage into an article of belief, will be seen from the evidence which has already been adduced" (B. F. Westcott, *A General Survey of the History of the Canon of the New Testament* [MacMillan: Cambridge, 1889], 478).

173 Proclaimed a dogma in 1950.

174 Proclaimed a dogma in 1870.

175 Proclaimed a dogma in 1854.

176 *The Catechetical Lectures,* Lecture IV, Art. 17.

177 Ibid., Lecture V, Art. 12.

178 Ibid., Lecture XVI, Art. 24.

179 Ibid., Lecture XI, Art. 12.

180 Ibid., Lecture V, Art. 12.

181 Irenaeus, *Against Heresies* III.1.1.

182 Jerome, *Letter* LIII.6-10.

183 Rufinus, *Commentary on the Apostles' Creed* 36

184 *Ad Episcopos Aegypti Et Libyae Epistola Encyclica* I.4.

185 Ibid.

186 Ibid.

187 This is far different from ascribing infallibility to the ecclesial body itself!

188 Keating, 124-26.

189 So much so that if we were to disregard the authenticity of the biblical documents, we would likewise have to disregard every other ancient document, including those of Homer, Virgil, Plato, and Euripides.

190 Most uncertainties have to do with word order, or whether the text should read, e.g., "and Jesus said," or "and He said." In no case is there an uncertainty that affects doctrinal belief.

191 A case in point is Jim Jones and the Peoples' Temple. True, many people died in this episode of history; yet not because they were eye-witnesses of some great miracle, but because of their belief in Jim Jones. A similar and more recent example is the Heaven's Gate tragedy. The Apostles, on the other hand, give independent testimony that they saw the risen Christ. It is unlikely that so many people would give up their lives for something they *knew* was a hoax!

192 E.g., Luke 1:1-4.

193 Cf. such passages as John 10:35 and Matt 5:18 among a host of others (see in chapter four under "Evidence for a General Recognition of the Canon").

194 Keating, 125.

195 Cf. Matt 24:24.

196 Christ did not establish an "institutional church" in Matt 16:18. Rather, "church" is a term which represents the collective whole of God's elect.

197 Matt 24:35. See also Luke 21:33.

198 John 14:26; 16:12-13.

199 This is the earliest 1 Timothy could have been written. The latest date would be 68 AD.

200 This is especially true of such doctrines as the Assumption of Mary—a doctrine which finds support neither from Scripture nor from church tradition. It should be noted here that Catholic apologists deny that the Catholic church has "added" anything to the apostolic deposit. Yet Catholic dogmas such as the Immaculate Conception of Mary, the Assumption of Mary, and Papal Infallibility are not only conspicuously absent from Scripture, but were completely unknown in the early church. Just how Catholic apologists can maintain both (1) that nothing has been added to the apostolic deposit *and* (2) that these are legitimate apostolic teachings is really quite baffling.

Chapter Six: O.T. Israel— ### A Story of the Catholic Church

201 Such as John's knowledge that he was writing a "book of prophecy" (Rev 1:9; 22:6-7, 9-10, 18-19)—a probable allusion to the book of Daniel. Cf. also Paul's contrast of the Old and New Covenants (2 Cor 3:6, 14), as well as that of the writer of Hebrews (8:6-13; 9:15).

202 Compare the rapidity with which the early church abandoned New Testament practices and beliefs and adopted its own set of extrabiblical traditions (e.g., elders for priests, autonomy of local assemblies for primacy of bishops, etc.).

203 Compare this with such deeply set (yet unscriptural) practices of the Catholic church as veneration and prayers to Mary and the saints, the priesthood, and purgatory, among others.

204 E.g., David Palm, "Oral Tradition," states:

"But there is a notable difference between the magisterium under the Old Covenant and our teachers under the New Covenant. The successors of the apostles, and especially Peter's successor, have the Holy Spirit to guide them into all truth, and they have Jesus' promise that the 'gates of hell will not prevail' against the Church (Matt. 16:17-19)."

205   While it is true that some of the Magisterial Reformers committed these same atrocities against those of the more radical wing of the Reformation (such as the Anabaptists), these atrocities are roundly condemned by Evangelicals today. The Roman Catholic church, on the other hand, has never officially condemned the license to exterminate heretics issued at the Fourth Lateran Council. Indeed, extreme conservative Catholics (such as Gerry Matatics) uphold the decisions made at this council while pointing out that the softened stance of Vatican II could conceivably be overturned someday.

206   *Heresies*, 120.

207   Ibid., 122.

208   Ibid., 123.

209   It is significant for our discussion as a whole to point out that the only significant orthodox defenders of the faith at this time were found not in the Western church (Rome), but rather in the Eastern church (Alexandria). The significance of this cannot be overlooked, for there were many differences between the two churches then, and even more so now since the schism between East and West around the eleventh century. The East never accepted the absolute authority of Rome or of the pope. The great defenders of Nicaea were the fathers of the Eastern Orthodox church, not of Roman Catholicism; and (so far as an institutional pedigree is concerned) Catholic apologists can stake no more claim to the likes of Athanasius than can Evangelicals.

210   *Heresies*, 125.

Chapter Seven: The Myth of Catholic Unity

211   This figure—usually posited as 20,000, 23,000, 24,000 or 25,000—varies depending on which Catholic apologist one reads. I have personally asked for the source of this

figure from several Catholic apologists, including Patrick Madrid and Bob Sungenis, and to date no one has been able to provide an accurate source for these figures. Some have alluded to the World Council of Churches as the source; but even here bibliographic information is not forthcoming. Moreover, even if the figure is accurate, one must ask just how "Protestant" and "denomination" are being defined. Does this include all non-Catholic religious bodies that claim to be Christian? If so, then it is no wonder that the figure is so high—the sheer number of extant cults in the world must be at least this many! But, of course, this is far different from the number of Evangelical Protestant denominations in existence today, and the repeated attempt by Catholic apologists to use this figure as an argument against Evangelical unity is irresponsible at best and disingenuous at worst.

212   As we noted in an earlier chapter, Catholic apologists speak freely of the divisions in the Protestant church, the liberal influence, and the "bickering" between denominations (cf. Tim Staples, *Surprised by Truth*, 219; Bob Sungenis, ibid., 119); yet each one of these characterizations can be applied with equal force to the Catholic church itself. The differences that exist among most Evangelical denominations are the same kinds of differences found among the different Rites, Orders, and other persuasions of the Catholic church. Moreover, Catholic scholarship is just as plagued by liberalism as its Protestant counterpart (though the same cannot be said about Evangelicalism). As far as "bickering" is concerned, one need simply peruse through any issue of *The Catholic Answer* to find examples of Father Stravinskas "bickering" with other priests about finer points of dogma and customs (see, e.g., Vol. 7/Number 4, p. 24, or Vol. 7/Number 6, p. 19-20). Indeed, all major Catholic church councils (including Trent) were fraught with "bickering," and there has rarely been consensus on decisions reached at these councils even after they adjourned. See, e.g., the dialogue during Vatican I in which some of the bishops were heard

saying about their opposition "He is Lucifer, anathema, anathema. . . . He is another Lucifer, let him be cast out" (quoted in Küng, 126-27).

213 Bob Sungenis ("From Controversy to Consolation," *Surprised By Truth*) thinks so. He compares the Protestant "rebellion" to the Israelites who rebelled against Moses in the desert (131-32). The difference, of course, is that Moses was not involved in adultery, indulgences, idolatry, and other corruptions when the Israelites opposed him— the Catholic church was involved in *all* of these when the Protestant Reformation opposed it.

214 *Catechism*, Art. 818-819.

215 Chapter III, *Sacred Scripture, Its Inspiration And Divine Interpretation*, 1.1, 4-5.

216 Fn 31, *Abbott* edition, cited in *Roman Catholicism*, 98.

217 Ibid., 99.

218 Marshner ("What Still Divides Us?") dismisses this charge against Catholic unity by asserting that there are "bad apples" within the Catholic church that have not yet been reproved. But if the pope himself has not clarified the issue, so that his words and those of the councils can be interpreted in a variety of ways, on what basis does Marshner label centrist and leftist Catholic scholars "bad apples?" How can he be certain that it is he who has the correct interpretation of official Catholic teaching, and that the liberals are incorrect? How can he know for certain that *he* is not the "bad apple"?

219 *The Decree Concerning the Canonical Scriptures*, Fourth Session, Council of Trent.

220 *The Mother of Jesus in the New Testament* (Garden City: Doubleday, 1975), xxxii.

221 Although one is hard-pressed to find even a kernel of belief regarding the Assumption of Mary, the Immaculate Conception, and the infallibility of the pope.

222 Ironically—and seemingly unwittingly—most Catholic apologists vacillate from one position to the other

depending on which point they want to make. For instance, in a debate with James White, Patrick Madrid claims to hold to the material sufficiency of Scripture, insisting that the Scriptures contain all teachings necessary for salvation, and goes to great lengths to ensure that we do not misunderstand "the Catholic position" ("Does the Bible Teach Sola Scriptura," available through Reformation Press). Yet, amazing in the same debate, he later points to the canon of Scripture as an example of an essential teaching *not* found in the Scriptures!

223 The Pontifical Biblical Commission of 1909 states: "Genesis 1-3 is historical, not a fictional or mythological narrative, nor derived from pagan mythologies nor are they allegories, nor partly historical and partly fictional." However, centrist Catholic scholars are convinced that Vatican II granted freedom to use critical methods for interpreting the Scriptures. Indeed, in light of John Paul II's recent endorsement of evolutionary theory (which *necessitates* a mythical reading of the Genesis account), it is difficult to disagree with these scholars.

224 This is according to Catholic apologist David Armstrong, from an internet debate on the Sola-L list.

225 Cf. "To Men of Thought and Science," *Closing Messages of the Council.*

226 *Dogmatic Constitution on the Church (Lumen Gentium)*

227 *Declaration on Religious Freedom.*

228 Bob Sungenis, for instance, believes the Byzantine to be the correct text, while most of his Catholic colleagues subscribe to the Eclectic text.

229 The following text appeared on the *Saint Benedict* Center web page:

An Open Challenge to Karl Keating: On October 26, 1995, Saint Benedict Center sent a debate challenge to Karl Keating, of Catholic Answers. We hold that, though he has the reputation as a conservative, Mr. Keating is, in fact, quite liberal. This is because of his consistent denial of Extra Ecclesiam Nulla Salus. After a series of e-mail exchanges,

Mr. Keating backed out of the debate, while persisting to malign us and our doctrinal position in his publication, On This Rock [sic]. A member of his staff also suddenly backed out of a similar debate, just as we were working out the details. Our challenge to Mr. Keating stated, in part "... we challenge you to debate us, on the Internet, regarding the issue of Extra Ecclesiam Nulla Salus, the doctrine of the Faith that our Founder defended and that you reject in your publications. We could both agree to a set date which would allow time to publicize the event for your supporters and our own." Over a year has passed since the original challenge, and the e-mail exchanges and other information we formerly had posted under "The Keating Files" seemed to be a bit untimely. For now, we will leave posted this simple challenge to Karl Keating, excerpted from our response to an editorial he published about us. This challenge, distinct from the original one, has gone unanswered for over a month and a half now: "I would like to end this already too-long reply with another challenge to Karl: Will you debate? The personnel, the format, and the exact protocol to follow are negotiable, as they were from the start... Will you do it...?" You can E-Mail Karl to suggest that he debate us. If you do so, please give him your name and e-mail address, so you can get a response from him.

230 See the *Catholic Answers* web site for details of this.

231 *The Catholic Answer*, a bimonthly publication from *Our Sunday Visitor*, Huntington, IN.

232 This text appeared in an advertisement placed in *The Catholic Answer*, 10, 3 (July/Aug 1996): 61.

233 Some Catholic apologists will no doubt cry foul at the suggestion that the pope be utilized in this way. But their objection would be unwarranted. While I am well aware that infallibility is said by Catholic apologists to be only a negative protection against error, and that it does not imply, for instance, that the pope will always ace math tests, this seems to be a case of special pleading in regard to the present suggestion. Why indeed could we not ask the pope to arbitrate all theological disputes within the church? If infallibility guarantees that the pope

will never err in any official *ex cathedra* pronouncement, then why could we not force the issue? Why not have the pope spend one day (one week or one month) simply proclaiming *ex cathedra* statements about all matters of dispute and be done with it? After all, infallibility guarantees that he will not err in an official capacity. Technically, then, there can be no objection to this request.

The Catholic apologist who objects to this scenario is simply guilty of holding a view of papal infallibility that does not accurately reflect the positive aspects of the papal proclamation given at Vatican I. The text states that the pope is infallible, "when he speaks *ex cathedra*; that is, when—fulfilling the office of Pastor and Teacher of all Christians—on his supreme Apostolical authority, he defines a doctrine concerning faith or morals to be held by the Universal Church." There is nothing in *that* definition that would preclude the pope from arbitrating all theological disputes. Nor is it simply a negative protection (not that that would matter in our scenario—all we are asking the pope to do is speak; if he is infallible then he would be negatively protected from error and we would have furthered our theological pursuit), but a protection against error when he *positively* "proclaims" a doctrine. Nor is it relevant that Catholic apologists do not happen to take infallibility to its logical conclusion (i.e., asking for clarification on every theological dispute). That fact does not militate against the notion that the pope, being infallible, should indeed be able to do this. There is simply no reasonable or logical objection to this proposal.

234 Cf. 1 Cor 1:13-15 and 11:17-18 for a classic example of ecclesial disunity in the New Testament. Although it must be admitted that disunity by way of factions is wrong, does Hahn really want to argue that the Corinthian church ceased to be the "true church" simply because of differing opinions?

235 This is amply illustrated by the schism in the Old Testament between the Northern and Southern tribes at the bad decision of Rehoboam (1 Kings 12). In the Catho-

lic schema, there cannot be more than one visible, unified institution of God since schism is a mark of illegitimacy. Yet it is undeniably the case that God not only worked through both the Northern kingdom and the Southern kingdom during different phases in Israel's history, but actually decreed the schism in the first place (1 Kings 11:11-13; 29-39)! As much as each kingdom would sometimes have liked, neither one could claim exclusive rights to Yahweh. If the Catholic apologist insists that there must be complete institutional unity in order to be legitimate, then he must also tell us which of the two kingdoms of Israel constituted "true" Israel. Given the Catholic definition of an undivided church, it certainly could not have been both.

Chapter Eight: Beliefs About Mary

236 Properly called an A proposition ("all S is P").

237 The teaching that the human and divine natures of Christ were synthesized into one.

238 Properly called an I proposition ("some S is P").

239 One must forgive the use of terms such as "some of Jesus," "non-God," etc. These are not intended to be irreverent; rather, the author is simply making use of the language of logic.

240 Indeed, the very title *Theotokos* given to Mary at the councils of Ephesus and Chalcedon was given out of a concern to uphold the divine *nature* of Christ, not to establish his personhood. Catholic apologists, when considering the title "mother of God," consistently ignore the original purpose for that title.

241 Properly speaking, God is not a person, but a being that subsists in three persons. God is a Trinity; yet it cannot be said that since Jesus is God then Jesus must be a Trinity! Catholic apologists have not made the necessary distinction between person, nature, and being. Some Catholic apologists have argued for an exception in the case of Jesus, asserting that Jesus is a "divine person" who took on a human nature. Such an argument, however,

encounters innumerable difficulties. First, the instant one uses the phrase "divine person," one has already violated the distinction above: "Divine person" is just another way of saying "person with a divine nature." Yet, the instant the incarnation occurred, the "person" in question was something more— namely, he was a "person with a divine nature and a human nature"; and it was to this person Mary gave birth. Moreover, if one insists that we must regard Mary as the mother of God based on the fact that Mary gave birth to a "divine person," we then must ask some probing questions: Jesus "grew in wisdom" (Luke 2:52); since Jesus is God, are we then to conclude that God grew in wisdom? Jesus did not know the precise day and hour of end-time events (Matt 24:36). Since Jesus is God, are we to conclude that God did not know this information? Jesus was "tempted in every way just as we are" (Heb 4:15); since Jesus is God, are we to conclude that God was tempted? Jesus died on the cross; since Jesus is God, are we to conclude that God died? The biblical view, of course, is that God has always possessed all wisdom, that God knows all things, including the timeframe for end-time events (Matt 24:36), that God cannot be tempted with evil (Jas 1:13), and that God cannot die since dying is a corporeal condition, affecting humans (1 Cor 15:22; "in Adam, all die") but not God (Ps 82:6-7; "I said 'you are gods.' . . . but you will die like mere men"), nor even angels (Luke 20:36; "they can no longer die; for they are like the angels"). How is it then that Jesus grew in wisdom, was limited in knowledge, was tempted, died— and, yes, was born? Quite simply, only by virtue of his human nature, and not by virtue of his divinity. God cannot be conceived and born anymore than he can die. Mary cannot, therefore, be said to have borne God (and hence, be designated the "mother of God") anymore than the Jews can be said to have killed God (and hence, be designated the "killers of God"). Jesus in his humanity had a mother; Jesus in his divinity was "without father or mother, without genealogy, without beginning of days or end of life" (Heb 7:3).

242 In spite of the insistence of Catholic apologists to the contrary, the Bible explicitly and repeatedly affirms that one gives birth not only to a person, but also to a nature. "And the earth brought forth . . . plants yielding seed *after their kind.* . . . 'Let the earth bring forth living creatures *after their kind.*" (Gen 1:12, 24). Jesus was the "son of David *according to the flesh*" (Rom 1:3), Abraham is "forefather [to the Jews] *according to the flesh*" (Rom 4:1). "It is not the children *of the flesh* [i.e., descendants by human nature from Abraham] who are children of God" (Rom 9:8).

243 *Heresies*, 182.

244 Ibid., 174.

245 Mark's account (3:31-35) is even stronger in this regard, for it includes Mary within the "family" who thought Jesus was insane (v. 21).

246 *Catechism*, Art. 967.

247 Ibid., Art. 969.

248 Ibid., Art. 492.

249 After all, he goes out of his way to give John the Baptist a particularly high status (Matt 11:11).

250 It is significant that, without exception, whenever Mary requests something of Jesus it is always met with a distancing rebuke (cf. Luke 2:48-49; 8:19-21; Mark 3:31-35; John 2:4; as well as the present passage).

251 Matt 8:29; Mark 1:24, 5:7; Luke 4:34, 8:28, and the present passage.

252 Also interesting to note is that John chooses to record this rebuke in the first place. One must ask why he felt this was important for his readers to know. The only reasonable explanation is that John wanted to show clearly that Jesus was indebted to no one—not even to his mother. This is significant since John is the apostle who took Mary in to live with him after Jesus' death (John 19:26-27). If anyone knew Mary on an intimate basis, John

did. Yet, far from venerating Mary, John portrays her in a decidedly unflattering light!

253 Judg 11:12; 2 Sam 16:10; 1 King 17:18; 2 King 3:13; 2 Chron 35:21.

254 So J. Cortés, *New Testament Abstracts*, III (1958-59), 247. This rendering is fraught with difficulties: (1) contra the proposed rendering, there *was* a change—since this was Jesus' *first* miracle (v 11), he could not have granted this kind of request before; (2) Mary gives no indication that she detected a change in relationship, so what need would there be for Jesus to ask "what has changed between us?"; (3) this rendering does not account for the fact that in *every other instance*, this Greek construction is a rebuke. If it is argued that this cannot be a denial of Mary's request since Jesus *does* eventually grant it, it must also be pointed out that Jesus denies requests elsewhere, only to grant them immediately thereafter (Matt 15:22-28; John 7:3-10).

255 So M. Lagrange and R. Schnackenburg, quoted in D.A. Carson, *The Gospel According to John* (Leicester: IVP, 1991; Grand Rapids: Eerdmans, 1991), 171.

256 See Carson's discussion in *John*, 170.

257 So Pheme Perkins, notes on John 2:4, *Catholic Study Bible*.

258 Ibid.

259 Again, *gunai* (γύναι), "woman" is used, not *mêtêr* (μήτηρ), "mother."

260 *Catechism*, Art. 964.

261 Most commentators agree that by this time Joseph was dead.

262 1 Tim 5:1-16 (esp. vv 3 & 8); Rom 16:2, 13; Phlm 2, among others.

263 See Gal 1:19; 1 Cor 9:5.

264 "Mary, the Saints, and Sacerdotalism," *Roman Catholicism*, 126.

265 Although there is nothing impure about marital relations.

266 See also Mark 3:31-32; Luke 8:19-20.

267 See also Mark 6:3.

268 Keating, 282.

269 D. A. Carson, *Exegetical Fallacies* (Grand Rapids: Baker, 1984), 34-36.

270 David Palm ("Oral Tradition") is guilty of the same error when he writes: "A specific application of [relying on Catholic Tradition] is the doctrine of the perpetual virginity of Mary. The data of the New Testament concerning the 'brothers and sisters' of Jesus are ambiguous by themselves, although I would argue that the biblical evidence leans toward the Catholic interpretation."

271 Carson, *Exegetical Fallacies*, 34-36.

272 For instance 1 Cor 12:1; 14:20, 26, 39, etc.

273 See e.g., Paul's use of this word toward unbelieving Jews whom he wanted to win over in Acts 22:1.

274 Keating, 283.

275 Ibid.

276 Mark 6:3.

277 Keating and other Catholic apologists are in the minority here. The majority of Catholic scholars today reject the notion of a previous vow of virginity by Mary because of the unlikelihood of a betrothed girl making such a vow; and because Jewish culture looked to the bearing of children as a great blessing and considered childlessness a disgrace (Luke 1:25; cf, the cases of Rachel, Sarah, and Hannah) (John McHugh, *The Mother of Jesus in the New Testament* [Garden City: Doubleday, 1975], 179-180).

278 This is also suggested by Leo Trese, *The Faith Explained* (Manila: Sinag-Tala Publishers, 1986), 62. If Keating does not believe this, then on what basis does he argue that Mary planned to remain a virgin through

marriage *before* she knew of the virginal birth of Jesus (283-84)? Even so, Keating seems to change the priority of this a few pages later when he states that Mary remained a virgin *because* of the announcement that she would bear a son while a virgin, arguing that "the circumstances [of the virgin birth] demanded" that Mary and Joseph remain a "special" family (286). But Keating can't have it both ways. Does he believe Mary made a vow of married virginity *before* she knew of the virgin birth, or *because* she knew of it? Keating, by arguing both points, gets more mileage from his argument.

279   The Greek word *opheilên* (ὀφειλὴν) means "that which is owed."

280   We must keep in mind that the writers of the gospels are not so much quoting the crowd's responses verbatim as they are recording the gist of what was said. For these writers, Jesus is indeed the unique son of Mary.

281   J. Harold Greenlee, *A Concise Exegetical Grammar of New Testament Greek* (fifth ed., revised, Grand Rapids: Eerdmans, 1986), 22.

282   This point is well illustrated by the lack of respect Jacob showed Esau and even his own father when he deceived both of them (Genesis 27). Another example from the Old Testament is that of Joseph who was rebuked by his father, Jacob, for implying that all his older brothers (and even his father) would one day bow down to him (Gen 37:5-10). Do we conclude that Moses was disrespectful because he not only gave advice to his older brother Aaron, but also told him what to do? All of these examples (which could be multiplied many times over) render Keating's argument about Hebrew culture moot.

283   Keating, 285.

284   See my unpublished doctoral dissertation, *The Role of Mary in the New Testament* (available at my website, www.ntrmin.com). See especially chapters 1 & 2.

285 Many Roman Catholic apologists engage in dubious

exegesis of Old Testament passages to support their belief that Mary had other children. For instance, in my public debate with Catholic apologist Gerry Matatics on this very issue, Matatics appealed to Ezek 44:2, which speaks of a "gate" which is to "remain shut," and which "no one may enter through" because "the LORD, the God of Israel, has entered through it." Matatics argued that this refers ultimately to Mary, who, as a virgin, was to "remain shut." Interestingly, Matatics also argued that a phrase such as "children of Mary" would "clinch" the Evangelical view that Mary did not remain a virgin throughout her life. Amazingly, though, whereas viewing Mary as the "gate" in Ezek 44:2 is completely without warrant, there is a passage in the Old Testament that says just what Matatics says would "clinch" the Evangelical argument. In Psalm 69, a psalm that speaks about the suffering of the messiah, is the following passage: " I am a stranger to my brothers, an alien to my own mother's sons; for zeal for your house consumes me, and the insults of those who insult you fall on me" (69:8-9). John 2:17 cites the first part of v. 9 as being fulfilled in Jesus' clearing of the temple. The last part of v. 9 is cited by Paul in Rom 15:3: "For even Christ did not please himself but, as it is written: 'The insults of those who insult you have fallen on me.' " Later in this same psalm, the Psalter writes: "They put gall in my food and gave me vinegar for my thirst" (69:21), a passage alluded to by all the gospel writers when recording the attempt by some to give Jesus vinegar to drink while on the cross (cf. Matt 27:48; Mark 15:36; Luke 23:36; and John 19:28-29). All of this points to the highly messianic content of Psalm 69. Yet, v. 8 specifically refers to "my brothers" and "my own mother's sons." Granted, there are portions of this psalm that cannot be applied to Jesus (e.g., v. 5, "You know my folly, O God; my guilt is not hidden from you"), but this is extremely rare in this psalm, and v. 5 may in fact be the only exception.

285a Such as the Assumption and the Immaculate Conception. The belief that Mary is Mediatrix, although not yet officially defined as an infallible dogma, is nevertheless an assumed belief by the majority of Catholics, and will likely become a dogma in the near future.

286 E.g., the title "Mother of God."

287 As even Keating himself admits: "devotion to Mary of a sort seen today was not common until the Middle Ages" (280).

288 Ibid., 260-61.

289 Patrick Madrid (*Any Friend*, 98-102) quotes me on this counters that both praising and bowing down to human beings have biblical precedent, citing such examples as Gen 49:7 (Judah will be praised) and Gen 27:29 (nations will bow down to Jacob). However, by comparing these acts of praising and bowing down to the current Marian practice, Madrid equivocates badly. He has attempted to classify these examples *and* the practice of bowing before Mary *as all of the same kind*. All of the examples he cites are instances of Hebrew cultural acts of humility shown to perceived superiors, whether those superiors are godly or not (cf. David's bowing down to Saul, 1 Sam 24:8; or the bowing down of Jacob and his brood to Esau). The modern day equivalent of this would be to bow down before Bill Clinton. Yet I know of no Catholic today, including Madrid, who would ever consider bowing before Clinton, or any political leader for that matter. This in itself illustrates that Madrid (and all Catholics for that matter) tacitly assumes there is a difference between the *kind* of honor afforded to Mary and that afforded to mere earthly dignitaries. Moreover, none of Madrid's examples include homage based on *religious* or *spiritual* greatness (as is clearly the case with Marian veneration). Both saints (Acts 10:25-26) and angels (Rev 19:10) absolutely reject homage of this kind. Madrid's objections to my statements are therefore little more than a smoke screen to cloud the real issue.

290 Keating sees no difference between the Catholic practice of bowing down before a statue to pray and the Fundamentalist practice of holding a Bible during prayer

(261). The difference, of course, is that the Fundamentalist is not bowing down *to* the Bible.

291 Council of Trent, Session XXV, "On the Invocation, Veneration, and Relics, of Saints, and on Sacred Images."

292 Clement of Alexandria *Stromata*, Book II, XVIII.

293 Ibid., Book V, V.

294 Tertullian, *Apology* XII.

295 Origen, *Against Celsus*, Book III, LXXVI.

296 Ibid., Book VII, LXIV-LXV.

297 Ibid., LXX.

298 Ibid., Book VIII, XX.

299 Lactantius, *Divine Institutes*, Book VI, XXV.

300 Council of Trent, Session XXV.

301 Athenagoras, *Apology* [*To the Emperors Marcus Aurelius Anoninus and Lucius Aurelius Commodus*], XVIII.

302 Ibid.

303 Arnobius, *Adversus Gentes*, Book VI, XXIV.

304 Ibid., Book XI, XVII.

305 Lactantius, *The Divine Institutes*, Book II, II.

306 Ibid.

307 Irenaeus, *Against Heresies*, Book I, XXV.6

308 Clement of Alexandria, *Exhortation to the Heathen*, IV.

309 Clement of Alexandria, *Stromata*, Book VII, V.

310 Ibid., Book V, VI. Ironically, many Catholic apologists use this same biblical passage to justify the current practice of Rome.

311 Tertullian, *De Spectaculis*, X.

312 Tertullian, *Elucidations*, XII.

313 Tertullian, *De Spectaculis*, XIII.

314 Keating, 269.

315 "This grace . . . is at once permanent and of a singular kind," Ibid.

316 Cf., e.g., John 14:29: "I have told you now before it happens, so that when it does happen you will believe." The word "told" here is in the perfect tense, but certainly does not mean that Jesus has told them from the beginning of their lives, but rather that he just now told them. Cf. also Acts 7:56, 10:45, and Matt 13:46, all of which use the perfect tense, but none of which implies a *permanent* state of existence.

317 Bauer, Arndt, Gingrich and Danker, *A Greek-English Lexicon of the New Testament* (Chicago: University of Chicago, 1979).

318 Keating, 279. Interestingly, in "What Still Divides Us," Bill Marshner suggests that Mediatrix is not an official title for Mary, by which he means there is no infallible proclamation regarding it, presumably suggesting (though he does not say explicitly) that it could be an erroneous title. This in spite of the fact that it is a title given to her in the *Catechism of the Catholic Church* (Art. 969), which Catechism the Pope has "declared" to be "a sure norm for teaching the faith," "a sure and authentic reference text for teaching catholic doctrine," ordered and approved by virtue of the Pope's "apostolic authority" and title as "Successor of Peter," and is to be used to instruct those who wish to know "what the Catholic Church believes" (*Catechism*, 5-6).

319 Keating, 279.

320 Eph 3:12; Heb 4:14-16; 10:19-22.

321 Even if, as many Catholics believe, Mary never died, she still must be counted among those who have departed from this earth. Whether she died or was assumed into heaven matters not; she is still in a place where those on earth are prohibited to tread.

322 Christ himself, of course, is excluded from this category; for though Christ experienced death, he can and is to be prayed to because he is God. No *creature* has this prerogative.

323 Madrid, *Any Friend*, 62-63.

324 Ibid., 63.

325 Ibid., 62.

326 Madrid ends this chapter with another piece of advice to his readers: "A good question to ask a Protestant who claims that Christ absolutely forbids *any* contact between saints on earth and saints in heaven is: 'Why did the Lord make a special point of appearing to Peter, James, and John on the Mount of Transfiguration in the company of Moses and Elijah—two "dead" saints?' (Matt. 17:1-8)," [emphasis his] Ibid., 63. It hardly needs to be said that this is not a very good question at all. In the first place, Moses and Elijah were no longer in heaven during this episode, but on earth. Second, the transfiguration was an apocalyptic event choreographed directly by the Son of God to give the apostles a glimpse of his eschatological glory—not an ongoing practice for the church (cf. Matt 16:28: "I tell you the truth, some who are standing here will not taste death before they see the Son of Man coming in his kingdom." In each case where the transfiguration is recorded it *always* follows on the heals of this promise—cf. Mark 9:1 ff., Luke 9:27 ff.). Third, Madrid has baited the question with his qualifier *"any,"* and thereby confuses the issue. Evangelicals do not argue that there was never any legitimate contact made between inhabitants of earth and inhabitants of heaven (there are many instances of angels who communicated with people on earth). But this contact was always initiated by the heavenly being—never by the earth dweller. What we deny is that any inhabitant of earth ever legitimately attempted to contact someone who had physically died. Madrid seems to have resorted to grasping at straws on this issue.

327 Ibid., 57.

328 Ibid.

329 Madrid does attempt to offer biblical support for the enhanced ability of the saints by pointing out that Christ in his resurrected body could walk through walls

(*Any Friend*, 58; cf. John 20:19), and that we are promised this same kind of glorified body in eternity. But Madrid has mixed apples and oranges here. The ability to walk through walls and to disappear and reappear somewhere else does not require attributes of deity. Even the angels can do these things—but they cannot be in more than one place at a time; nor can they hear different people speaking at the same time from opposite sides of the world! Note the words of Augustine to this effect:

> And [Jesus] will so come, on the testimony of the angel's voice, as He was seen going into heaven, that is, in the same form and substance of flesh to which, it is true, He gave immortality, but *He did not take away its nature. According to this form, we are not to think that He is everywhere present. We must beware of so building up the divinity of the man that we destroy the reality of His body.* It does not follow that what is in God is in Him so as to be everywhere as God is. . . . God and man in Him are one Person, and both are the one Jesus Christ who is everywhere as God, *but in heaven as man* (Augustine, *Letter* 118.8-10). [emphasis mine]

330 Madrid, *Any Friend*, 59.

331 Ibid., 59-60.

332 Ibid.

333 Ibid., 59.

334 See Richard Manning, "May Catholics Pray to the Patriarchs and Prophets," *The Catholic Answer*, 11, 5 (Nov/Dec 1997): 8-9. Manning answers in the affirmative. If this is true, however, then it is indeed odd that we never find the slightest hint among the biblical writers of such a practice.

335 Keating, 264.

336 Madrid, *Any Friend*, 35.

337 Madrid does this later as well when dealing with the biblical passages that indicate that those in heaven are aware of what is occurring on earth (e.g., "there will be more rejoicing in heaven over one sinner who repents

than over ninety-nine righteous persons who do not need to repent." Luke 15:7, cf. v. 10). Here Madrid asserts: "Ultimately Svendsen must still contend with the clear biblical evidence that God does in fact permit the saints in heaven to be aware of the acts and thoughts of people on earth" (*Any Friend*, 60). But, once again, the biblical passage posited does not support the contention proffered. In each of the scenarios given by Jesus to illustrate the repentance of the sinner (the first a shepherd who finds a lost sheep, the second a woman who finds a lost coin) the "rejoicing" is prefaced by the statement, "Then [he/she] *calls* [his/her] friends and neighbors together and says, 'Rejoice with me!'" Clearly, the "friends and neighbors" can know about the find *only because the owner has told them*. In the same way, the angels and saints can know about the conversion of a sinner *only because God has told them*. The heavenly host rejoice because they hear the *announcement* of God to the effect that a sinner has repented; not because they can hear that sinner repent.

338 Keating, 265.

339 Contra Keating, the rich man did not *pray* to Lazarus, nor to Abraham; he simply spoke to them. Praying implies speaking to those not of the same realm and dimension.

340 Although the title has not yet become official, the concept is nevertheless a popular one.

341 Keating, 279.

342 Matt 16:21; 26:24, 54; Luke 13:33; 18:31-33; 24:7, 44-46, etc.; contra Keating (275) who thinks that Christ did not have to die in order to pay for our sins.

Chapter Nine: The Catholic Priesthood

343 This same observation, of course, can be made about the pope.

344 Both the Mass and the Eucharist will be addressed in the next chapter.

345 *Catechism*, Art. 1552, 1554.

346 Ibid., Art. 1547, "they differ essentially." It is clear,

then, that when the Catholic church speaks of the ministerial priesthood they mean a special class that necessarily excludes the laity, both in title and in function.

347 See e.g., Eph 4:11; 1 Cor 12:28, Acts 20:17; etc.

348 See e.g., Acts 20:17, 28; Tit 1:5-7; 1 Pet 5:1-2.
Some Catholic apologists have argued that the word "priest" comes from the word *presbuteros*, which is a designation for a church leader in the New Testament. But this is incorrect. The word *presbuteros* in the New Testament always means "elder" never "priest." There is a word that means "priest" in the New Testament (*iereus*), but this word is never applied to a church leader.

349 It certainly does not have the meaning intended by Paul.

350 Cf. Keating, *What Catholics Really Believe—Setting the Record Straight* (Ann Arbor: Servant Publications, 1992), 134-35.

351 Ibid., 134.

352 Implied by Paul in 1 Cor 9:5.

353 Keating, *Catholicism and Fundamentalism*, 41-42.

Chapter Ten: The Eucharist and the Mass

354 Mark Shea, *This Is My Body: An Evangelical Discovers the Real Presence* (Front Royal, VA: Christendom Press, 1993).

355 Ibid., 16-17.

356 It is difficult to know how Shea, as an Evangelical, could have posited the notion that "God forbids human sacrifice" as an argument against transubstantiation while at the same time considering himself an *informed* Evangelical. Christ's sacrifice on the cross itself was clearly a *human* sacrifice, and one which Evangelicals unequivocally deem as legitimate. This betrays a deep misunderstanding of the Evangelical position by Shea.

357 But if this is true, then what about the Last Supper, which is upheld by Catholics as the original Mass? Was that a "re-presenting" of the sacrifice on the cross? How could it have been a re-presenting of something that had not yet occurred (Christ had not yet been sacrificed)? The Last Supper would then have to be seen as a "sacrifice before the sacrifice" instead

of a re-presenting of the sacrifice on the cross. But, if the Last Supper is not a re-presenting of a sacrifice, nor a sacrifice in itself, then (since the Last Supper is the institution of the Eucharist) on what grounds does the Catholic church hold that the Mass is a sacrifice or a re-presenting of one?

358 See Shea, 23-25.

359 In spite of Shea's insistence to the contrary, it will not do to postulate that Christ's sacrifice is outside of time, since the writer of Hebrews clearly has in mind a sequence of events—Christ sacrificed himself once, and then "sat down."

360 This same point can be made about Paul who, although expounding extensively on the eucharistic tradition he received (1 Cor 11:23), never once mentions the concept of a *sacrifice* in connection with the Lord's Supper. It is also interesting to note that in chapter 11 of his book, the writer of Hebrews places so much emphasis on faith in that which is "not seen" (Heb 11:1-3). The reason he includes this here is to contrast the "new and living way" (10:20) of the new covenant (according to which Christ's sacrifice has "perfected forever" [10:14] those who are his) with the old way of the levitical sacrificial system (according to which there is a daily and annual reminder of the sins of the people [10:3, 11]), which are called mere "shadows" of the realities found in heaven (8:5; 10:1). The old way was attractive to the Jew, who in turn was tempted to return to Judaism because of the tangibility of the sacrifice. The new way is based on a sacrifice that, although it happened in history, is now completed and therefore intangible (i.e., its benefits are not yet "seen"). Ironically, the Roman Catholic, in his quest for a tangible sacrifice, falls into the same error as the apostate Jews who were returning to Judaism.

361 Or *Accidents*.

362 See also Mark 14:22 and Luke 22:19.

363 Although it does not seem to occur to them that the reverse is also true; viz., since Catholics are not known for taking Scripture literally, they are inconsistent for taking this one literally!

364 Shea, 47-48.

365 Although Cyril of Alexandria, one of the framers of Ephesus, seems to have been inconsistent with his own principle in regard to the flesh of Christ in the Eucharist (See his *Cum Salvator Noster*).

366 Augustine, *Letter* 118.8-10

367 Shea, 32-33.

368 In fact, John does not record the Last Supper at all in his account.

369 Augustine, *On Christian Doctrine* III.16.24

370 Contra Keating (*Catholicism and Fundamentalism*) who thinks there was no attempt by Jesus to clarify that he was not speaking of literal bread. Keating asks, "If they had [been confused], why no corrections?" (233). But Keating ignores the fact that neither were there corrections by Jesus to the woman at the well in John 4. Yet, are we to take Jesus' words there literally?

371 In a recent internet debate, Catholic apologist David Palm asserts that *trôgô* is never used symbolically in the New Testament. But this is simply not the case. The only other time this word is used in John it is clearly in a symbolic sense: "He who shares [*trôgô*] my bread has lifted up his heel against me" (John 13:18). This is a quotation by Jesus of Ps 41:9 to show that Judas' betrayal fulfills the Scriptures. The phrase "he who eats my bread" is no more "literal" than that Judas literally "lifted up his heel" against Jesus. The former symbolizes that the betrayer would be an intimate friend, while the latter symbolizes the betrayal itself.

372 *Catechism*, Art. 818-819.

373 "The Sola Scriptura Debate," available through Reformation Press, Lindenhurst, New York.

374 Bettenson, 147-48.

375 Irenaeus, *Against Heresies*, IV.28.5-6.

376 Contra Keating (*Catholicism and Fundamentalism*, 238)

who makes the odd contention that "there is no record in the early centuries of any Christian doubting the Catholic interpretation." It is also important to note that many of the citations quoted by Catholic apologists, while affirming a "real" presence, do not thereby affirm transubstantiation. Most are concerned with the simple affirmation that the bread and wine are the body and blood of Christ, nothing more.

377 Augustine, *Letter* 98.9.

378 Augustine, *Expositions on the Psalms*, Psalm XCIX. VIII.

379 Bettenson, 147.

380 Ibid., 148.

381 Theodoret, *Eranistes*, Dialogue 2.

382 In spite of the assertions to the contrary by Shea and others.

383 *Catholicism and Fundamentalism*, 253.

384 1 Cor 11:20-21. It cannot be argued here that the Corinthians were able to become drunk because, as Paul says, it was not the Lord's Supper they were eating—for Paul makes the exact opposite point; viz., it was not the Lord's Supper *because* some were becoming drunk. This bespeaks the fact that the eucharistic wine was alcoholic to begin with.

The Mission of Reformation Press

The ministry of Reformation Press was established to glorify The Lord Jesus Christ and to be used by Him to expand and edify the kingdom of God while we occupy and anticipate Christ's glorious return. Reformation Press will seek to accomplish this mission by publishing Gospel literature which is biblically faithful, relevant, and practically applicable to many of the serious spiritual needs of mankind upon the verge of a new millennium. To do so we will always seek to boldly incorporate the truths of Scripture, especially those which were largely articulated as a body of theology during the Protestant Reformation of the Sixteenth Century and ensuing years. We gladly join our voice in the proclamations of—

Scripture Alone, Faith Alone, Grace Alone, Christ Alone, & God's Glory Alone!

Our ministry seeks the blessing of our God as we seek His face to both confirm and support our labors for Him. Our prayers for this work can be summarized by two verses from the Book of Psalms:

"And let the beauty of the LORD our God be upon us, And establish the work of our hands for us; Yes, establish the work of our hands." —Psalm 90:17

"Not unto us, O LORD, not unto us, but to your name give glory." —Psalm 115:1

Reformation Press is a not-for-profit (501 C3) institution and therefore can and does appreciate monetary donations from anyone who shares our burden and vision for publishing literature combining sound Bible doctrine and practical exhortation in an age when too few so-called Christian publications do the same. All donations will be recognized by a tax-deductible receipt. We thank you in advance for any assistance you can give us in our labors to fulfill this important mission. May God bless you.

For a catalog of other great
Christian books including
additional titles by
Eric Svendsen contact us in
any of the following ways:

—*write us at*—
Reformation Press
160 37th Street
Lindenhurst, NY 11757

—*call us at*—
631. 956. 0998

—*visit our website at*—
www.reformationpress.com *or*
www.greatchristianbooks.com

—*email us at*—
reformationpress@email.com

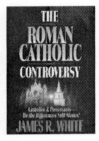

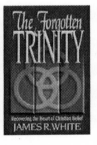
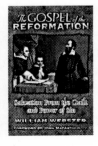

Geese in their Hoods– *Writings on Roman Catholicism* by C. H. Spurgeon

This is a wonderful compilation of Spurgeon's comments on the Church of Rome by Timothy F. Kauffman. It serves to remind us that theology has consequences, and that the threats to eternal peace with God from Rome are as real in our day as in Spurgeon's. Many today would like to sugar-coat historical truths and blind us to the realities of an institution corrupted by power, influence and ill-gotten gains. *$10.99*

Salvation, the Bible & Roman Catholicism   by William Webster

Have the basic doctrines of Rome changed since the Reformation? Many, even Roman Catholics, think they have. This book shows that the R.C. Church still officially promotes the same sacramental/works-based salvation protested by the Reformers. It extensively compares the dogma of Rome with the teaching of Scripture, as well as giving a proper explanation of the gospel. *$8.99*

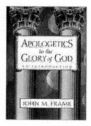

Apologetics To The Glory of God   by John M. Frame

In this informative introductory book on apologetics Frame sheds needed light on the message and method of genuinely Christian apologetics. Giving special attention to application of the truth, he insightfully examines apologetics as proof, defense, and offense. If you want an overview and explanation of Apologetics as a whole we would strongly recommend this as a great place to start. *$14.99*

Defense of The Faith   by Cornelius Van Til

This classic work in apologetics was designed to stop secularists in their tracks. *Defense of The Faith* explores the roles of authority, reason, and theistic proof, while contrasting Roman Catholic, Arminian, and Reformed methods of defending the faith. Written by the father of modern apologetics this book is an essential text for the library of every Christian, whether clergy or laity. *$9.99*

Truth Under Attack   by Earl Davies

This comprehensive handbook on cults and false religions provides a very practical guide for Christians. It is complete with helpful facts on heretical churches, cults, and other aberrant religious movements. Each chapter contains useful background information followed by a handy reference guide to the specific doctrines each group espouses and how these conflict with the Scriptures and orthodox Christianity. *$16.99*

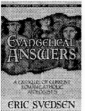

Evangelical Answers by Eric Svendsen

While many modern evangelical leaders are encouraging a peace with Rome, a new breed of Catholic apologists have mounted a calculated campaign to convert evangelical Protestants to Rome. Their tactics are dubious at best and decidedly intellectually dishonest. Svendsen carefully exposes their agenda, fallacies, doctrinal errors, and unbiblical argumentation. John MacArthur Jr. considers this a must read. **$16.99**

Drawn By The Father by James R. White

A thrilling study of Christ's teaching in John 6:35-45! Ponder anew the marvelous grace and sovereignty of God in salvation. A simply laid-out treatise on the Father's eternal plan to elect, call, and irresistably draw souls to Himself throughout the ages. Learn what the infallible Scriptures reveal about the Father's will, the Son's work, and our role in the gracious redemption plan of God. **$5.99**

The Pilgrim's Progress *The Accurate Revised Text* by John Bunyan

Dr. Barry E. Horner, an authority on the literature of Bunyan, judiciously crafted a modernized version which is sensitive to retain all the glorious language and compelling doctrines of God's grace to sinners that Bunyan labored from a Bedford prison to impress upon men's hearts. Extensively footnoted and illustrated with classic 19th-Century engravings this is the only edition of this timeless treasure you ever need to own. **$11.99**

Outlined Study Manual *of The Pilgrim's Progress* by Barry E. Horner

This extensive study manual is clearly the best guide for understanding *The Pilgrim's Progress* available today. It is carefully laid-out in a manner which lends to easy reading and study. Left pages include the entire text of *The Pilgrim's Progress* (Accurate Revised edition, see above) while right pages hold the corresponding study outline. A must for any worthwhile study of this immortal classic. **$21.99 *(18.99 ea. in 5 packs)***

Themes and Issues *from The Pilgrim's Progress* by Barry E. Horner

This apologetic examines in detail the evangelical themes and issues woven throughout the *The Pilgrim's Progress*. You will marvel to discover the extent to which Bunyan deliberately incorporated deep Bible truths everywhere within his allegorical tale of the journey of Christian to the Celestial City. You'll benefit from decades of Dr. Horner's study and seminar teaching combined in this incredible commentary. **$18.99**

Reformation Press— A Great Christian Books *Bookstore*

YOU CAN ORDER NOW 3 WAYS!

1) **MAIL TO:** *Reformation Press 160 37th Street Lindenhurst, NY 11757*
2) **FAX TO:** *(561) 892-6131* **or** 3) **CALL US:** *(631) 956-0998*

quantity	item #	description	unit $	total $

Dear Canadian friends—

Please add $10 U.S. to the standard shipping rate to include proper amount.

If paying by check please pay in U.S. funds drawn from a U.S. bank. Thank you!

N.Y. State residents add 8.25% sales tax	
order sub-total	
shipping & handling	
ORDER TOTAL $	

name _____

street address _____

city, state, zip _____

telephone _____ email _____

[shipping & handling charges]

Add $2.95 for 1 book
but when you order 2 or more
SHIPPING is FREE!

add'l services: 2nd-Day Air = add $10 to above rate   Next-Day Air = add $15 to above

☐ check enclosed
make check payable to:
Reformation Press

exp. date ☐☐ ☐☐

card type ☐ visa ☐ mc

credit card # ☐☐☐☐ ☐☐☐☐ ☐☐☐☐ ☐☐☐☐

name as appears on card _____

✓ *Send a catalog to my friend:*
name _____
street address _____ city, state, zip

✓ *I'm not purchasing now but keep me on your mailing list!*
name _____
street address _____ city, state, zip

Note: Prices are subject to change without notice.